STO   NONFICTION   May 16, 1978

4.11.78

DID SOMEBODY PACK THE BABY?

THE FAMILY MOVING BOOK

Barbara Friedrich
Sally Hultstrand

PRENTICE-HALL, INC., Englewood Cliffs, New Jersey

Credit:
Rainy Days and Mondays
Lyrics by Paul Williams © 1970
Almo Music Corp. All rights reserved.
Music by Roger Nichols (ASCAP)
Used by permission.

*"Did Somebody Pack the Baby?": The
Family Moving Book* by Barbara Friedrich
and Sally Hultstrand
Copyright © 1978 by Barbara Friedrich
and Sally Hultstrand

Printed in the United States of America

Prentice-Hall International, Inc., London
Prentice-Hall of Australia, Pty. Ltd., Sydney
Prentice-Hall of Canada, Ltd., Toronto
Prentice-Hall of India Private Ltd., New Delhi
Prentice-Hall of Japan, Inc., Tokyo
Prentice-Hall of Southeast Asia Pte. Ltd., Singapore
Whitehall Books Limited, Wellington, New Zealand

10 9 8 7 6 5 4 3 2 1

Library of Congress Cataloging in Publication Data

Friedrich, Barbara,
    Did somebody pack the baby?
    Includes index.
    1. Moving, Household.   2. House buying.   3. House
selling.   I. Hultstrand, Sally, joint author.
II. Title.
TX307.F73   643   77-16136
ISBN 0-13-210906-9

To Blaze, with love

ACKNOWLEDGMENTS

Our thanks to June Nadler, Ginny Shafer, Ann Livermore, and Muff and Jacquie Maskovsky, who read parts of the manuscript and offered helpful suggestions; to Kathy Edelin, our intrepid typist; to Gerry Huey, who gave us sustenance; to Bertha Eller, a friendly face in the crowd; to Roy Winnick, for his taste and wit; and to our mothers and dads, Judy and Bob Mulrooney, Peg Wolfe, and to all those friends who shared their experiences, offered encouragement, and sparked our memories. Of course, we thank Don and Steve, and Jodie, Barb, Ande, Jen, Donny, Steffie, Mary, Sue, and Hank who all are so much a part of our story.

CONTENTS

PROLOGUE

We were comparative strangers. Our daughters were friends, but we had only a nodding acquaintance. We had both been invited to lunch by a mutual friend, but at the last moment the luncheon was cancelled. It was a bleak February day, and neither of us had anything else to do, so we decided to go out for lunch anyway, just the two of us.

We settled ourselves in a little French restaurant at a table behind a pillar, shrugged off our winter coats, ordered a glass of wine, and began exchanging pleasantries. It didn't take us long to discover that not only were we two lonely women in a new town, but that we had a lot more in common: between us we had moved our households a total of twenty times in as many years.

The waitress came to take our order, but we hadn't looked at the menu yet. We ordered another glass of wine, put our elbows on the chic little table, and started really getting our teeth into things.

We discussed the problems of moving with teenagers and how to deal with their very real suffering, how we happened to buy the houses we did, and the difficulty of getting acquainted with people in our new town. One of us had remodeling problems, and the other had six inches of water that mysteriously appeared in the basement the week after she moved in. One described unloading the moving van at the height of the worst ice storm in the history of the Midwest, and the other described the time her family was stalled in a blizzard on the way to Massachusetts and couldn't locate the van for a week.

The waitress appeared again to take our order. We had another glass of wine.

We compared the merits of the school systems in the places we had lived in, and tried to decide which city had the best restaurants. We discussed the difficulty of unearthing a good doctor in a new community—and dentist—and plumber—and hairdresser. One described her first move, from a Quonset hut on a college campus, and how the movers had carefully packed the garbage that she had wrapped in a newspaper. The other described the sinking feeling in the pit of her stomach when, after the family had wearily settled into the packed car and was driving through the outskirts of town, she suddenly realized that her youngest child had been misplaced.

When we noticed the waitress standing over us again, we gave the menu a perfunctory glance and ordered the French diet plate. Between bites we laughed a lot and cried a little over our disjointed lives, and the strengths and weaknesses they had developed in us and our families. We compared notes on all the little tricks of the trade we had learned in twenty moves, and the frustrations of trying to launch a family in a new town. The winter afternoon was growing dim and most of the little round tables were empty when one of us said, "We ought to write a book," and so we did.

A Note To Our Readers: All the incidents and situations we describe in this book are actually true. If they didn't happen to one of us, they happened to someone we have known. It became apparent early in the writing that it was awkward to refer to ourselves individually; hence the composite family headed by the composite "Blaze." Some of the other names in the book have been changed to protect the innocent—or the guilty!—with the notable exception of the illustrious Newton D. Baker.

Barbara Friedrich
Sally Hultstrand

PLAYING THE CORPORATE GAME

Life by Parker Brothers ⌂ You can't tell the players without a scorecard ⌂ Laid off or worse! ⌂ How to read the omens ⌂ How to tell the children you're moving ⌂ Coping with your own emotions.

In these confusing days of women's lib, independence, and the search for the definition of the female self, there are still a substantial number of women who learned at their mother's knee the tenet of Ruth, "Whither thou goest, I will go." Certainly, today many of us are getting the chance to put this into practice. For every liberated woman whose husband follows her around the country in pursuit of success, there are millions of others who must pick up chick and child, pack the bedding and family silver, and accompany their husbands wherever the job might take them.

Sometimes I think the reason behind the long-lived popularity of Parker Brothers' best-selling game, Monopoly, is its remarkable resemblance to real life. You start at Go, and with a toss of the dice you move to an inexpensive apartment on Mediterranean or Baltic Avenue. On your next turn you might move on to Oriental Avenue with its tiny look-alike houses arranged in neat rows. Some people are lucky enough to throw doubles, and they move ahead rapidly. Before, you know it, they land on New York Avenue! Another player may land on Chance and be sent back to the beginning and have to start over. And have you ever noticed how the real estate gets more expensive as you make your way around the board? If you really hit it big, you might end up owning Boardwalk or Park Place. One player might finish with a row of apartments on St. James Place and another with a couple of houses in Marvin Gardens. Some players are sent to jail—they are the only ones who don't keep moving! Moving on, buying and selling real estate is a way of life for millions of Americans.

We live in a mobile society. Depressions and recessions, booms and busts, centralization and decentralization cause job changes and the attendant relocation of families. And most of us are familiar with the demands of corporations, in which one often goes simply "up or out." Gone are the days when a couple could expect to remain in their hometown to see their children and grandchildren born and raised in that same hometown. Lovely as this would be, it is the rare exception today, rather than the rule.

Etched with excess stomach acid on my memory are the years in which we moved three times. That's happened to us twice. At one time we owned a house in Wisconsin, and one in Connecticut, while my husband was living in an apartment in

Manhattan. That year we paid taxes in Massachusetts, Wisconsin, New York City and Connecticut. That was the first year we had to hire an accountant to figure out what we owed Uncle.

The shortest stay we have ever had, so far, was six days in one house. I had just finished hanging the last curtains when my ecstatic husband came rushing in to tell me about the marvelous opportunity being offered to him—in Philadelphia! I don't know who was more upset—I, who had spent three days hunched over the sewing machine making curtains, or my mother-in-law, who had been cleaning out the old occupant's dirt while I sewed. She had come to help with the move because I was pregnant. So on we went to Philadelphia where—you guessed it—another toss of the dice, and we were transferred to Boston the week before the baby was born.

Some of the players in real-life Monopoly may be familiar to you. You may even be related by marriage to one of them.

THE CORPORATE MAN OR THE MAN ON THE MAKE   This is that dynamic fellow who knows that in order to succeed and reach the elusive but beckoning summit, he must be willing to pack up the wife and kids and necessary accouterments—dogs, cats, gerbils, *et al.*—and push onward and upward whenever and wherever the company desires. In most cases this type of move is considered a promotion, both titular and financial. The eventual payoff can be big and beneficial to the whole family. At least that's what your husband told you while delivering the big sales pitch designed to make you share his enthusiasm.

THE RESTLESS WARRIOR   This is that rugged individualist who becomes bored and discontented in his present situation and firmly believes that there is no reason for anyone to stay with a job that is anything less than Utopian. He fairly devours *The Wall Street Journal*, and keeps his resumé up-to-date and at the ready, just in case! He requires a saint for a wife.

THE STATUS SEEKER   We are all familiar with this player who moves on to a more prestigious address as soon as he gets enough money together. This move may take him and his family to another neighborhood or another town but usually within the same locality. The house is always bigger, as is the mortgage.

THE VISIONARY   This is the man who is engaged in an eternal quest for his elusive "self." This search may take him from one college campus to another, or from a dry-cleaning business in Ohio to a health-food shop in California to a farm in New Hampshire. He is a dreamer, and his dreams generally involve packing up and moving on.

THE MILITARY MAN   When his wife signs on as a partner, she at least knows what to expect. Every couple of years, whether she needs it or not, he has a new assignment at a different post. The military transfer is unique, though, in that one post is much like another, and the social network encompasses the world, providing built-in support wherever the assignment may be.

THE YOUNG AND THE RESTLESS   Today's new breed has hit the road in search of an ecologically sound, unpolluted, antiestablishment way of life. Moving for these young people is relatively simple, because they don't have too many worldly goods. What they do own can be stashed in their backpacks or tossed in the beat-up van that will carry them back and forth across this wide land seeking their own personal Valhalla.

THE SOCIAL SECURITY SET   This group is known as the golden-agers, the senior citizens, the Gray Panthers, or by any of the many euphemisms we coin to refer to the older members of our society without calling them old. Some have reached their personal dreams of success; some have not. But like the young and the restless, they may divest themselves of material goods. Furnishings and possessions gathered over a lifetime may be junked in favor of a new life-style. They flock to retirement settlements in Arizona, condominiums on the Florida waters, and the golf courses of California. Some take to the road in cozy-sized or superluxurious motor homes. Some opt for a ski lodge in Aspen or a log cabin on a Minnesota lakeshore. Others take to the waters, and home for them becomes a vessel making its way up and down the intracoastal waterways, six months to the north and six months to the south. Wherever it may be, this can be the very best move of all if it is the culmination of a lifetime dream and the last word in the sentence, "Someday we're going to _____ !"

THE DISPENSABLE MAN   For reasons perhaps beyond his control, a man may suddenly find himself on the street. Budget cuts, elimination of entire departments, company bankruptcy, or simply his failure to do the necessary job may result in his being handed his walking papers. Pity the nonsupportive wife who alludes to any chink in the armor of her mate out loud. If she intends to spend the rest of her life with this man, she had best learn to follow his lead and stifle!

Unemployment is a sad and frightening situation. Because of the economic ups and downs of recent years, a staggering number of people are finding themselves suddenly out of work. Unfortunately, this can occur when we least expect it, at a time when our expenses are at their greatest, when our standard of living has risen, or when the spirit and body are flagging. For instance, how many of us want to explore new pastures, tear up roots, and begin a new future in our forties, a time when so many of us want out of the rat race and long to prop up our feet and begin to enjoy the fruits of our labors? However, there is no job and no income, and we must survive. In order to eat, we must work and earn, and that means job-hunting, and that may mean moving on.
  I vividly remember my husband walking into the kitchen one evening a few years ago and greeting me with a throat-cutting gesture instead of his customary peck on the cheek. Clever and intuitive as I am, and knowing my husband as I do, I quickly surmised that something was amiss! My heart pounded, my blood raced to my head, and the pot of noodles I had been stirring boiled over. When I composed myself, in my most calculated-to-reassure and good-sportsy voice, I squeaked, "My God, what's wrong now?" "We're on the beach," he replied. He told me that the company had filed for bankruptcy. There was to be none of the usual two weeks' notice and no severance pay. The beautiful

balloon has burst without warning. Visions of my lovely home, my "dream house," and all the terrific plans that we had made for it, shattered into a million pieces. Like the good and understanding wife that the *Ladies' Home Journal* and *Good Housekeeping* trained me to be, I assumed a stiff upper lip. (I only cried in the bathroom at two o'clock in the morning.) We would work it out together, and we did. Helen Gurley Brown be damned!

The entire adventure (if you invoke the power of positive thinking, even looking for a job during a recession can be an adventure), took a long seven months, but we survived, and were even strengthened by the experience. During that span of time Blaze, my indefatigable husband, never lost faith and kept all of us thinking *up*, and we learned a great deal about ourselves and one another and the strength of our family unit. I, the sheltered and rather pampered wife who had never really held a paying job, embarked to find work in the marketplace. Surprisingly, to *me* most of all, I landed the first position I applied for. Selling shoes in one of the local department stores was not the career of my dreams, but my salary, low as it was, at least covered the grocery bill.

I strongly advise any woman who finds herself in this economic and emotional difficulty to seek some kind of job. It goes without saying that any money added to the family coffers is important. Psychologically the benefits are enormous. There is nothing to be gained by having a husband and wife both waiting for the phone to ring or the mail to arrive with hoped-for job offers. The two of you will become more and more depressed, and battles are likely to take place because of the tension and strain. By having a routine to follow, our lives continued in a somewhat normal manner. My husband had the house to himself and conducted the business of job-hunting much as he would have from an office. He researched businesses that might be interested in his qualifications, sent résumés and cover letters; contacted friends, business recruiters, and headhunters; answered ads in the city and national newspapers. (You can obtain out-of-state newspapers somewhere in most cities. Check in the yellow pages of the phone book under "News Dealers." The Sunday *New*

York Times and Tuesday's *Wall Street Journal* are usually filled with ads.)

I would arrive home later in the day filled with little anecdotes about my experiences in the shoe department. It was great to have a fresh topic of conversation rather than dwelling on our mutual problem. You both must make every effort to keep busy and active and not allow yourselves to become negative. Help one another in every possible way. I must mention at this time that afternoon TV has got to be a no-no. This is not the time to have your man become addicted to the "soaps." Avoid getting yourselves in a rut.

Our five children pitched in with the household chores. They learned to do the food shopping, planned and prepared meals, dusted and vacuumed, and did the laundry and the ironing. We learned that each of us had a responsibility to the family. The right job offer finally came, and yes, we would be moving. We all greeted this long-awaited announcement with mixed emotions. Our lovely home would have to be sold, we would have to leave the community that we had come to love and had become a part of, and our oldest daughter would have to say goodbye to her very first beau. (Remember how traumatic that can be when you're sixteen?) But we as a family had come to realize the importance of our basic needs. We all discovered how much eating meant to us, among other things. Our five clothes-conscious children had developed a real appreciation of their creature comforts. The new opportunity was, of course, the only answer. We were still in the game, and we plunged ahead.

With a little experience you can learn to read the signs that tell you when a move is in the offing. For instance, you know you'll be moving:

> when you finally finish decorating the house.
> when you've just ordered a five-year supply of personalized stationery with your address on it.
> when your husband's salary finally grows into the mortgage payments.
> when you've just installed new carpeting.

when your name is finally at the top of the two-year waiting list at the tennis club.

when the supermarket cashier unflinchingly cashes your personal checks.

when your college-bound child is accepted at your state university.

when your hairdresser will fit you in at a moment's notice.

when your homely daughter finally hooks a boyfriend.

when the perennial garden you planted is in its prime.

when you have finally found all the good shortcuts in town.

when you attend Open House at the school and know your way around the building.

when you land a terrific part-time job with just the right hours.

when you are finally invited to join the exclusive garden club.

when the store clerks start calling you by name.

when your built-in range has given up the ghost, and you've just made the down payment on a new one.

when you have developed a good list of baby-sitters.

when you have finally found a repair man you can trust.

when you have met the parents of most of your children's friends.

when you finally have coordinated towels and bed linen.

That's life! Once you know you are going to be moving—whether it's the result of a long job hunt, a fabulous offer from out of the blue, or the unceasing military or industrial transfer—you as husband and wife are committed to pulling up stakes and in effect starting over again. Now how do you tell the children?

In most cases when children have reached the age of reason (whenever *that* is!), it is best to include them in your discussions and plans. After all, you're in this thing together. The key word in all relocations must be "share." Children of almost any age are going to feel threatened. Their security is being tampered with. They are faced with the unknown—a new home, a new town, a new school, and new friends. They are likely to toy with the idea, even at an early age, of chucking the whole family, expanding their baby-sitting jobs and paper routes, and setting up housekeeping in a neighbor's garage. To be perfectly honest, I'll bet there are plenty of wives and mothers who entertain the same idea themselves.

To be sure, it's difficult to paint a rosy picture of an unknown, but you should try. If your move is to be to an area that is relatively close, try to take a long weekend with the family to look over the new town or city. Write to the Chamber of Commerce and the real estate board to glean as much information as you can about the community and what it has to offer—community activities, schools, housing, and prices. You might be able to narrow your sights to one particular area or suburb and familiarize your family with it before you move. You may all be pleasantly surprised to find that you like it after all, and that can be a very nice dividend.

If you, the wife and mother, can assume a positive attitude, swallow the lump in your throat, and try your darndest to make the whole experience as pleasant and hopeful as you possibly can, your feelings will be contagious to the rest of the family. We all have a little Sarah Bernhardt in our makeup, and this is the time to put your acting abilities into action for the sake of your husband and kids. On the other hand, you cannot overlook the very real fears of those you love. Talk it out with one another as a family and individually. I recall some very special moments with some of my children when I would hear the sound of sobs in the pillow late at night, and just the two of us would talk quietly of our thoughts. Never forget that your husband has some fears and misgivings too, and he needs to have an understanding and loving ear. When we share our fears and worries, our load is always lighter.

O.K., you're on your way. You've faced the inevitable, and you really are moving. It may cheer you up to know that you are not alone. Vance Packard in his informative book, *A Nation of Strangers*, tells us that one-fifth of all Americans move every year. Horrors! Or how about these statistics from the telephone company: the "average American moves fourteen times in his or her lifetime," and "forty million Americans change their home addresses at least once every year; one-third of these people cross a county or state line." There should be some comfort in these numbers.

And so the stage is set, and the roles have been cast. Your own personal production can range from gloomy Greek tragedy to low camp comedy—maybe all in the first act! The star of the scenario is you, whether you sought the part or not, and the responsibility for a guaranteed long run will rest on your slender shoulders. Your role has been played countless times throughout history by the likes of Abigail Adams, Mary, Queen of Scots, Eleanor Roosevelt, the nomadic tribeswomen of the desert, the Eskimo women of the Arctic, and Mrs. Attila the Hun. It's a hard act to follow, but your family is counting on you to win a Tony.

SHARPENING THE SHEARS FOR THE FLEECING

How to turn the tidiest profit when selling your house⌂Recognizing eyesores and what to do about them⌂Emphasizing the good points⌂Throwing a good garage sale.

In these days of soaring real estate prices, it's not only nice to turn a tidy profit on your old house, it's necessary. In spite of what you've heard, prices are always higher in the town to which you are moving. This is an unwritten law! So the question is, how to con someone into paying more than you did for the same property.

First, clipboard in hand, you and your husband should tour the whole place from attic to cellar, including the garage and yard. You are looking coldly and critically for eyesores. By eyesores, I don't mean the couch from Goodwill in the family room or Aunt Katie's paint-by-number nasturtiums in the bedroom. Those go with you. I'm referring to the broken knob on the kitchen door, the caulking pulling away from the bathtub, the loose railing on the front porch, the dripping faucet, those rusting old bikes behind the garage. You know what I mean—those things you've been planning to get around to one of these days—the things that make the place look tacky.

If your husband is unavailable for this tour, you might enlist the aid of a friend, but this is risky if you are the least bit sensitive. What she considers eyesores might be construed by you as hints of sloppy housekeeping or criticism of your interior decorating talents. As I said, it's risky. Better to involve your husband if you can, because he's the one who will have to take care of much of the fixing anyway.

Do not, I repeat, *do not* plan large redecorating projects. Decorating usually does not sell a house as the buyer will probably change it anyway. The important thing is that the house is sound and clean, and everything is in good working order. Big projects take too much time and money, and you have other fish to fry. Just tidy up. Wash the finger prints off the staircase wall, give the floors a good waxing, and if there's a big grease spot on the kitchen wallpaper, remove it. You can get the stuff to do the job at any hardware store.

Try to look at the house as if you were seeing it for the first time. When one of our houses needed painting at selling time, I just painted the front door in a contrasting color, and the whole house looked fresher. If the season is right, a tub of flowers on the doorstep perks things up. Trim the shrubs if they are looking scraggly, and pull the weeds in the foundation planting. Spreading a bag of peat moss around the plants really helps. Your whole aim in this exercise is to make your home look cherished and well cared for. Surely homeowners as meticulous as you are would never let plumbing problems go untended, or neglect having the chimneys cleaned regularly, or forget to change the furnace filters. And heaven forbid that you would ever let the Dutch attack any elm of yours!

In a suburban Connecticut town where houses turn over frequently, one man considered this spruce-up such an important part of selling a house that he started a flourishing business of putting houses in shape for sale. He called his work House Cosmetics, and that's an accurate description. Pluck an eyebrow here, and apply a little rouge there. Just remember, nothing too ambitious. You are not after a face-lift. That's too expensive and time-consuming.

Now is the time to get rid of any junk you don't want to take with you to the new house. Weed out the outgrown overshoes and snowsuits, drag your mother-in-law's floor lamp down from the attic, and make up your mind to part with the leaky rubber boat you were always going to patch and the exercise equipment you've used twice. Your closets and storage space will look much bigger with all that stuff removed.

One of the few good things about moving every few years is that if you do it right, you may never have to clean closets and cupboards in between. My old friend Judy, who moved all too often in the early days of her marriage, called me excitedly one day and said, "Now I know we're really putting down roots. I had to clean out the linen closet!"

Don't get carried away with this clearing-out project, though. Another friend was delighted to be transferred to sunny California. "Hurray!" she said as she quickly gave away all the family's winter coats and sold the Flexible Flyers. Eighteen months later they were shivering in their new home in Minneapolis. Use a little foresight.

Now that you have all your castoffs piled in your garage or driveway, there are two ways you can go. You can call the Salvation Army or Goodwill, and they will come and haul the discards away. They will do it for nothing. Or you can put an ad in the paper to invite your fellow townspeople to come and pay *you* to let *them* haul it away. I'm talking about a tag sale, garage sale, or rummage sale, the terminology depending on where you live. Of course, this is a little more work, but if you can keep a straight face, it can be remunerative. I have only done this once myself because I kept having to lock myself in the bathroom with an uncontrollable case of the giggles brought on by the sight of my friends and neighbors paying me cold cash for all that junk!

When you hold your sale, get your children to help as salespeople, if they're old enough. If you don't have kids the right age, enlist your bowling team or best pal. You do need a couple of extra salespeople to keep track of things. Even Bloomingdale's has a clerk at every counter. Some communities require a permit for a garage sale, so check with City Hall. Also, if you plan to sell mattresses or box springs, make sure it's legal in your locality. Sale of used bedding is banned in some states.

Let your youngsters clear all their own junk out of their rooms and the playroom and put it in the sale, and, as an incentive, let them keep the proceeds. You get a lot more stuff cleared out that way, and you don't have to listen to them wailing afterwards, "Why did you sell my G.I. Joe?" (or "my Hot Wheels," or whatever). Many people will come with their children, and all the neighborhood kids will be hanging around all day enjoying the festivities, so have a big kiddy box. In it go old toys, children's books, costume jewelry, games, etc., all priced for a few pennies. This keeps the kids busy, and helps you get rid of a lot of junk. Let *their* mothers get rid of it when *they* move.

If you are foresighted, this would be a good opportunity to rid yourself of the plants that you won't be able to take with you and to turn a little profit on them at the same time. If you are concerned about what to do with the goldfish and your son's burgeoning family of white mice when you move, put a price tag on them, too. Not too high, though!

Throw all your old paperback novels in a box to sell for a dime or a quarter apiece. Go through your old records and do likewise. Do make sure, however, that you are willing to part with everything you put out for sale! A delighted neighbor bought my children's outgrown rocking horse, the springy kind, that we had given our eldest on her second birthday. All of our children had bounced their little bottoms on it, and when I saw it going down the street, I got a big lump in my throat and my eyes started to sting. I made a fool of myself running after her and buying it back, but now it sits in the attic of our new house, patiently waiting for grandchildren.

There are a few things for which I should prepare you. The first is the possibility of rain on the day of the sale. It's much nicer if you can display your wares in the driveway, but if you can't, you can't. You'll have to stack things up in the garage as best you can. I definitely would not hold any part of the sale in the house itself. The next thing you know, someone wants to use the bathroom, and then customers are all over the house, asking if you want to sell your davenport or your dining room set, or "How much is that sweater you're wearing, lady?" In some parts of the country, clever burglars have used the tag sale as an opportunity to case the joint prior to a robbery, so don't let anyone you don't know inside.

If you have advertised the sale to start at 9 A.M., you should know that there will be a rush of customers at eight. The real shoppers don't want to miss out on the good stuff. They will queue up at least an hour early, if not the day before. You should also be prepared to greet the local secondhand or so-called antique dealer checking for "sleepers," some real treasure that he or she can buy cheap and sell to someone else at a big markup. A few really needy people will arrive, old ladies going through your pilly cardigans, and young couples with seven children under the age of five looking longingly at your old stroller. Be generous. After all, your objective is to get the stuff out of the house. Whatever is left at the end of the day—and one day of this madness is enough—the Goodwill will come and get, bless them!

Once you have the house all cleaned up and cleaned out, it should look so nice that you may wonder why you are going through with this move. Put all those doubts aside, because in one month of normal living, believe me, you'd be right back in the same old mess.

BRINGING THE LAMB TO THE SLAUGHTER

Whether to use a realtor or sell it yourself ⌂ How to determine your asking price ⌂ What to include in the sale ⌂ How realtors operate ⌂ Tricks to showing the house to good advantage ⌂ Timing your move correctly.

So the time has come to put the house on the market. The first decision has to be whether to do it yourself or hire a professional. You can save yourself that big fat commission if you handle the deal, but there are drawbacks. If a friend-of-a-friend hears you are moving and is interested in the house, great! But if you have to advertise, you must be prepared to show it to anyone and everyone who asks, even the Boston strangler. That's the law. People will want to see it early in the morning on their way to work, and at suppertime on their way home from work, and in the evening after the baby's in bed. You must be prepared to listen to snide remarks about the color of your carpeting, and your choice of bathroom wallpaper, and the number and kinds of weeds in your lawn. If you find this too embarrassing, you'll have to turn total strangers loose in your house to snoop in your closets and kitchen cupboards by themselves.

If you are up to this, you must determine what price to ask. In recent years prices have escalated so rapidly that what you paid for the place may have no bearing on its present worth. In some areas houses are escalating 10 percent annually. What comparable houses in your neighborhood have recently brought is usually a good guide if you have access to accurate figures, *not rumors*. Or you can hire a professional real estate appraiser, for a fee. The appraiser will give you a written appraisal of the property as well as a suggested market value. This is sometimes a good document to show to a prospective buyer. The fee will vary according to the locality, but if you're selling the house yourself, it's a good bet. Whatever you do, don't price your house so high that the sale drags on for months and months. The house can become a "dog," even if there's nothing wrong with it. People wonder why it hasn't sold and imagine the worst. On the other hand, if it sells immediately, your husband will torture himself for weeks, muttering even in his sleep, "We didn't ask enough!"

Another thing you will have to decide for yourselves is what you want to include in the sale of the house. Carpeting, draperies, chandeliers, portable airconditioners, water softeners are all negotiable items. Generally, it is assumed that anything attached to the house goes with it unless otherwise specified. Therefore, if you're particularly fond of your dining room chandelier and really want to take it with you, take it down before you ever show the house, and replace it with another fixture. You can get something inexpensive and put it up, and no one will ever know the difference. Once a customer has seen it, though, she may insist on having it, or the deal is off. I guess it's human nature to want something as soon as you're told you can't have it. A multithousand-dollar deal can go sour over a ridiculously inexpensive item. I have a black cast iron eagle given to me by my kids one Mother's Day. You can buy one like it for under ten dollars in any hardware store in the country. We nailed it over the front door, and I loved it because of the little givers who had picked it out themselves and paid for it with their allowances. You guessed it! When I took it down for packing, the angry buyer called and insisted that I put it back up. I vehemently resisted, and she insisted, and I think we would have gone to court if my smart husband, Blaze, hadn't sashayed down to the hardware store and bought another eagle and nailed it up.

Sometimes excluding a couple of items when listing your house is smart business. It leaves you a little leverage for negotiating the deal. The buyer may make an offer under your asking price, and you can counter by throwing in the items you originally excluded. Well, sometimes it works. Last time though, Blaze threw in our new bedroom rug which I really wanted to take with us because it was painstakingly selected to match our bedspread. I'm still grumbling, but he was tickled pink with the clever deal he made. I'm also now washing my clothes in hard water because he negotiated away my water-softening equipment. It's hard to get used to dealing with bathtub ring once you've been spoiled by the Culligan man!

You should also have a little knowledge of real estate law and contracts so that when a prospective buyer says, "We'll take it," you will know what to do next before the fish gets off the hook. By all means, if you're not using a realtor have a lawyer handle the transaction and draw up the contracts for you. Some states require that lawyers represent both parties at the closing, even if real estate brokers handled all the negotiations.

If you advertise your house for sale in the newspapers, be sure to specify "Principals only" or you will be inundated with calls from realtors wanting the listing. But be advised by doing this you may also be excluding your house from the major portion of the out-of-town buyer market. Most out-of-towners work through agents.

If you show the house yourself, you must also come to terms with your conscience in the case of any defects that are impractical or impossible to correct. Maybe you have a basement wading pool every time there's a heavy dew. Here the principle of "caveat emptor" applies—let the buyer beware! In other words, don't bring it up. What should you do if the buyer looks you in the eye and asks, "Do you ever get water in the basement?" Don't ask me. That's why we use a realtor.

A real estate agent will take about 6 percent of your selling price, but will handle a lot of these problems for you. She will schedule all appointments to show the house, and you can bet your sweet bippy that she will try to show it during normal working hours. You will be told when to expect her to bring a client, and you can absent yourself, your family, and your pets from the premises when the house is being shown. The place will look more spacious and serene, and you won't have to answer any embarrassing questions or listen to unkind remarks about your furniture arrangement and the state of your medicine chest.

If you decide to have an agent handle all this for you, which firm do you call? First you need a little knowledge of how realtors operate. Generally, there is an office provided by the head of the firm. He—it usually *is* a he—has a desk in a private room at the rear where he deals with the contracts and arranges his lunch and golf dates. There may be several desks in the larger front office, mostly manned by women working varying degrees of part-time. Each has some "floor time," meaning that she is to be at a desk, answering the phone, at a certain specified time during the week. Any live ones, customers, who call or drop in at the office during that time are *her* clients. This means that if she successfully negotiates a deal with this client, she gets to split commission with the boss in the back room. However, if she shows the customer everything in her file, and there's no sale, all is not lost! She can pass the client on to another agent with another firm, setting up an appointment for them to meet. If that agent scores, the commission is split with the first agent, who, of course, splits her share with the boss in the back room. Got it? The pie can be cut into as many pieces as there are people who have had their finger in it.

If you have a friend in the business, and you want to remain her friend, let *her* know first that you want to sell your house. If she lists it, it means money in her pocket whether she sells it or not. Otherwise choose a firm that seems to do a lot of business in your neighborhood. You can tell by the signs in the yards and local newspaper listings.

You may want to consider giving your listing to a firm allied with one of the rapidly multiplying national referral services. More and more out-of-towners are availing themselves of this kind of service. A couple in Albuquerque may call a local broker whose firm is a member of such a group. He will make an appointment for them with an associated realtor in Portland, explain their requirements, and the broker in Portland will make a hotel reservation for them, line up a few houses, and perhaps even meet them at the airport when they arrive. This service doesn't cost the buyer a penny. Member firms in these realty networks usually pay a substantial fee to become affiliated. It's rather like buying a McDonald's franchise, but they stand to gain in increased referrals and to benefit from nationwide advertising campaigns. As a seller, you will probably expand your chances with out-of-town buyers if you list with a broker affiliated with one of these firms. You may also want to keep this kind of service in mind when it's your turn to be the looker in your new town.

You have the right to give a firm an exclusive, if you wish. This means that you give them a certain period of time to try to sell the property before you give it to another firm or put it on multiple listing. If they fail to sell it in the specified time, they relinquish their exclusive right to show the property. Presumably they will try very hard to sell it before their exclusive expires.

Most communities offer a multiple-listing service. This means that a house on multiple listing is carried in the files of every firm in town that is a member of the Multiple Listing Board. Any of their agents can sell it. However, the agent taking the listing originally splits the commission with the agent closing the deal, and both of them split their share with their bosses in the back room.

What usually happens is this. You decide to call a realtor whose firm is a member of the Multiple Listing Board, and you tell her that you want your house multiple listed. The board, a loose association of local realtors, will send two or three representatives to your home to offer their appraisals of what the house will bring on the local market. This is not a binding figure, however. You set your price.

Next, an open house will be scheduled when all the multiple listing members can come and see your home so they will know what they are selling. In large communities there is often a certain morning each week for these showings of all the new offerings on the market. Of course, all agents can't view all the houses, but they will try to cover the areas or neighborhoods in which they operate. A picture and a fact sheet on your property will be on file in every multiple listing real estate firm in town.

Open house morning can be a good dress rehearsal for the main performance, when a potential buyer is actually scheduled to arrive. It can't hurt either to whet the appetites of the agents who will have to do the selling, so you will want to have your house looking its best. There are a few tricks to showing your home to good advantage. I always pretend to myself that I'm entertaining and try to have the house look the way it does for a party.

Certainly you want the bathroom to be at least Howard Johnson clean. Close the toilet lid, put out fresh towels, scrape out the soap dish, and give the room a spritz of scent. Likewise, your kitchen should not be a candidate for imminent closing by the local health department. Clean the range and the oven, and be sure the floor is shiny. These are two areas which, if they aren't squeaky clean, can really turn prospective buyers squeamish.

Turn on the lamps, especially if it's a dull day. This is very important in creating a warm atmosphere. Have fresh flowers and greenery, a bowl of polished apples, and a fire in the fireplace if it's chilly outdoors. Soft music playing is nice if it can be arranged so it doesn't seem too hokey.

Just before we showed our first home, I sent Blaze to the florist for an armful of rhododendron leaves and a pot of yellow mums. He grumbled about the expense, but the first couple who looked bought it. Not because of the greenery, of course, but it didn't hurt.

In the afternoon I try to have something that smells good in the oven. Pot roast beats Glade air freshener every time. Most of our houses have sold quickly, but one dragged on for months. I got tired of cooking fragrant things every time someone was coming to look, so I devised a couple of shortcuts. Sprinkle a little nutmeg on a warm burner, and they'll think you just baked an apple pie. Or simmer some bouillon in a pan on the back burner.

What's even better is boiling up a batch of Castle Spice. This is a concoction that was reportedly used in medieval days to combat the odors of goats and chickens and chamber pots in the old chateau. The enormity of the problem of Ban-less knights and unrefrigerated joints of mutton ripening on the sideboard was somewhat moderated by the fresh breezes blowing in all seasons through the slits that served as windows but, nevertheless, the lady of the manor needed a lot of help with housitosis. Brew up a batch and simmer it on the back of the stove when lookers are expected. It will boil down, so add some water each time you use it. Store it in a covered jar until you need it again, and with any luck, it should last until the house is sold. Here's the recipe:

Castle Spice

- 4 cinnamon sticks
- 16 whole cloves
- 1 teaspoon pickling spices
- 4 teaspoons ground ginger
- 2 quarts water

Combine in a large kettle, bring to a boil, and then simmer as long as needed.

I always make this at Christmas time too because it smells so great, but it's confusing for the children. When the aroma of Castle Spice wafts through the house, they don't know whether to start packing or write to Santa.

None of these tricks will work if they want four bedrooms and you only have three, but the idea is to create a warm, inviting atmosphere. Then take the kids and get out of the house. (I say "warm, inviting," not hot and noisy!) Take the pets with you or shut them up in the car. They'll piddle on the upholstery and chew the knobs off the dashboard, but it's worth it if you sell the house.

You may say that this is going to a lot of trouble. Not if you sell the house quickly! There are few experiences as traumatic as having your house on the market. You feel so vulnerable. People come through who exclaim that they "just love it!" and "it's just what we've been looking for!" and then you never see them again. Hypocrites! It's a severe emotional strain. Nobody likes rejection, and every time someone looks at your house and doesn't buy, it hurts. It's a little like being rushed by a sorority and not being pledged. The realtor will tell you polite little lies like the house was too far from the husband's job, or they needed more space for their room-sized loom, but in your heart you feel that your style and taste have been impugned. You also feel as though you're constantly standing inspection, like having your mother-in-law coming in daily to give the house her white glove test. You get sick of hearing yourself telling the kids not to mess things up, and they get sick of it too, as they will be certain to tell you.

You also have most of your life's savings tied up in this little deal, and you're not going anywhere until you get the bread for the new house. This becomes particularly excruciating if your husband has already gone on to the new job, and you've been left behind holding the bag—I mean the house. Therefore, any little touches you can provide to hurry the process along are well worth the effort.

This brings up the subject of what to do if, heaven forbid, your husband is due on the new job in another city before you can join him. In my opinion, more than thirty days' separation should be avoided like the Swine Flu. I spent one whole Wisconsin winter in a house with five kids while Blaze was living it up in a bachelor pad in New York City. While I was trying to shovel four feet of snow out of the driveway so I could get to the grocery store, he was making like Joe Namath in Fun City. The climax of that fiasco occurred when he decided to throw a cocktail party for all the people who had entertained him. The first news I had of this fun affair was when, during the course of the party, someone suggested calling good ol' what's-her-name out in Wisconsin. The phone rang just after I had put out a small inferno in the basement caused by lint build-up in the clothes dryer and taken the temperatures of two children confined to their beds with chicken pox. This sort of situation is not calculated to give you the jollies. Only my unholy fear of being stuck alone with five kids permanently kept us out of the divorce courts that time. Move together if you possibly can.

Occasionally you may find yourselves for a short period with two mortgages, one on the old house and one on the new. This is not ideal, but it's not as catastrophic as it sounds. Generally, you can arrange with the banks to pay just the interest and insurance for the duration of the emergency.

You hear a lot of conversation around about a house selling better if it's furnished. This may be true in the case of older homes, but a fairly new house without too many eyesores to cover up should be just as marketable standing empty.

A friend of mine had to make this kind of decision when her husband was transferred from the Chicago area. They had a beautiful traditional home on a prime lakefront lot, and she elected to leave their furniture in it so it would show to best advantage. Neighbors told her later that after it was sold and the furniture had been shipped to her, the new owners gutted the interior, stripped the exterior of shutters and carriage lanterns, and completely redesigned it in a starkly modern style. With its new glass window walls the house was completely unrecognizable. The lot was what the buyer was interested in, and this house could just as well have been left empty.

Some sellers feel, however, that showing an empty house puts them in a poor bargaining position. Presumably the buyer will have the brains to realize that the family has already gone on to the new city, and the owner is quite possibly desperate to get this house off his hands and some money into the hands of his new banker. The buyer may automatically start computing how low he dares to bid on the house.

Incidentally, this friend rented furniture in her new town to use in the interim. Most large cities have furniture rental firms.

Just let your fingers do the walking if you find yourself in need of this service.

Many people prefer to sell the old house before buying a new one, simply because they need to know how much money they are free to spend on their new home. After you pay off the old mortgage and legal fees and commission, what's left is your equity. This becomes the down payment on the new house, although you may want to put some aside for improvements of one kind or another. One advantage to making several moves is that by buying and selling wisely, you are often able to upgrade your housing more quickly than would otherwise be possible.

Many corporations have very good programs to help you get rid of your old house. Some buy them outright, some have alliances with large national real estate firms that will buy your home from you and then sell it themselves. In this case, two or three professional appraisers give the house the once-over, and you are offered the average of the prices they suggest. You can always sell it yourself if you feel you can do better, but this does give you a good out and can possibly alleviate a bad case of nerves.

You should be sure to check carefully into your company's moving policy. There are many different kinds of benefits provided, varying from one corporation to another. Most pay the moving company, some pay real estate commissions, inspection costs, and/or legal fees; some pay an extra cash allowance for relocating in a new town. This is intended to cover such expenses as refitting of carpets and draperies, appliance hook-ups, baby-sitters, auto registration, and the multitude of minor expenses associated with moving to another house. Some people strip a house of absolutely everything when they move out, even the lightbulbs in the ceiling fixtures. Even such minor expenses add up.

If your personal good fairy is pleased with you, you may find that you have two offers at the same time on your house, praise be! Some realtors go through a lot of folderol about submitting sealed bids which must be opened simultaneously. This happened to us once when Blaze was out of town. I had to arrange for him to be on the phone long distance at the time of the opening of the sealed bids. As it turned out, one bid was too low, so there was no choice to be made, but there was a real Academy Awards atmosphere about the evening as we breathlessly awaited the opening of the envelopes. I even had my acceptance speech memorized.

When a person decides to make an offer on your house, a contract is submitted, accompanied by a check, which is called "earnest money." This is intended to show the buyer's good faith in negotiating the deal. The money is held in "escrow," or in safe keeping, until the completion of the transaction. The amount may vary up to 10 percent of the price of the house, according to local custom or the wishes of the seller.

So now you've got a deal! Date of occupancy becomes the next issue. The buyer wants to know when he can get into the house. Unless there are unusual circumstances, give yourself plenty of time. Moving is a chain reaction. *You* have to find a new house, the people in that house have to find a new house, and so on, and on, and on. Everyone's move is just a link in a chain of moves stretching across the country and sometimes reaching overseas. Many people make the mistake of insisting on moving during the summer, when schools are not in session. There are two reasons to avoid this.

First, it's often harder for kids, especially teens, to make friends in the summer when they are not thrown together with others in the classroom. They hang around your neck like albatrosses until school begins. If a child comes into school in the middle of the term, he is more likely to be noticed instead of being overlooked in the mass confusion and excitement of your average opening day in any school in America. In fact, even if we have been transferred in the summer, I sometimes don't send my children to school until the second or third day of the term so the teachers and students will realize that they are newcomers.

Second, summer is the busiest season for moving companies, and it stands to reason that you are likely to get better service at any other time of the year.

If at all possible, give yourself *at least* two months' leeway from the time your old house is sold until you move into the new one. It's much easier to move directly from one house to another without any way stations in between. That's extremely unsettling for the whole family. Kids make friends in one neighborhood, and then you move them again, and even your pets are more disoriented than need be. Besides, the only time I have ever lost anything in a move was that time when we put our things in storage. We had had to evacuate our old house, so we moved temporarily into a tiny ranch style with no basement, few closets and no stove. We put most of our things in storage except the beds and the davenport, which was scheduled to go to the upholsterer. I had a few boxes of linens, dishes, and other necessities stored in the living room, and we borrowed an electric rotisserrie and a hot plate from friends. We expected to camp in this fashion for a month or so while our new house was being finished. The month turned into four months, and the camp-in turned into a disaster.

In order to spare them an extra transition we enrolled the children in a school near the house-under-construction. There was no lunch program, so they had to be driven back and forth across town a total of four round trips a day, most of which interfered with the baby's naptime. Then they picked up a revolting case of pinworms, and the doctor advised boiling all the sheets and underwear daily. This on a hot plate! Tiny little ants got into all the cartons standing around on the floors and into my portable dishwasher which was eventually going to be installed in the new house. The dog who had been raised in a town with no leash law now barked incessantly at the end of a chain in the backyard. If I brought her into the house, she watched cunningly for a chance to slip out when a child opened the door, and then the only way I could get her back was to pretend I was going someplace in the car. She would hop willingly into the back seat and spent most of her time sitting expectantly in the car in the driveway, waiting to go.

The weeks dragged by, school was out, and the weather turned unbearably hot. My mother came for a visit, and one day she was helping me catch up on the ironing. As I picked up a stack of clean clothes and turned to hang them up, she wiped her perspiring face with her shirttail and said, "Never mind putting them away. Pack them in the suitcase. We're going home!"

When we finally moved into the new house, we could really

appreciate its roominess and comforts. It was great, except for the tiny little ants who hitchhiked along in all those big yellow cartons. We exterminated those, but when we sold the house, the dishwasher and the ants in it, were part of the deal. I never had figured out how to get rid of them, and I had no intention of taking them to our next abode. Moving can be survived, but only a fool would make it any harder than necessary.

FINDING A HOUSE THAT'S A HOME

The house hunting expedition⌂ How to find the kind of house you want⌂Knowing what you really need⌂Getting the lay of the land in neighborhoods, schools, prices⌂Mistakes I have made and lived with⌂What to do if you can't find a house you like.

Back in Happy Acres many years ago when we were all young, hardworking couples with our 3.2 children in diapers, the most exciting events that we had to look forward to were a big night out at the local movie or a rousing game of bridge with a few neighbors. When one couple in the neighborhood announced that they would be moving, our reactions were mixed with happiness and a lot of envy. Veda and Roc were being transferred all the way to San Francisco, which as everyone knew was the perfect city.

Roc had to start his new job almost immediately, leaving Veda and the babies until a new home could be found and the old one sold. She would handle the children, the bills, and all the business details. He would contact the realtors before he left, but Veda would carry the burden of showing the house and handling any problems that came her way. She willingly assumed the tasks presented to her. She was very proud of Roc and loved him very much and wanted him to be proud of her, too. We all offered to help her out in any way we could, but Veda coped and came through with flying colors.

Because of the great distance separating them and the expense of air fare, Roc was seldom able to get home, so Veda's problem, more than anything else, was loneliness. She prayed that Roc would find them a suitable place in San Francisco, the sooner the better.

We could all see that she was becoming more and more miserable. When finally the phone call came telling her to make plans to get out to California next weekend, we were all relieved. Roc had lined up a few houses that he thought would do, and they would be able to see them all during her visit, make a decision, and begin their trek to the West.

The children would be taken care of by one couple, a neighborhood boy would walk and feed the dog, and all of us who were Veda's size tore through our wardrobes seeking our best cocktail dresses and smartest suits for our friend to borrow so she would look terrific if she happened to meet the new boss. She treated herself to a bottle of Shalimar. We were almost as excited as she was as we helped her pack her suitcases.

Three of us drove Veda to the airport and waved goodbye

as the plane took off. Five days later we waited for the returning plane bringing her back with wonderful stories of the sights she had seen and the house that would be perfect for her. Would she have an ocean view or a mountain view? Well, we'd know soon enough, because the plane was unloading. We looked expectantly for Veda's familiar face. There she was, but she looked terrible! She was pale and shaky as she walked rubbery-legged across the ramp. When she drew near we noticed the dark circles under her eyes. Something awful must have happened. As she reached us, Veda smiled and suddenly began to sparkle. She mumbled the words as if in a daze, "Fantastic, amazing, really amazing." We guided her to the car and began to question her. Was she all right? Had something gone wrong? Did they find a house? Veda looked up, blushed a deep crimson, and said, "What house? We never left the hotel! It was amazing—really amazing!" Veda was taken home by the three most jealous women in Massachusetts.

Packing your bags for a trip alone with your husband to a distant city to buy a new house can be exciting. Should you put in a long dress for dinner? A sexy new nightgown? Your new T-strap heels? Forget it. Veda's story was the exception! Pack your old flannel pj's and some Sominex. Also comfortable shoes and a pair of pants for climbing around construction sites and into attics and cellars. For most of us this will be no second honeymoon. In fact, after three or four days of househunting, you may be in the market for a marriage counselor!

One important precaution to take before boarding the plane: Do not make any definite promises to your kids about what they're going to have in the new house. This includes bedrooms of their own, swimming pools, a place for a horse, a playroom, or whatever. The only thing you're certain of is indoor plumbing! You don't want to be bound by promises that are too hard to keep. You may find a house with a great pool, but you can't sit on the patio without watching the cars whiz by on the freeway. Or you may come across a big old house with bedrooms to spare but only one bathroom and a leaky roof. There is a great tendency to blackmail kids into moving with promises of the glories to come, but it generally backfires. Your children are going to have enough prejudices against the new town in the days ahead without being disappointed in their new home because you promised something you couldn't deliver. If you can find a place that fulfills all your dreams, great! But usually compromise is the order of the day.

From a woman's point of view, the most exciting thing about the transfer, apart from the raise that hopefully goes with it, is THE NEW HOUSE! I don't know what it is about those words that makes the blood race and the skin prickle with excitement. I guess it's the prospect of starting fresh—like an artist with a new canvas. You can leave your old mistakes—the paneling that made the den too dark, and the drapes that never quite matched the carpet. Or maybe this time you'll get a laundry room on the first floor and a shower stall in the bathroom. Or, glory be, an attached greenhouse! Whatever it is that you've been craving, now's your chance! Just don't have too many preconceived ideas or you may be disappointed.

Hopefully, your husband will have been able to get the lay of the land in the new town prior to your trip. Sometimes he will have to go on ahead to meet the people in the new office or take part in orientation of some kind. If he can arrange a day or two to look around at different neighborhoods or suburbs, it can be extremely helpful in narrowing things down.

Once my husband commuted for months before we were able to sell our home and join him. During the time he was away from us, he did a lot of househunting in the new town. If he came upon a likely prospect, he would get out the Polaroid camera and take a bunch of pictures to bring home to the family on weekends. If he thought the house was a real winner, he would make it a point to get shots of the local schools, tennis clubs, shopping center, and other highlights to pique our interest. Blaze is a born salesman. Having those pictures to mull over at our leisure made the whole family feel they had a part in the house-picking decision.

Blaze has the instincts of Craig Claiborne, and he enjoyed exploring the suburbs of the new city for gourmet delights in the long evenings after work. By the time I arrived to househunt seriously, he knew where to locate the best pizza in town and which Baskin-Robbins was about to run a coupon special. The neighborhood that most appealed to him was an easy commute to those gastronomic emporiums. Airport and office proximity was incidental to Mocha Almond Swirl.

Getting hold of a few issues of the local newspapers in advance can be extremely helpful. Not that you will be able to locate a house from the ads. Real estate ads are notoriously optimistic. For instance, some terms in current use and their literal translations:

"beautifully maintained"—you won't believe how old this house is!

"scenic"—miles from the nearest store

"cozy"—tiny

"modern kitchen"—running water

"prestigious area"—overpriced

"must be seen to be appreciated"—doesn't sound like much, and it isn't!

"rustic" or "quaint"—falling down

"for the handyman"—ditto

"horse country"—the residents all speak with a broad A

"reduced to $ . . ."—overpriced to begin with

"intimate"—one bathroom

"authentic Colonial"—rambling wreck

"antebellum"—ditto

"commuter special"—under the El

"expansion possibilities"—an attic into which you pour money

"cottage for two"—midgets!

"quiet and secluded"—you can be raped in your yard without drawing the attention of nosy neighbors

"impeccably" anything; (decorated, restored, etc.)—you'd better be loaded

"a lot of potential"—likewise, only in this case, you get to provide the "impeccable"

"11 subdividable acres"—swamp

"cute"—Oh, Gawd!

However, the newspapers can give you a line on price levels and which realtors handle what kind of property. Do you want a small lot in a subdivision, or do you want to be in a town with sidewalks

---

and street lights? You can get a good idea of the flavor of the different suburban towns and of the core city itself from the local news, society, and sports pages. An important consideration will be the proximity of your husband's business—also of the airport, if he is the traveling kind.

This brings us to the question of how to locate a good realtor. Reading the newspaper ads, as I said, is one way. In large cities, most agencies specialize to some degree. Some do most of their business in large estates, some limit themselves to smaller properties in subdivisions, and generally there are some invisible geographical lines drawn whether they admit it or not. Friends or business acquaintances in the new town will make recommendations if you ask or even if you don't ask! This can sometimes be hazardous to a budding friendship. Occasionally you and your realtor may not hit it off, and it may be necessary to break off the relationship. Your business friend may develop a case of hard feelings if the realtor was his favorite Aunt Phoebe.

Perhaps you are already lined up with an agent through one of the nationwide referral services in your old town. These firms are multiplying like rabbits throughout the country, and as I said earlier, they will be happy to make an appointment for you with an allied realtor in your new town. For this service they will get a piece of the pie if that agent sells you a house.

This may be a good time to give some hard thought to the question of seeking a home in a neighborhood inhabited by your husband's business associates. The advantages to this are obvious. You will probably be welcomed with open arms and included in the social activities of the wives. But beware of the drawbacks. If your dog Spot tries to make a lunch out of the neighbor's cat Bitsy, and Bitsy belongs to the boss, a tense situation may be in the making. Each to his own, of course, but you should consider all the options.

Arm yourself with two good maps of the new city before you start househunting. This is vital, even if you are under the protective wing of a realtor with a badge in Girl Guides. One map should be a *broad overview* of the area, including all the *major* streets and highways, parks, country clubs, and other landmarks. The second should be a detailed map showing each and every street, school, shopping center, and public building. Incidentally, if you're looking for a house surrounded by a bit of property, circle the areas on the map that show winding streets with a reasonable distance between them. These areas might bear further exploration. The ordinary road maps handed out at gas stations usually don't fill the bill, unless you are neurotically concerned about where you can get your next tankful of Texaco. I've found that the local auto clubs generally have superior maps. Otherwise you can buy good maps for under a dollar at local bookshops, airport magazine stands, drugstores, and sometimes hotels and motels. The Chamber of Commerce is a good lead in small towns. Try to arrange to have the maps in hand before you start out.

We were given a map by a real estate agent the last time we moved, and it was very good in every way except one—the top of the map was actually west, and the bottom was east. Most Americans would be as surprised as we were to see the Mississippi River running east and west! Two years later Blaze still goes into a nervous sweat when anyone says, "Go west for five blocks and then turn south on Jefferson Boulevard." He was never very good about directions, but this was a needless handicap. If you can find the time, orient yourself a little in terms of the airport, your hotel, and your husband's new office before you leave home. Mark these locations on the map, along with the places where any friends or acquaintances are living at present, for reference points.

So you're on your way, armed with the name of a good realtor, and, hopefully, an appointment to do business, your maps of the area, a notebook and a pencil, and your high hopes. Now you may ask, "What do I do with the notebook and pencil?" Easy! You make notes. At least you *or* your husband does. One of you will ride in the front seat with the realtor making animated conversation, and the other rides shotgun in the back, writing like crazy in the notebook.

You may make notes on the house you just looked at if it was at all interesting to you, or you may jot down names of likely-looking subdivisions you pass by in your travels. If you are getting desperate, you may note names of good-looking apartment buildings, or even names of builders taken from signs on construction sites. Avoid, if at all possible, having a realtor show you brand new housing, or houses being built for speculation by a contractor. Often you can save yourself money by dealing directly with the builder—no commision. If you're not driving by too fast, note his name and phone number, and you can call him in the evening from your motel. Evenings are usually the only time you can reach a builder by phone anyway.

If you have your maps handy in the back seat, you can mark the locations of houses that interested you. Then you and your husband can drive by again later when you are alone and give the neighborhood the once-over.

Again, a Polaroid camera is a handy item to have along. With all the houses that you will see, your mind is apt to become fuzzy when discussing them later. A few pictures can ensure that you and your husband are at least arguing about the same house.

Anyone who has ever put her house on the market can curl your hair with horror stories of the *animals* who came to look. You were probably left infuriated or in tears a few times yourself when you were selling yours. Be a courteous looker. Here's the unofficial househunter's code of conduct:

1. Always keep your appointments, unless a genuine disaster strikes. Even if a house looks ghastly from the outside, someone on the inside may have been cleaning since dawn. Don't embarrass your realtor by refusing to even have a quick look.
2. When the owner is on the premises, keep your uncomplimentary comments to yourself—at least until you are back in the car. The walls have ears!
3. If you do come face to face with the owner lurking in a dark hallway, thank her for the opportunity to see her house, and search your mind for something nice to say about it. Examples: "Terrific plastering job," "It must be very convenient to have your bedroom right off the kitchen," or "How clever of you to knit shades for your chandelier!"
4. If you are genuinely interested in the house, and the owner is within earshot, restrain yourself from going on about your master plan for remodeling, doing away with the atrocious color scheme and the icky carpeting. Once the house is yours, do with it what you will, but if you antagonize the owner, you

are apt to set the stage for an unpleasant transaction.

5. Put off having that cigarette until you're back in the car. It's rude to walk through someone's house, dropping cigarette ashes and using her clean ash trays. She may have other lookers coming later, and your smoke will overpower her "Castle Spice" atmosphere. Many people cannot tolerate the odor of cigarettes. Cigars are also taboo, whether you're liberated or not.

6. Be subtle about toilet flushing to check the water pressure and stamping on the floors to see if the joists are sound. It's embarrassing if you crack the plaster.

7. Don't use the brass knuckle technique when grilling the owner about the idiosyncrasies of the house and the makeup of the neighborhood. You can ask almost anything if you do it the right way, but this is where your best tea party technique comes into play.

8. If you must take your offspring along, keep them firmly in hand. Don't allow them to run up and down stairs chasing the owner's cat, pound on the piano, or open the refrigerator. Promise strangulation if they come up with any comments such as "This house stinks!" or "We're not going to live *here*, are we?"

9. If it's the monsoon season, offer to leave your muddy shoes at the door. Quite possibly the seller has her floors freshly polished.

10. Don't overplay your role as enthusiastic prospective buyer, especially when you know the house is not for you. It's just plain cruel to raise the seller's hopes when you have no intention of darkening her door again.

Assuming that you have children, they must be a big consideration in any move that you make. Aren't they always? A new start can be traumatic for kids. With this in mind, it's a good rule of thumb to screen the prospective neighborhood. We once bought a house in an area of relatively substantial homes, lots of rooms sheltering lots of kids, or so we thought. We naturally assumed from the size and newness of the neighboring houses that our children would find loads of other kids in all sizes and ages. Not so! After two or three weeks of total silence in the area during the summer months, we unhappily discovered that we had moved onto a childless street. Oh, there were a few babies and some college age kids, but a fat lot of good this did us with our subteens. Perhaps with the start of school, our five children would find some friends and be happy again. In the meantime they were ready to kill one another, and I was ready to hand them the necessary weapons. Have you ever spent a summer in a hot and humid Midwestern town with no friends and five miserably unhappy offspring? Suicide City! They eventually did meet other children through school, but I spent the year driving from one end of town to the other so that they could have companionship. Fortunately for all of us, (we never did learn to like that town), a terrific offer for my husband from another firm came within a year, and we happily left this pristine, childless neighborhood behind. We had learned another lesson the hard way.

During our next househunting safari, before making a definite commitment on the house that we fell in love with, my husband and I literally knocked on doors of nearby homes, introduced ourselves, explained our situation, and inquired about the child population. I remember Blaze rolling down the car window to question two teenage girls passing by the house we were considering and asking them where they attended school, what grade they were in, and where they lived. I'm sure they thought he was a dirty old man, but he obtained the information that we needed. Another good idea, and not quite as incriminating, is to make a phone call to the local Board of Education and ask for a headcount of children in your prospective area. School personnel can be helpful in this type of situation and are usually very willing to help newcomers.

One suburban town we were considering used a private bus company to transport students to and from school. After checking with the company, I was able to determine just how many pickups were made within surrounding blocks of our prospective new home. I was also able to learn the age groups, as the buses made separate trips to the elementary, junior, and senior high schools. One or two phone calls can help you obtain much information and eliminate a great deal of loneliness for your youngsters later on.

Your real estate salesperson may be helpful with problems

such as these, but let's face it, if she is not personally involved in the workings and makeup of the neighborhood, she just won't have all the answers to your particular and unique problems. Better to be a do-it-yourselfer in some situations.

Along the same lines, it may be important to you to be close to the church or synagogue of your choice if you are a one-car family. The kids can walk or ride their bikes to church activities and you may be able to leave your chauffeur's cap on the hook for a few hours. It may be helpful to call the church or synagogue office and ask if there are families from the neighborhood in attendance. This personal call can provide a twofold benefit. One, you gather information concerning the religious makeup of the neighborhood, and two, you have introduced yourself to the church. They will be aware of your arrival and will most likely make an effort to seek you out and welcome you into the fold.

Before it is assumed by the reader that I am advocating that your children are to be the most important consideration in a move, let me set you straight. Yes, it is indeed important that your children be happy and contented in their new home, and you should do all in your power to insure that this be so. At the same time, there is a purely selfish motive. Any of the millions of women who have moved many times has surely learned that if the family traumas are lessened, the husband enjoys his new position and surroundings, and the children become busy and active members of the young social structure, the mother/wife role becomes that much easier and more satisfying. A trait that mothers of the world have in common is in evidence here. We are more likely to be happy and contented when those we love are happy and contented. The converse is also true. There is nothing quite so heartbreaking as seeing a young child, or for that matter, an older child, dreading the coming school day because no one talks to him, and he feels completely alone. Children can be cruel to one another, as we all know, and everyone in the family hurts when one member is hurting. If, by making a few well-directed phone calls to the proper sources before making a final commitment to a house and a neighborhood, you are able to alleviate this loneliness for your child, it's well worth the little time and effort. Practically speaking, too, the neighborhood that houses future friends and schoolmates for your offspring no doubt contains future social contacts for you as parents and adults.

As I have mentioned, sometimes even before you start your househunt, you may be able to narrow an area down. Suburbs have sprung up all around our cities. By getting in touch with the local Chamber of Commerce and obtaining all the available literature pertaining to the various suburbs outside the city proper, you can determine property values, tax rates, school ratings, community-sponsored activities, recreation facilities, and so much more. You should know what your economic situation is and what you can afford for living accomodations, so you will not embark on a househunting expedition in a state of complete disorientation.

I recently talked to a woman who was moving to Atlanta. She had pretty much settled on a particular suburb within commuting distance of her husband's office, with several attractive homes that suited her family's needs. After a busy morning of househunting she and her real estate agent stopped off for a quick sandwich and a cup of coffee in a small shopping center that served the neighborhood she was interested in. The luncheonette was crowded with high-school students who were apparently cutting classes. The real estate agent told her that the local high school maintained an open campus policy and that the students were allowed to come and go and assume responsibility for their own actions. The woman had already had problems with her teen's school attendance, so she knew this was not for her and decided to look elsewhere. You can usually pick up the flavor of a neighborhood and its residents by browsing around its stores and keeping your eyes and ears open. A little eavesdropping while you sip a Coke can often give a clearer insight into the character of a town than hours of touring with a realtor.

We once fell head over heels for a house in one of Cincinnati's loveliest suburbs. We knew that we would be reaching, pricewise, but the intended house was really a dandy. The choice had been narrowed down to three houses; this one was a bit over our budget, and two others that were attractive and would satisfy our family needs and pocketbook. Unable to come to a decision, Blaze decided that it would be a good idea to bring our teenagers to town for the weekend and listen to their comments.

It was a beautiful spring Saturday—the kind of day for working in the yard, planting, readying flower beds and cleaning up winter's discards. The kind of day in which our family enjoys grubbing in our oldest jeans and sneakers in the yard.

As we drove along the winding road that led to our number-one choice, we opened the car windows and listened to the birds and sound of mowers doing their thing on greening, growing lawns. In the driveways of the neighboring homes stood well-equipped lawn maintenance trucks. No teenagers manned the mowers to help out good old Mom and Dad. Only pro's worked this area, it seemed. As we neared the house to be considered, we passed a distinguished elderly gentleman led on a leash by his impressive Afghan hound. The gentleman was nattily attired in a Brooks Brothers houndstooth jacket and sported a jaunty Swiss walking hat. He was quite debonair and reminded me of Walter Pidgeon in *Mrs. Miniver*. A voice from the back seat said, "Molly would really hate this place!" "Yeah, and so would Dad!" said another. They were right. Molly is a large black Newfoundland, short on manners, who loves to chase rocks and stalk butterflies, and is a true "klutz." Well-behaved Afghan hounds would never be Molly's cup of tea! Dad's idiosyncracy and also his greatest pleasure is grubbing in the yard on warm weather weekends. He dons the most bedraggled outfits that Goodwill refuses to accept and generally causes embarrassment to all family members if he should be seen by outsiders who don't know how well he cleans up! (He has built beautiful and lasting stone walls from Massachusetts to Missouri, laid sod by the yard and brick patios by the foot, painted and pruned wherever we have landed.) Without a word we turned the car around and drove out of the lovely neighborhood and bought one of the other houses, where we lived happily ever after for two or three years. Molly continued to stalk the butterflies and carry her rocks and Dad happily continued his spring projects getting as grubby as he wanted.

You know better than anyone else just what you require in housing, and you must tell the realtors what you need rather than having *them* tell *you*. Always keep in mind that the agent's primary interest is her commission. You are the buyer. You must stay in control of the situation. We once had a realtor who drove us from one end of the city and back again and never really took the time to find out just what we, the buyers, wanted. She had houses to show, particularly those that she had listed, and she was determined to show them to us regardless of our requirements. Finally, after a few futile, frustrating hours, Blaze called a time-out, pulled into a coffee shop, and on a paper napkin drew a plan of the house that we were regretfully leaving, down to room sizes and layout, lot size, and style. We told her about our school needs and community interests and, of course, price range. We packed her off to her office and asked her to call us when she found something comparable. Having a large family and a small zoo and assorted paraphernalia, ranging from a nine-foot grandfather clock to a collection of large rocks gathered in the Smoky Mountains, we needed quite a bit of room. This agent had stubbornly insisted on showing us small houses that we could add onto or large ones needing massive remodeling. Our tastes are traditional rather than contemporary—we are nuts about center-hall Colonials—yet we looked at some terrific cantilevered places that Frank Lloyd Wright might have designed, but not for us! The following weekend this well-intentioned lady had discovered four houses for us to look at that approximated what we were searching for, and we were able to make a final decision quickly.

Of course, you may want a complete change of style, or perhaps you need something larger or smaller than what you are leaving. Fine. But be firm; stick to your guns, and get what *you* want. Real estate people often feel that if you see a house, maybe you'll fall in love with it, and they'll have a sale. Generally, their listing books are jam-packed with property, and you can spend days on wild-goose chases and accomplish nothing. I have always thought that if I were in real estate I would take the time to get to know my customers, their wants and needs in a home, and something about their family situation and age groups. Actually, this can be done over a cup of coffee in a short span of time and, in fact, can speed up the process for all concerned. After all, a house is probably your largest and most important purchase, and the search for it should involve a great deal of thought and care—but not necessarily time!

One more word about your realtor—try to avoid getting too chummy! No matter how friendly and interested she seems, remember that this is a business deal. Just because you've practically lived together for a week and your sisters went to the same college, don't think you *have* to buy a house from her, like it or not. You don't need to feel indebted. This is the realtor's *business.* If you find yourself calling in the evenings to get ideas on remodeling the kitchen of the last house you looked at, you've gone too far. One agent that I worked with for a week became such a pal that we saw each other after we moved in. Until she made a pass at Blaze, that is! That was unusual, though. Usually you will be ignored after the papers are signed, no matter what buddies you thought you were. Regardless of what she implied, you'll never be invited to her bridge club! Remember that she is in this for money. Don't ask for too much advice. *You* and *your family* will have to live in the house you buy. Check out facts on schools, club memberships, neighbors, etc. yourself, at the source. Some friends of mine bought a house with swimming privileges at a private beach in the neighborhood, or so they were told. After the closing they discovered that it was going to cost them a bundle to swim because their house was on the wrong side of the street. Don't rely too much on hearsay.

Pay a visit to the school your children will be attending. *Who* says it is "triple A rated," and exactly what does that mean? Most principals welcome your visit and are only too happy to tell you about the wonderful opportunities awaiting your children in their school. One reliable indicator of a good school system is class size, the average number of children in each classroom. (This differs from the "teacher-pupil ratio" where all the supplementary teachers are counted, such as gym, art, music, remedial reading, etc. Not that these teachers aren't indicators of a good school. They are, but they don't reduce class size.) High teachers' salaries are usually another indicator of a good system. Even good teachers are subject to the profit motive, so the system that can pay most usually gets the pick of the crop. *If* you have some basis for comparison, achievement test scores can be informative. Many schools administer the same standardized tests, and the school system's scores can be compared with national averages, as well as with the median scores of the system from which you are coming.

Have the principal give you an informal tour of the building, including a visit to a class or two in operation, and you will be able to tell more about the system than any discussion of educational philosophy can tell you. Every parent with children in school has a particular interest in some phase of education, even if it's just the hot lunch program. You can ask casually about these things as you walk through the building. The last time we were househunting, we had narrowed things down to a big old house that I loved in a quiet suburban town. I went over to have a look at the elementary school my children would be attending if we bought that house. As I walked through the hall on my way to the principal's office, I was immediately impressed with one thing— SILENCE! My footsteps echoed down the empty corridors. The principal gave me a tour of the building, and in each classroom the children sat in orderly rows busily working—QUIET! The teachers ruled their domains from big desks at the front of the rooms, and they all seemed to be approaching retirement age. My kids were coming from an open classroom, team-teaching situation where there was lots of freedom, and noise, and movement, and I feared that they might find the adjustment to a self-contained classroom too difficult. Once you let the genie out of the bottle, it's hard to put him back in! This is not to say that one type of teaching is better than another. Highly informed people have been debating that question for years. It was just a matter of what my kids would feel comfortable with. We went to House Number Two on our list which was in a neighboring town, where I found a more relaxed atmosphere in the schools.

Even if you have no school children in your family, and no plans for any, it's smart to have a home in a town with a respected school system. It pays off when it comes to that old familiar villain, RESALE. For the family that is subject to transfer, a prime consideration in the choice of house has to be the likelihood of quick resale. You don't want to be stuck with a house that won't sell when it's time to move on again. Some friends of ours, a childless couple, having learned from bitter experience, now always buy in a town with a good school system. They once were stuck for over a year trying to sell a house in a town with school problems.

It's wise to check out the condition of the existing school buildings. If they resemble the set of the Towering Inferno after the fire, a move may be under way to build new ones. Are the schools on double sessions? Even in these days of declining enrollments, rapid expansion of a town may mean a school building program and a subsequent tax increase.

There's an old realtor's bromide about the three most important factors in the sale of a house—location, location, and location. Homes in some communities move faster than those in others for many reasons. You just have to know which are the desirable neighborhoods, not all the reasons for their popularity.

After you have found a house that is *you*, and you are sure that this is the home you really want (and to be honest, this can happen in a day or can go on for months, much like falling in love), take ten. Don't allow yourselves to be rushed into a quick decision. Invariably, the agent is going to tell you that there are at least two other customers on the verge of submitting a contract. This has been the case with every house we have ever been interested in, whether it has been on the market for six years or is still in the process of being built. Don't be panicked into making an offer. You and your husband should sit down quietly together, preferably in a cozy cocktail lounge and, without any outside interference, weigh your decision carefully. Suppose the house oozes with charm, has lovely old shade trees and a great yard for kids, but is rather old, and needs lots of paper and paint, and a general sprucing up? Are you good at papering, painting and sprucing? What about the size of that lovely yard? Does your touch mean death to geraniums and are you allergic to yard work? If so, can you afford a lawn service? And what about the tranquility of the location? Complete quiet and serenity can become pure unadulterated hell if you are married to a traveling man and long for the sound of adult voices. Maybe you are a one-car family, and the closest grocery store is miles away. How do you manage when you need a loaf of bread? On the other hand, some people, though basically very congenial, just don't want to see neighbors every time they step out the door. If all the houses literally share a common backyard, this can be a problem.

As a young wife and new mother with a husband who had

just completed his two-year stint of military duty, and after living in tiny quarters on an air force base, I eagerly looked forward to our first civilian home. Blaze accepted a fine offer from a small company with good potential—and very low pay—in Massachusetts. Out of financial necessity, we decided to rent. We longed for a house after our confining apartment, and we located a big, old, sixteen-room frame house with a view of the ocean from the master bedroom—if the wind was blowing and the trees leaned the right way. We had passed with flying colors a complete interrogation by the very proper and ladylike owner of the house and came to a satisfactory agreement, or so we thought. We were ecstatic! Moving day was in November, as dreary a month as there can be in New England. The house was cold on that day, and it became colder—and colder—and colder! We soon discovered that this house had been used as a summer home and had very little insulation. But we were young, and it was romantic to huddle by the fireplace every evening and make a mad dash to the bedroom in our flannel pajamas. There were a few other hitches to the deal, and they soon began to wear us down. My young, ambitious, moving-up-the-ladder-of-success husband had to do a great deal of traveling. To be precise, he would leave early Monday morning and return late Friday night. I occupied my time with exhilarating, stimulating conversations with two babies. There were no neighbors to speak of. The lovely rambling house just across the road turned out to be a rest home for the aged and infirm, and the house next door was used strictly as a summer home. Winter arrived, and it snowed, and snowed, and snowed, but somehow we survived. When our lease was up, we promptly bought a smaller house in a development with other young couples where we lived happily—and warmly—for several years.

A converse situation arose some years later. Our children were all well past the toddler stage and growing quickly, rapidly approaching their teens. Unable to find an adequate house to buy in the new city, we located a very nice rental. Eager to be together after months of commuting, we took the house fortunately on a no-lease basis. (We had learned *something* from prior experiences, after all!) The house itself was great, and it fit us beautifully. The fly in the ointment was *too much* neighborhood. There were children wall-to-wall, and since it was summertime, these "flies" were always out *en masse*, and the noise was constant. The older children were outside at ten or eleven at night, playing basketball and shooting BB's at the newly installed picture windows of nearby homes under construction. The younger neighborhood kids were sent out to play at 7 A.M. I would awaken to the sound of Big Wheels, go-carts and minibikes thundering and clattering under our bedroom window. There was constant turmoil, and the noise level was unbelievable. After two months we gave notice to the landlord, found another house to buy, and preserved our sanity.

These two houses were bad choices on our part. In the first instance, being young and naive, we thought of the excitement of living in a large house, and neglected to consider the drawbacks. In the second situation we again let our emotions be our guide. The family had been apart for a number of months, and we all wanted to be together at any cost. A noble thought indeed, but we had neglected to think of the little idiosyncracies that were present in our family makeup, and let's face it, we all have them. We particularly enjoy a sense of privacy. We like friends and companions, but we also enjoy doing things together as a family. I mention these two instances to illustrate again that each family is unique, and that during a moving period the qualities that are important to you as a family should be considered.

Once in a lifetime, however, you may stumble across a house that seems to select you instead of your selecting it. It may be a cozy New England hip roof nestled in the hills of Vermont, or a pink adobe hacienda surrounded by curious-looking cacti in New Mexico. No matter. The one thing that can make all the moves worthwhile is to live in THE house. Now THE house for us, unfortunately, was not my THE house. Oh, it was a beauty—lovely, charming, and gracious—historic, too. It was the kind of house that Sunday drivers passed very slowly, hoping to catch just a glimpse of the interior. They took pictures and pretended to take the wrong turn so that they could drive along the circular driveway and under the magnificent portico. A big house, a huge house, a hard-to-clean house that yearned for a staff and gardeners but had only me and whomever I could grab to carry a load of folded laundry up "the servant's" back stairs. It was Blaze's THE house and always will be.

The love affair began after fruitless weeks of househunting. We had looked at everything on the market, new and old, loved and neglected, compact or spacious, even houses that were much more than the budget would allow. We had begun to rationalize on this point. We were reaching the desperate hours that all would-be house buyers suffer through if they have been at it long enough. I had returned to our already-sold home with a heavy heart, sore feet, and a conciliatory pat on the cheek, and the words I have come to know so well, "Don't worry, honey. I'll find something for us soon."

The following days changed the course of my husband's life. It came about quite by accident. Blaze was in the real estate office going through the listing sheets with a fine-tooth comb when someone said, "Did you hear that the Baker house came on the market this morning?"

"It's a great house," someone else said, "but it's so big. Nobody in his right mind would buy it today with the cost of heat and upkeep. It needs so much updating!"

Those magical words piqued the intrepid Blaze's interest. With a gleam in his eye he quietly asked our agent to check it out. She made an appointment to see the house that very afternoon.

It was destiny. As in all great love stories, Blaze had yearned in his heart for this very house as he made his evening rounds looking for a place to live. The house was the unattainable lady, the dream of the young man that still lingered in the heart of the domesticated, middle-aged man. Here was success. This was what would make all the struggles worthwhile. And now it was within arm's reach!

The present owners had lived in the house many years, raising five children, and the now-elderly gentleman was leaving his house with mixed emotions. He loved to work in the spacious gardens, growing and tending his fruits and vegetables and specimen flowers and trees, but now the family's needs had dwindled as the children had grown and scattered, and they felt that it was time to move on. They loved the house that held so many happy memories, and they wanted it to be loved and cared for as they had cared for it, to house children again, to be enjoyed for all its comforts. A rapport sprang up between the two men the moment that Blaze was introduced to the gardens. (Blaze has such a kelly-green thumb that I live in fear that it will spread to the rest of his body!)

That evening my phone rang, and I knew immediately that this was it. "I found it!" he said. "It's got 6600 square feet of living space, and it stretches 106 feet across the front. And you should see the gardens!" I hadn't heard that tone of wonder and love since Blaze had whispered in my girlish ears the first tentative words of affection, "I'm nuts about you."

As he described THE house, I learned that it was unbelievable and big, charming and big, architecturally perfect and big, and he had to have it. I was to fly up the next day and take a look at this wonder. "Honey, you're really going to love it!"

Mother Nature was on Blaze's side that momentous day. The sun was shining brightly (something it didn't often do in this midwestern city on the shore of one of the gloomier Great Lakes). The roses were beginning to open and the scent was heavenly. (I didn't get even a whiff of the steel mills until later when the wind changed direction.) The rare cherry tree given to the first owner of the house by the Japanese government fifty years before was in full dress to greet me. The sunshine glittered on the multipaned windows, and inside the crystal chandeliers gleamed. The wide stair treads squeaked comfortably in welcome. There was a butler's pantry with a hammered pewter sink used by a real butler in the house's heyday. A servant's call box on the kitchen wall intrigued me. There were crown moldings and sculptured ceilings in the dining room and a maid's bell on the floor. The thirty-five-foot sunken living room had three sets of French doors opening onto a beautiful awning-covered terrace paved with imported quarry tile. The garden was a green thumbers' dream, with its flowering apples and Damson plums, rare poppies, and peonies in shades of pink bordering a flagstone walk leading down through the back lawns. There were asparagus beds and Brussels sprouts, a huge grape arbor, and even a few rows of corn hidden in a corner of the grounds. What lovely weddings we would give in this perfect setting!

Our realtor had taken to her bed after a few weeks of trying to find a pleasing house for the crazy man I live with, so our tour guide was the last remaining daughter of the family. She had been raised in the house and was not happy that it was to be sold. She warmed to us gradually as she realized that we had succumbed to the charms of the house. She showed me the secret panel in the phone room tucked beneath the stairs where she and her sisters had played and hidden from their mother. This had been a happy home, and I began to feel that its good fortune would shine on my family too. We spent almost two hours taking in all the details of the house and enjoying the stories that had taken place here. It was one of the most pleasant afternoons I have ever spent. As we were about to leave, the young woman handed me a well-worn book and said, "Take this with you and read it tonight. It will tell you more about the history and the original owner of the house." I thanked her and glanced at the title, *The Life and Times of Newton D. Baker*. As we drove under the massive portico and down the driveway, I reached for Blaze's hand, smiled warmly and said, "Dear, I love it too. But who the hell is Newton D. Baker?"

We made the best offer we could afford, and I still think it was accepted for sentimental reasons, since it was way too low. We spent three happy and proud years enjoying THE house, even though we all worked harder than we ever had to work before or since. We painted and papered, freshened up and modernized, and gardened and gardened and gardened. I learned how to make Damson plum preserves for Christmas gifts for my neighbors. I served fresh asparagus from our garden during the spring, and we lived on zucchini all summer long prepared in a hundred different ways. (Since then I've often wondered why the United States government doesn't send zucchini seeds to India? A few plants could feed all of the starving hordes of the world!) And I had fresh flowers in almost every room from early summer to late fall. It was a thrill and a privilege to know that it was our home even for a short time. I didn't live there long enough to put on one of those weddings, though.

We still have the original set of blueprints, and every once in a while Blaze will spread them out and lovingly look at each page for hours at a time. If it's very quiet, and I tiptoe past the room, I can just make out the words, "Damn!" Sixty-six hundred square feet of living space! And a hundred and six feet across the front!" I know that Blaze will never fully recover from the love affair, and I also know that no other house can take the place of THE house. I can only say to him, "After all, it's better to have lived in it and left, than never to have lived in it at all." Newton D. Baker, by the way, was at one time mayor of Cleveland, and later, Secretary of War under President Wilson. But crowning all his other accomplishments, he sure knew how to build a sensational house.

Seldom does the right house fall into your lap as this one did. It usually takes a lot of digging and some compromising. Keep a list of the possibles, and arrange them in numerical order—first choice, second choice, third choice. Keep revising this list as you look. If you are given listing sheets with pertinent data and pictures of the houses you are interested in, keep them handy and go over them in the evenings in your motel. Make notes of any questions you have about them to ask your realtor the next day.

Generally three or four solid days of looking should be sufficient for most areas if you have been shown the kind of thing you're looking for. After four days, the mind and body won't absorb more, and it's time to get down to the nitty-gritty. That is the business of making an offer, and then making a deal.

What to do if you really can't find a house that you can stand? Hopefully this won't happen to you, but if it does, there are four ways you can go:

1. Most companies give the wife just one house hunting trip, and that is usually limited to a week, but you can come back later at your own expense, of course.
2. You can go home and leave the house buying to your husband.

Very risky. I've never done this, but I've known people who did. It puts the husband in a very vulnerable position. The wife may never stop telling people that she hates the house he bought. I think it's better to make your mistakes jointly. If you go home and let your husband keep on looking, be sure to come back to put your seal of approval on the house before he signs the papers.

3. You can look for a place to rent on a short-term basis. This is a bad deal if there are children involved. In effect it amounts to two moves with all the attendant hassle. By the time you are finally settled somewhere, you'll probably be transferred again, so keep the moves to a minimum. Of course, renting does give you a chance to familiarize yourself with the area before you buy, if you think there's a chance you might be "permanent," whatever that is!

4. This brings me to the forth alternative—you can build a house. Having done this twice myself, I can tell you that it has its pleasures and pains. Among the pleasures is the chance to be really creative and to get the kind of home you've always wanted. Building takes longer, however. You need an honest contractor and an ironclad contract, and you must be a good enough sport to leave your creation when the next transfer comes.

The one thing to remember during this trauma is DON'T PANIC! There's got to be a house for you somewhere in this town!

WHAT EVERY WOMAN SHOULD KNOW

About appraisals The mysteries of the contract About contingencies and negotiations The ins and outs of mortgages The thrills and chills of the closing.

I really do feel sorry for realtors facing several days with "out-of-towners," as we are known in the trade. It's grueling, to say the least. They have to be up every morning and in the office to check the new listings, and then pick up the clients at their motel after grabbing a cup of coffee on the run. They show houses all day, stopping only for a quick lunch and a sprint to the phone booth to make some more appointments. They work until darkness falls or client exhaustion sets in, whichever happens first. Family needs and personal life have to be set aside until the clients find a house or bolt for another agent. If the clients do find a house that satisfies them, then the stomach-churning, ulcer-producing process of offer and counter-offer begins. The only people on whom this ordeal is harder than on the realtor is the couple who needs the house! This is really a harrowing experience for the buyers because they have much more than a commission to gain or lose. They are not only about to take a flyer with their financial security, but also with the future comfort and happiness and well-being of all members of the family.

It's tempting to jump at the first habitable piece of property you see, but don't be too eager to write out a check. If you have any doubts about the true value of the property, get a quick appraisal before you make an offer. A good appraiser will inspect the house and then estimate its worth as compared to that of other property that has recently been sold in the area. His appraisal will be based primarily on the square footage of living area, resale value, replacement cost, structural quality, condition of the exterior and interior, and neighborhood. An appraisal is an especially good idea if you are considering an older home. Their true worth is usually more difficult to discern than that of a spanking new house in a subdivision of homes that are selling like hotcakes.

If you don't have time to get an appraisal, here's a simple guide for figuring a realistic price for the house you're considering. Find out from your realtor or a local contractor the current buildings costs per square foot of housing in the area. Multiply this figure by the square footage of the house in question and add the price of the lot.

Example:

Square footage of house	2,300
Local building cost per sq. ft.	×$30.
	$69,000
Cost of building lot	+$10,000
	$79,000

There are, of course, variables. If the house is in first-class condition and has lots of extras, you will have to pay more. On the other hand, if the porch ceiling is about to tumble down and there are water stains on the dining room ceiling, and you tripped over the warped parquet flooring in the hall, your offer should be much lower than your thumbnail appraisal.

If you are considering any additions or alterations to the property, such as a pool, a fence, or a garage, now is the time to investigate the local building regulations to make sure they will be allowed.

While you are being objective, decide once again whether you can truly afford the house you are considering. As a general rule of thumb, the experts agree that the price of the home should be no more than two and one-half times your annual income. And bankers advise that your mortgage payment (including insurance and taxes) shouldn't exceed one-fourth of your monthly take-home pay. These are not hard and fast rules, and prospective lenders will consider your other assets as well as your financial obligations when you go shopping for a mortgage.

If, after a sleepless night of agonizing over the alternatives, you decide to make an offer, a contract is drawn up and submitted to the seller's agent. A time limit is specified—generally twelve to twenty-four hours—during which the seller may accept the offer or reject it, or he may counter with an offer of his own. This is a period of negotiation, and it is nerve-racking for everyone concerned. Husband and wife may retire to their motel to fight about the choice, or they may want to keep looking at other houses as insurance in case this one falls through. Of course, meeting the seller's asking price and conditions avoids a lot of this stress, but that is not always practical or advisable. Many sellers tack a much higher price on a house than fair market value dictates, just to "test the water," so to speak, so don't be afraid to bid low. Some sellers aren't afraid to ask an unconscionable price! The process of offer and counteroffer helps you determine the true worth of the property.

Not all sellers are realistic, so don't waste too much time if they won't entertain your offer. Once, after deciding that the run-down condition of an older home warranted only a moderate square footage bid, we offered exactly half of the asking price of the house. (It did have possibilities, if one was handy and determined.) The owner, an elderly widow who thought her house was still in great shape and was emotionally wrapped up in the place, refused to counteroffer. That negotiation took place over three years ago. The house is still on the market. Some buyers submit an offer labeled as "final." Then the seller just has to say yes or no. This shortens the negotiations, but it also cuts off your options. I doubt that Henry Kissinger would approve.

What is this mysterious contract, anyway? It is the initial purchase agreement, and it is usually drawn up on a standard form agreed upon by all the realtors in the area. It contains blanks to be filled in with the pertinent data. The essential information should include:

1. The price you offer to pay for the property.
2. A legal description of the property. This is not just the address, but also exact dimensions and location of the lot in surveyor's lingo.
3. The amount of earnest money you are offering as a binder. As I have said, this money will be held in escrow until the closing, when it will become part of your down payment.
4. Any items you expect to be included in the sale, such as carpeting, portable air conditioners, fireplace equipment, appliances, or whatever. Don't make too many assumptions in this area. Some people take everything with them, including the curtain rods and the light bulbs!
5. The date you wish to close the deal and take occupancy of the house.

6. The date and exact hour of the day when your offer expires.
7. Any contingency clauses you wish to include, such as termite inspection (which is standard in some areas), building or structural inspection (including electrical and plumbing systems, roofing, etc.), and your ability to arrange financing for the mortgage.
8. Provision that your earnest money will be returned if the deal falls through for any reason except that you didn't live up to your side of the agreement.

The contingency clauses are an extremely important part of the contract. They protect your earnest money and, in some cases, they can help you pull out of a deal that for one reason or another has lost its attractiveness.

Let's be honest. When you were selling your house, you went through all sorts of gyrations to cover up or hide some of those eyesores that you had come to know and hate. Well, didn't you quickly paint the basement walls to conceal the water marks from the last gully washer? Or how come you told the kids, "No flushing unless absolutely necessary!" This was no time for the septic tank to back up. Admit it, there is probably a little larceny in all our souls, and even though the present owners of the house you are considering are lovely and helpful people, keep in mind that there are very few so-called perfect houses. Let us work from that premise. Your prospective home also has its kinks. The problem is to find out just what they are before *you* are the owner.

I once looked at a house that was to my eyes a dream come true. It was a large, pillared Southern Colonial set on a lovely knoll, shaded by big old trees. Before my eyes floated visions of myself as an older but no less fascinating Scarlett O'Hara (*before* the siege of Atlanta), gliding grandly down the circular staircase to my adoring family. My enthusiasm was contagious, and Blaze agreed to submit a contract, but he specified a building inspection contingency clause. The inspector duly arrived, and he was quick to point out the ceilings that didn't quite meet the walls at the corners, the dark stains on the bedroom ceilings, indicating a leaky roof, and the sub-substandard electrical wiring. The termite inspection revealed that my majestic pillars were on their last legs and were ready to crumble if anyone leaned against them! We got our check back.

There is a definite need to be a bit hard-nosed when you are buying a home. *Any* home, old or new. Inserting these inspection clauses is a good way to alleviate a great many problems, both emotional and financial. If there is a swimming pool on the property, get a reliable pool contractor to look it over. If the worst is discovered—the darn thing leaks like a sieve—maybe you should have second thoughts. If you are wild about the house, and after careful thought and reliable estimates of what the cost of repairs will be, you decide to buy it anyway, you are in a terrific negotiating position.

In some areas the seller won't entertain any other offers while your contract is under consideration, but this is not true everywhere. You should know the local procedure before you make your offer, especially if the traffic is heavy with other people looking at the house. That could affect your strategy.

If the seller should make a counteroffer, you will be allowed a specified period of time to consider that offer and respond. Once both the buyer and seller have signed the contract, though, it becomes a binding agreement, and you will be ready to locate your mortgage money.

Many couples suffer from an attack of cold feet the morning after they have signed the contract. Realtors recognize this as the "buyer's remorse syndrome." Young couples buying their first house are most subject to this affliction, but even experienced home buyers have been known to come down with a bad case. If you feel the symptoms coming on—sweaty palms, difficulty drawing a deep breath, and a tendency to huddle in a corner with your legs drawn up in the fetal position—try to recognize it for what it is, a normal reaction to the prospect of signing away your life's savings for the next thirty years!

If you truly feel that you've made a bad mistake, you may be able to bail out of the deal on one of the contingency clauses. If not, you may lose a few thousand dollars of earnest money after some harrowing negotiations for a release from the seller. He can legally force you to conclude the purchase.

Blaze once bought a house on his own after spending a

grueling morning at the dentist's having a root canal job. His appointment to see the house with the agent was at one o'clock. At one thirty, sitting in the car outside the house, he scribbled an earnest money check, handed it to the ecstatic agent, and took off in a swirl of dust for the airport and a weekend home. My woman's intuition was working overtime, and I suggested that I fly back with him on Sunday to take a look at the new house, just in case.

It didn't remotely resemble the description that Blaze had painted for me. The "spacious" rooms were actually grand broom closets; there were a few spindly twigs that would be trees— someday in the very distant future—and a few tufts of onion grass in what passed for the front yard. The house did have a view, though not one to tickle my aesthetic fancy. We would be able to pass the warm sunny days sitting on the back porch, picking out license plates on the cars as they made their way along the interstate to Chicago. Poor Blaze was stricken.

My reaction is better left undescribed. We realized that the pain killers that Blaze had been given for the root canal had obviously given him a lovely "high," and everything had looked wonderful to him. Thank the Lord for contingency clauses! Luckily the bank showed a slight hesitation in granting the loan. They felt the price was a little steep, Blaze didn't press the issue, and we were able to bail out on the mortgage contingency. Incidentally, that was the first and last time Blaze bought a house on his own.

I am admittedly no financial wizard. I follow my husband around the country signing my name wherever he tells me to, and thanking God that I have him to put those little x's on the lines where my signature goes. (The one drawback to this very convenient arrangement is that someday I may unwittingly sign myself into a mental institution!) Nevertheless, by repeated exposure and the miracle of osmosis, I have absorbed quite a few bits and pieces of information concerning the mysterious world of mortgage financing that I will now pass on to the uninitiated.

Basically, there are three types of mortgages— conventional, FHA, and VA. Conventional mortgages are the easiest to get because the interest rates are higher, and so the banks like the business. Sometimes when money is tight, even

---

conventional loans are hard to obtain. In order to secure a conventional mortgage, you may have to cough up as much as 20 percent of the purchase price as your down payment, sometimes more. This is a lot of money, but you don't necessarily have to have it in the bank. It can come from the equity you have in your old house, assuming you have a house to sell.

FHA stands for Federal Housing Authority. They do not loan money. Their function is to insure a loan that you get from a bank or other lending institution. FHA makes it possible to buy a house with as little as 10 percent down payment, if the borrower is considered a good risk. Because the government stipulates a low interest rate on the loan, banks have a limited number of FHA mortgage dollars available. Conventional loans pay them a better return on their investment, which is what banking is all about.

The third type of mortgage, the VA loan, is similar to the FHA loan, except that it is granted only to eligible veterans or servicemen. The Veteran's Administration insures the loan, and it, too, is made at a lower rate of interest than conventional loans and requires a smaller down payment.

Our first experience in home buying provides a good example of mortgage financing. We had found a tiny new Cape Cod that we could just barely afford. We had a nest egg as big as a hummingbird's for the down payment, so since Blaze was eligible, we applied for a VA loan. So far, so good. When we arrived on the scene with our furniture, our two babies, and our handful of cash, prepared to close the deal, the builder was ready, we were ready, but the VA wasn't. The property had failed to pass the inspector's perc test, meaning that the drainage for the sewage disposal system was inadequate. (Later we realized that this was a problem shared by the whole neighborhood. Our subdivision became known around town as Cesspool Hollow, a fitting epithet if one were to judge by the odors wafting over our patios on a warm evening.)

Young and naive, we were unruffled by this minor detail. Besides, we needed a place to lay our heads, so when the builder offered to rent us the house for a nominal per diem figure until the hang-up could be worked out, we readily agreed. Weeks went by while the builder wrangled with the VA over the particulars of filling and grading and drainage. Looking after our interests, the VA wanted him to install a septic tank, but the crusty Nova Scotian couldn't justify the expense at the price we had contracted to pay. Besides, he had planned cesspools for the rest of the subdivision, and he couldn't afford the expensive precedent. Meanwhile we squatted in the house with a growing sense of concern.

This state of affairs stretched into five long months, until April, when at the height of a violent spring thunderstorm the house was struck by lightning. Even a blithering idiot could recognize that as some kind of omen!

"Get me out of here!" was my response. We didn't own the house and didn't even have a lease. Now it was a shambles, with a burned-out roof and floors sloshing in water from the combined efforts of the fire department and Mother Nature. We moved in with a neighbor, and I started househunting immediately.

That stroke of lightning was just the kind of catalyst we needed. Overnight, the builder became cooperative. He didn't want the property on his hands either, now that it was uninhabitable. It might take months to find another pair of buyers and his business was in urgent need of an injection of funds. He offered to put the house back together again, redecorate it completely (what woman could resist that?) correct the drainage, and lend us the extra money we needed for a down payment on a conventional loan—at no interest. Sold!

Through pure dumb luck, that disaster turned out to be one of the better deals we have ever fallen into. With a larger down payment, we were able to build up equity in the house more quickly, and when we were transferred again and sold the house, we came out of it with a nice little bundle of cash to put down on a bigger house. As everyone knows, that's the name of the game!

It's considered good form to shop around for mortgage money to make sure you are getting the best deal. Interest rates can vary a bit. In some places it is customary to pay "points." This sounds confusing, but it is simply a commission you pay to the bank for lending you the money. Then they give you a little passbook and allow you to pay interest on the money for another twenty-five or thirty years besides! When money is tight and mortgages are hard to arrange, your corporation may be able to direct you to a bank where it has some influence. Consider this a fringe benefit.

It's a very common practice for a bank to impose a "prepayment penalty" on a mortgage loan. This means that if you should pay off the loan before the twenty-five years or whatever is up, you have to pay extra for the privilege. This is not for corporate gypsies! Be sure to insert a clause waiving the prepayment penalty in the event of a transfer.

If you can arrange an "assumable mortgage" or one that can be transferred to a new owner, this may make the property more marketable, if you have to sell in one of our recurring periods of high interest rates.

When all the names are signed on the contract in the right places, and you've found a banker willing to lend you the money, you will probably want to make an appointment to see your new house again before you leave town. It's nice to take some pictures to show your kids and friends back home, and for you to dream over at odd moments in the next few weeks. Otherwise, you might be unable to recall what the house even looks like!

You may want to take some measurements or draw a quick sketch of the floor plan. (One considerate seller gave us the blueprints for the house we had just contracted to buy.) Then you can ponder your furniture arrangements when you have more time without bothering the sellers.

This is a good time, too, to have a friendly off-the-record discussion of any idiosyncracies the house might have, if the owners are receptive. If you have to stamp the floor in a special spot before the furnace will go on, its nice to know the technique.

Make a list of your questions and get them off your chest in one fell swoop. After we had signed the contract for the sale of one home, the buyers came by for a last look before leaving town. I tactfully made myself scarce by going down to the basement to tend to the laundry while they looked around. The couple tracked me down though, and after hearty assurances that they were going to go through with the deal "no matter what," they suggested that I come clean about the little faults of the house, whatever they might be, so they would know what to expect. I truly couldn't think of a single idiosyncracy I felt free to describe, but they kept insisting. Finally, backed up against my washer like the subject of a CIA grilling, I made one up.

"There's no way to open the upstairs bathroom door from the outside if it's locked," I said. I explained that when their little one inevitably locks himself in, they could rescue him through the skylight—if they had a long ladder and weren't afraid of heights.

Satisfied that they knew the worst, they went home happy. You can't get blood from a turnip, so don't press for details if they don't seem to be forthcoming. How could I tell them that the roof leaked like a sieve?

Practically everyone involved in the buying and selling of a home will do his best to make the transaction an amicable one. Of course, those most concerned are the buyer and the seller—at times a dynamite combination. Whenever emotions are involved, there are bound to be sparks. Sparks are fine and to be expected. It's the explosions that must be avoided.

A few years ago I had a neighbor in her mid-forties, the capable and prudent mother of three teenagers and a credit to the fine man she had married, who midway up the ladder of success suddenly found himself out of a job. Any one of these situations could cause even an emotionally stable, mature woman to go bananas—menopausal moodiness, teenage tension, or breadwinner blues. Put them all together and they can spell N-E-R-V-O-U-S B-R-E-A-K-D-O-W-N!

Everything passes eventually, and after six months that seemed more like six years, the husband found a new job in another state. The teenagers grew up a bit with the passage of time, and, well—two out of three solutions isn't bad. But of course they had to move.

Their house sold quickly and for the asking price. A younger couple who loved it were the buyers, and for a while everything was rosy. The couple were local, with family and friends abounding in the area, and none of them could wait to see the new house. Mothers and fathers, aunts and uncles, golf and tennis partners, the parents of the children's friends, along with carpenters, decorators, and plumbers, and electricians who would be working on a planned new addition arrived in a steady stream at Lou's door. Day by day the traffic traipsing through the house increased, and day by day Lou's ladylike demeanor deteriorated until she believed herself to be rushing headlong into the big N.B. she had avoided since her problems first began.

Needless to say, Lou's husband had gone on ahead to the new job, and she was left to handle the bulk of the final moving details, along with maintaining Open House for the new buyers. Returning home one weekend, Lou's husband took one look at her and decided to put a halt to the house tours. He phoned the couple and told them to plan on making a final visit/inspection the next weekend, when he would be home. If they had any questions he would gladly answer them at that time and please, please, they were not to drop by again until the closing. And that was that! Lou, who is a good-natured lady, felt sorry that the circumstances during those last few weeks were not more pleasant between the two couples. The buyers had no comprehension of the emotional problems that my neighbor and her family were facing but, more than likely, they may someday find themselves in the same boat!

During a move as seller, you must think of yourself and the welfare of your family. Allowing the prospective owners to come and go at will is thoughtful but surely impractical when done to the extreme. Establish mutually satisfactory guidelines in the beginning of the deal. As buyer, if you must check measurements and decide on colors, be considerate of the harassed owner and arrange a convenient time.

Once the whole purchasing hassle is over, you can go home and repent at your leisure. Devote yourself to the nitty-gritty of getting your family ready to move, and forget all about the world of high finance until the day of "closing" rolls around.

Participating in a closing is comparable to the thrills and chills of *Jaws* or *The Exorcist*. I have admitted to an inadequacy in financial matters, but I failed to mention that any kind of business dealings leave me in a state resembling shock—cold, clammy, and unable to look anyone in the eye. I am even embarrassed to return the soda bottles to the store for my deposit. I am constitutionally unable to take merchandise back to a store and lodge a complaint—the very thought makes me cringe. Consequently, put me in a chair at one of those huge tables in a boardroom at a bank or a lawyer's office, and I am so much jelly. Psychiatrists tell us that the mind tends to blot out unpleasant experiences that the conscious mind can't bear to remember. I guess that's why our closings are so foggy in my memory, but I'll do my best to describe what happens.

A closing is the ceremony in which the ownership of the property actually changes hands. Sometimes it's referred to as "passing the papers." You'll have to attend two closings, one for the house you are selling, and one in the new town to assume ownership of the house you are buying. The meeting may be held at the bank, a legal office, the real estate office, or a park bench. (Closing ceremonies usually occur at the height of the pandemonium on moving day; however, this does not have to be so. The actual passing of the papers may occur earlier with the contract specifying that the premises need not be vacated until a later date. You may be able to avoid the whole scene by sending your John Hancock through the mails, but that's really a cop-out. In my experience, the procedure has differed with every transaction!) All parties to the transaction will be there, including the banker, real estate people, lawyers (if you wish), and the buyers and sellers. Quite an imposing crowd. Now the money and the deed to the property will change hands. That sounds simple, but for some reason, it isn't. Assorted and sundry checks will be handed across the table with great ceremony, and the lawyers will check them off on their lists.

As I have pointed out, the earnest money you have already paid becomes part of your down payment. The rest of the down payment must be in the form of a certified check or cashier's check. That's because when the deed is handed to you, the deal is legally closed, and there can't be any waiting around to see if your check is going to bounce. Any other checks that are required can be personal checks.

There are a lot of little niggling fees and taxes to be paid that can range from various recording fees, sewer assessments, termite inspection costs, to a new hat for the banker. These vary somewhat according to the locale, and your lawyer or banker will fill you in on what's necessary. You will be notified at least twelve days prior to the closing just what the settlement costs will be. This is stipulated by law—the Real Estate Settlement Procedures Act of 1974.

The bank will require you to show proof that you have taken insurance on the house. Since the property is security for the loan, you can't blame them. I always used to be confused as to why the insurance coverage was never as much as the purchase price. Then my husband pointed out the obvious. If the house burns down, the land isn't going anywhere, so we don't have to insure that. There may be title insurance to be paid, though, to protect you from other claims on the land.

You may have to reimburse the old owners for fuel oil left in the tank or taxes that have already been paid on the property for the current year. If you are buying any of their personal goods, you will have to pay for them now too. I have a friend who sold his pool table to the new owners of his house for two hundred dollars. When I asked him why he wasn't taking it with him to Texas, he said, "I can't get it out of the basement." I asked how he got it down there, and he said, "I didn't. I bought it from the last owners for two hundred dollars." That's what you call irony. I wonder how many people will buy that pool table, not realizing that they are paying for what has become an integral part of the house!

Try to pay a visit to the new house before you go to the closing. If your timing is perfect, the old owners will have moved out, and if there is any unusual damage, or the dining room chandelier is missing, you can haggle about it *before* they get your money. This is vital even if you are buying a brand new house! You should meet at the property with the builder and go through the new house together, making note of any unfinished details. Then you can agree to withhold a sum of money to cover the unfinished work. This gives you some leverage to get the work finished up promptly. It's very annoying to be living in a house with bare bulbs hanging from the ceilings for months and months, and having to plead with people on the phone to come and finish their jobs. They are much more eager to cooperate if you owe them money!

You may find that there has been some misunderstanding

about details of the building. We specified a screened porch on the plans for a house we built long-distance. When we inspected the house on our way to the closing, we found a nice porch, but it wasn't screened. My husband inquired when the screens would be finished. The builder said, "What screens?" He maintained that if there were to be screens, they would have been indicated on the plans with some little interwoven lines up in the corner of the porch blueprints. "Oh!" said we. It was a simple misunderstanding, but a difference of several hundred dollars was involved, and it had to be negotiated at the closing. After some acrimonious discussion, we agreed to split the cost of the screens.

Incidentally, it's a good idea to be represented by your lawyer at a closing. In some areas this is required by law, but that's uncommon. The lawyer's fee will be an additional expense, but it will be a very small percentage of the money that is changing hands, and it's great to have someone with some clout in your corner. In some cases your company will even pick up the tab.

My one and only experience with attending a closing without Blaze was for me no worse than walking the last mile on Death Row. I set out early on a dreary Monday morning fortified with three cups of coffee and a bad case of colitis. The rain was pouring down in sheets as I made my way into the downtown area to the lawyer's office, the car radio humming the strains of "Rainy Days and Mondays." How apropos. My security blanket was beside me in the form of an overstuffed purse full of little reminder notes and irrefutable instructions from "on high," written by Blaze. Pressing business kept him from attending the ceremony! Could an organization meeting on the new job really be more important than this? By the time I arrived, I thought I had composed myself rather well, and I became more relaxed when I spotted my realtor talking with the buyers. I became unlaxed when I learned that the buyers were old family friends of MY realtor. Their entourage also consisted of an austere-looking lawyer carrying a Gucci attaché case. I'm sure he had a Gucci belt, wallet, and shoes to match, but I was too undone to take notice. The group was ushered into a paneled room and seated around an enormous conference table. I sat down with what I considered businesslike decorum and promptly spilled my bulging purse all over the rug. Attempting to maintain my dignity I stooped to retrieve all my little cue cards. The proceedings from then on are a blur. Mother Nature is kind in allowing us to suppress the memory of real pain. I do remember questioning a few items that Blaze had "suggested" I bring up. This was all carried out by rote, but at least I must have appeared to know what I was talking about. Checks were passed across the table and everyone got his, hands were shaken all around, and I remained seated for the benediction, which never came. It was finally all over, and I rushed out of the office and into the safety of my car, took a deep breath, turned on the ignition and heard some callow youth who probably never went through the rigors of a closing, still singing "Rainy days and Mondays always get me down." He should only know—

If your husband intends to leave you to handle the closing and other miserable business details, look for a handsome young lawyer to represent you. Hubby may find that he can arrange to be present after all. Of course, like everything else in life, this can backfire. You may discover that he is trotting around New Town examining real estate in the company of an agent who looks like Farrah Fawcett-Majors.

When the money and the deed have been exchanged, and you've shaken hands all around the table, there is one last little ceremony—Handing Over the Keys. If you are the seller, this may be accompanied by a little twinge of the old heartstrings. It's a very funny feeling to be giving up the keys to the house you've called home for any length of time. Usually we fail to think about this little detail ahead of time, and when the keys are called for, Blaze starts digging in his pockets, and I rummage through the used Kleenex in my purse to find them, and then there's a long, embarrassing pause while we struggle to get them off our key rings. This is hard to do with aplomb when your eyes are full of tears.

When we sold our first home, we had to go back to the house after the closing to pick up the barbecue grill we had forgotten on the patio. The new owners were already there, and when I saw their little boy come running from the swings in the backyard and hop up the steps and in the kitchen door, it was almost more than I could take. We were thrilled about our move and were buying a bigger and better house, but old attachments die hard. Try to avoid going back until a suitable period of time has elapsed and you have control of your emotions.

You really should not move any of your belongings into a house until it is legally yours. Likewise, when you are the seller, you are responsible for the property until the closing takes place. In the event that the house is empty, a good realtor won't turn the key over to the buyers until the papers have been passed, and she will accompany them on all visits to the property. Then there can be no dispute about who is responsible for the premises and the contents of the house.

A friend of ours had her house on the market for several months after she and her family had moved away. The realtor finally had a hot prospect, and the deal seemed assured. Then one Sunday she kindly let the prospect have the key so the family could pay a leisurely visit to the house to plan their furnishings. Unfortunately, one of the children left the tap running unnoticed in an upstairs bath. The ensuing water damage dispute queered the deal and resulted in a large repair bill for the owners. If anything is stolen or damaged, responsibility lies with the owner, so it makes good sense to go by the book. Don't move anything in until the house is yours. If you are the seller, don't risk being a nice guy at your own expense.

A few years ago, when we bought Blaze's dream house, in Shaker Heights, Ohio, we were so delighted with our purchase and the amicable relationship which had developed with the previous owners, that we outdid ourselves in being nice guys. "Mrs. Smith" asked if they could store some of their furniture with us for six weeks until their new and much smaller home would be ready for occupancy. Since the dream house consisted of seventeen of the largest rooms that we had ever seen and our furniture was meager at best, we readily agreed to the idea. The plan was for us to store some of their furniture, and some cartons containing books and sundries, at one end of the large living room, keeping everything out of the way of our day-to-day living. We scattered our own living room furniture throughout some of the remaining sixteen rooms and decided to start from scratch in the living room anyway, as soon as we had the time and the necessary funds. (The time arrived quickly; the funds were delayed.) A most satisfactory solution for all parties.

We had finally unpacked the last of our cartons and the house began to take shape. Our furniture was temporarily spotted in rooms that also held pieces belonging to the Smiths. These pieces would be carefully moved to the living room within a few days by the Smith's movers. When the designated day arrived, along with Mrs. Smith and a crew of five burly moving men, I hied myself and the dog and three cats into a separate part of the house and attempted to make all of us scarce. I casually sauntered through the main hall of the house at interims, pretending that I belonged, growing more and more horrified as I watched the size of my living room shrink from a baronial hall into the local storage room of the Red Ball Express Moving Company! Furniture and boxes were meticulously placed end to end and over and above one another until they reached to the top of the twelve foot ceilings. Mrs. Smith, that smart cookie, had quietly left the premises for a vacation to her farm in Vermont so her family could recuperate from the strain of the move! The moving crew worked quickly and before I knew what was happening the entire room was quite impenetrable by man or woman, dog or cat. I shouted at the foreman that he must stop. Not only was this against the local fire ordinance but Blaze and I didn't intend to play Tarzan and Jane for six weeks in the jungle being created in our living room. Perceptive as he was, and sensing my distress, the head honcho allowed that he could put some of the stuff up in the attic or down in the basement. "But it'll cost you, lady!" "It'll cost the Smiths," thought I. A path was gradually cleared down the middle of the room giving a narrow egress and exit; we were unable, however, to see the fireplace or any of the windows for six long weeks. I still have no idea where all of those huge cartons and that massive furniture came from. The Welcome Wagon lady summed up the situation nicely when she arrived five weeks later and said, "I guess I caught you at a bad time."

No matter how pleasant the relationship, try not to allow the new owners of your home to assume that you will be at their beck and call to solve their "new house" problems, of which there are bound to be a few—the ones you told them about and the ones you carefully forgot to mention. Every one of us knows someone who develops palpitations and breaks out in a cold sweat at the thought of turning on the dishwasher or raising the thermostat. We kindly refer to that individual as "not mechanically inclined." Should you happen to sell your house to one of these people, be sure to take the necessary precautions beforehand.

We had installed a beautiful swimming pool on our property in Cincinnati the summer before we were transferred to Cleveland. (This may also be one of the harbingers of a move in the offing!) A pool requires special care and maintenance, hence we had gone to great pains to explain the procedures involved to the buyers before we left town. Along with verbal instructions, we had left written diagrams showing the filter, how to backwash, vacuum, chlorinate, and all the details for keeping a clean, happy pool. The new couple grasped the instructions with amazing alacrity, and when we left town we were certain that all would be well. Well—

Six weeks later, in the middle of an August heat wave in Cleveland, in our new house with no swimming pool, surrounded by complaining children and a cranky wife, Blaze received a phone call from that nice fellow who bought our "estate with swimming pool" in Cincinnati. He and his family had just returned home from a two-week vacation. They thought it a good idea to turn off the pool pump, "to give it a rest" while they were gone. When they returned home they discovered that the sparkling aquamarine water had become bilious green and slimy! The fellow ranted that we had sold him a lemon with defective equipment and misrepresented the property to him. Keeping his cool, Blaze set him straight. (One never turns off a pool pump to give it a rest in the middle of a Cincinnati summer.) Chastened, the fellow called the pool maintenance man and read his instruction books once again. He called the next day to apologize and to vow that the pool would live again.

Be sure that you have supplied the new owner with all warranties, guarantees, operating instruction sheets, and most important, the names and phone numbers of service people that you have used. In a nice way, you must let the buyers know that the house is now their baby. You have your own new house to worry about.

6

DOING YOUR OWN THING

Building your dream house ⌂ The importance of the detailed contract ⌂ Financing ⌂ Guarantees ⌂ Buying a house under construction ⌂ Carrying on during a remodeling job ⌂ Storage of household goods.

If all else fails, and you've been unable to find a house you can stand, the alternative may be to build or remodel.

The first time we were bold enough to start from scratch, we built a very nice house in Wisconsin in which we managed to live for two weeks before we were transferred. (The company decided to centralize, and half of the town was being sent to New York.) Bloody but unbowed, we put out the "For Sale" sign and took off for Connecticut, where finding the right house was once again a problem. Our pocketbook was too slim for our plumpish tastes, so we decided to build again.

Incidentally, in both cases we found it it cheaper to build than to buy a comparable house. House building is often more economical in the long run because in selling and buying a house, everyone extracts his pound of flesh. This is only true, however, if you remove yourself from the scene so you don't succumb to the temptation to make a lot of costly changes.

The first step was to find a reliable contractor. In each case friends recommended local builders, and we were able to buy a lot from the builder himself. We told him how much money we could spend, what our requirements were, and what general styles we liked. Both times the builder was able to come up with a plan from his files from which we were able to work. We sat down at a drafting table and moved doors and windows and walls around until we had a plan that would work for us. The builder then figured an estimate based on a certain number of dollars per square foot. This is a common measuring tool, as I have said; the rate per foot, however, may vary widely from one locale to another.

A contract was drawn up, detailing the type of construction—plaster walls or wallboard, the grade of lumber to be used, types of doors and windows, ratio of sand to cement in the concrete, etc. The contract should be very detailed, specifying everything that goes into the house from insulation to kitchen cabinet allowance. You probably think this sounds too complicated—you and your husband know nothing about lumber or concrete mixes! You don't have to. Ask the builder to show you a few of the houses he has put up, and ask for some references. You can usually tell by looking if this is the quality you want.

Having an honest builder is the key to building whether it be local or long distance; if at all possible, however, get yourself a lawyer to look over the contract for you before you sign your life away.

The contract should specify the kind of flooring to be used, the kind of tile and where it should go, the allowance for light fixtures (which is never enough!), the kind of wall paneling to be used, the appliances to be built in, the kind of kitchen cabinets to be installed or the allowance for them, type of paint to be used and number of coats, and/or the wallpaper allowance. One of our contracts even included an allowance for carpeting to be laid over subflooring.

Choosing these components is the most fun! The last time we built, I spent one whole day with the builder, going from lumberyard to tile store, to cabinetmaker, to electrical fixture stores, picking out everything. Since I had just done the same thing six months before, it was easy. Then I went home, a thousand miles away, and in a little more than three months our house was ready, and I saw it for the first time. Loved it! You have to be decisive, though, and not allow yourself to stew over your selections after you get home. You can drive yourself and the builder crazy if you do, besides running up a tremendous telephone bill and increasing the building costs with changes.

Appliances and carpeting or anything else that is included in the building contract go into the mortgage, which saves you a lot of initial expense when you first move into a house. Of course, you've got to realize that you'll be paying interest on them for the next twenty years or so. Many people buy the basic home with plans for expansion later, but we had the upstairs finished into two bedrooms, and a garage and breezeway added on. We paid a little more in mortgage payments and down payment, but we were able to enjoy our time there without the hassle of working to finish the house on weekends ourselves, and trying to nickel-and-dime the materials out of the grocery money.

The type of grading and landscaping to be done should be specified in the contract. Whether or not a lawn is included varies according to local custom, but you should know what to expect. The contract should also state the condition the house will be in when it's turned over to you. "Broom clean" is the term which is often used. This generally means the sawdust has been swept into a corner, and that's all. In some cases, those pesky stickers will be removed from the windows if you put it in the contract. Some builders include window washing, but don't quibble on these little points. You don't want to antagonize the builder so much that he puts too much sand in your concrete mix!

Like everyone else, builders have their little idiosyncrasies. One of our contractors was a teetotaler, and when we told him we wanted a wet bar in the family room, he balked. We finally assured him that the sink was for flower arranging. He didn't believe us, but housing starts were down so he pretended he did and we got the bar. This fellow would conduct absolutely no business on Sundays because of his religious convictions. That was a little inconvenient at times, but, all in all, we found it reassuring!

The same builder was six foot six. He would have made a great guard for the Boston Celtics, but he had an annoying tendency to install fixtures at a height that would be convenient for him to use. The shower heads in that house were so high that the best shower caps were almost useless, and my mouth and chin were among the missing whenever I looked in the bathroom mirror. The makeup lights were high enough to give my hair wonderful highlights but did awful things to my face. I finally complained when I tore a muscle trying to hang my heavy winter coat on a closet rod that was over my head! A friend of mine toiled for several years in a kitchen with counters so low that she developed chronic backache. Her builder's wife was a tiny little thing!

Have a firm date for completion of the house in the contract with penalties to be borne by the builder in the event of default. A good builder can usually finish an average-size home in a hundred days. We gave our first builder six months, and since we were living in a house we rented from him, he took the whole six months. How dumb can you get? We thought he was doing *us* a favor!

What about financing? In one case we obtained a building loan from the bank, and they doled out the money as the builder needed it. The next time we simply gave the builder a down payment and he arranged his own financing for the construction. We paid him at the closing just as though we were buying a used house. In either case, be sure there is insurance on the house as it is being built. Unfinished houses are subject to damage from vandals as well as fire and the elements, so make sure that your investment is protected, either by you or by the builder.

Let me remind you again that if you deal with a builder directly you will save money. His costs are fixed, so any real estate commission is tacked onto his selling price, and you will pay it, no matter what the contract says. Some builders are already committed to a broker and, if that is the case, c'est la querre!

Check your contract for guarantees on such things as the heating and plumbing systems. Wiring and plumbing and some other aspects of construction are generally spelled out by local building codes and will be subject to inspection by local authorities. Our last builder even guaranteed a dry basement for six months, which is more than you get in a used home. A good builder will be available after you move in to fix up any little things that are wrong, but don't expect him to be your permanent maintenance man. That's what husbands are for, and besides, the neighbors will talk!

Even in a brand new home you will want to allow a day or two for a proper cleanup before you move in. You won't need all that Lysol that you use in an older home, but you will probably want to wax those nice new floors to keep them that way and to get the stickers off the plumbing fixtures and the sawdust out of the cabinets. Invariably, it's snowing or raining, and there's always a sea of mud around a new house. Try not to let it upset you. The movers should provide runners to protect the traffic lanes on moving day.

One way to get a new house without starting from scratch is to buy one already under construction. Some builders put up houses for speculation and stop short of the finishing details. The buyer can then select the tiles and flooring, colors, etc., and the house can generally be finished in six weeks. Of course you can't be moving walls around or changing the location of the bathrooms, but if the floor plan and the exterior suit you, you still have a chance to be creative. If you're in a hurry, and who isn't, it's a good shortcut.

Architect-designed houses are usually not for transients.

Too much time and money are involved, and resale is often more difficult. A good builder can save you money by using stock lumber sizes, stock trim, windows and doors, etc. As soon as you get into custom designs, time and money are rapidly spent, and the next thing you know, you're moving again!

An alternative to building a home may be remodeling an older one. There can be great satisfaction in buying a house of an earlier vintage, with that gracious charm of a bygone era. If you remodel, you are able to secure the best of both worlds—old-time quality construction with modern-day amenities, such as central air conditioning, air filters, central vacuum systems, intercoms, cook centers, and 220 voltage.

Our last home was sold within three days. Hurrah! That was all well and good, but we hadn't found a new one yet. The weeks flew by as they always do when you need all the time you can get, and we were nearing the new owner's date of occupancy. Sheer panic began to set in! The thought of no place to go when one has an entourage of seven people, three cats and a big hairy dog, can unnerve even the stoutest of hearts. The bottom really fell out when the new owner arrived to measure for drapes, and I realized that she was moving in and I was moving out but didn't know *where*.

Finally, just two weeks from moving day, either from desperation or resignation, we decided on an older home in a very nice neighborhood. The fly in the ointment in this less-than-perfect solution was that the house needed extensive remodeling, including a new kitchen, new bathrooms, walls knocked down, complete decorating—the works. We put our problem in the hands of one we believed to be a reliable and reputable contractor.

During the remodeling process, arrangements were made to have our children stay with friends in our former hometown. My husband and I went off to a pleasant hotel within a short distance of our new home. The children would join us in three or four weeks. Work on the house was to begin immediately. At least that's what the contractor told us, and that's when the trouble started, and that's also about the time I located a new doctor and a prescription for tranquilizers.

Living in a hotel sounds extremely glamorous after going

through months of househunting, house-selling, garage sales, list-making, sorting, packing, and wrenching goodbyes. It is. It's terrific for about three weeks. After that the kids arrive to stay in the hotel with you. Try walking through the sumptuous main lobby carrying plastic bags full of dirty clothes on your way to a local laundromat. Inevitably, a fancy reception is in progress at the time. People raise their eyebrows as you try to be inconspicuous, sideling behind the potted palms with your laundry bag slung over your shoulder, leaving a trail of Tide like Hansel and Gretel in the forest.

Room service is not always practical. Club sandwiches are a treat at midnight, but the company may become leery if the expenses grow to excess. With this in mind I tried to buy as many nonperishable groceries as possible for snacks. At night, I also managed to hide containers of milk and orange juice in the ice machine down the hall. In the morning I made a dash to retrieve them for breakfast. On one occasion the containers disappeared. I never did find out who the culprit was, though I surmise that a traveling salesman discovered them and enjoyed a late night snack on us. Perhaps he thought it was a service of the hotel.

As you may have deduced, our remodeling project took longer than expected—three months longer. By this time bloody murder was in all our minds. We were not only ready to go for the jugular of the contractor but for one another's as well. Togetherness may be great on "The Brady Bunch," but it somehow loses its charm when seven people are living in close quarters for four long months.

Never, never, never go into a major remodeling project without putting everything in writing—our first mistake. I don't intend to impugn the honesty of all contractors, but so often in a verbal agreement issues and instructions may be grossly misunderstood by either or both negotiating parties. A friendly handshake in good faith can be easily forgotten as time passes and tempers grow short with anxiety.

Our contractor provided only a generalized set of specifications and refused to commit himself to a specific completion date "because," he said, "we won't know what we have to rebuild until we tear out all the old walls and bathroom fixtures." Stuck again!

A contract for remodeling should be as exact as a building

contract. Materials to be used and a completion date for the project are essential. Contractors are apt to start one job and then go off to another so they can keep several balls in the air at a time. This seems to be a common business practice, but both you and the contractor should know when you expect the job to be finished, again with a penalty to be borne by the contractor if he fails to observe the time limit.

If you are having remodeling done on your home, be sure your contract also contains a *lien waiver clause*. If you pay the contractor for the work and he fails to pay off the individual subcontractors, they can without such a clause, legally prohibit you from reselling your property until they have been paid.

We encountered strike situations, kitchen cabinets lost enroute, a plumber who hammered through a dining room ceiling while installing an upstairs bathtub, and orders for flooring and materials that were never even placed. Every delay costs you, the owner, money and pain. You can cry and plead and scream and shout and kick your feet, but the only method of action that works is to cut through the middleman and call directly to the factory general managers, if necessary even the company president. Then, if you are lucky, you will get some action. We finally moved into that house with the kitchen still in the blueprint stage. Fortunately, I had a refrigerator and a new stove which were, happily, delivered on time. I had these two appliances hooked up in the utility room where there was also a laundry tub, and where I cooked some rather nongourmet meals. I eagerly watched my kitchen being studded in a dead heat with the arrival of winter's cold. Then there was another major setback—the contractor had forgotten to place the kitchen cabinet order. So I did without, and we made do with packing boxes and crates for months.

We decided to splurge on a lovely quarry tile for the floor. We received part of the shipment from the factory in the South, and the floor man installed it around the perimeter of the kitchen. Then we waited. Days passed, and still the final shipment failed to arrive. I made repeated calls to the supplier and was assured that it was on the way. Delivery dates came and went, and still no tile. Finally one innocent young clerk admitted that the particular pattern we had chosen had been discontinued. In a rage, I put in a call to the company president. The man fortunately had a sympathetic ear and decided to help this hysterical, babbling woman. After weeks of searching through warehouses, enough tile was found to complete the job.

A move such as this necessitates the storage of your furniture. Everything is double-packed and placed on huge wooden palettes, which can be loaded and unloaded onto the trucks, into warehouses, and back onto trucks with minimal handling and chance for breakage. In our particular case, because our house was not completed when we moved in, only a partial delivery of our goods was made initially. The trick to this kind of move is knowing which cartons you must have immediately, such as beds, linens, pots and pans, and clothing. (We had spanned two seasons while waiting for our house and a change of wardrobes was required.) A good inventory list is a must for both you and the movers. Of course, a halfway move demands good organization when you are moving out of your home. At that time it is necessary to list all the items that you will need immediately and designate which items of furniture are to be placed in storage. You can place red tags on the things going into storage, and green ones on those items to be delivered to the house.

Inevitably, you are going to misplace something. Our oldest daughter was to leave for her first year at college and had carefully and meticulously packed her trunks. They had been placed in a restricted area and were not to be touched. Wouldn't you know, they landed in storage somewhere in an enormous warehouse. Fortunately the trunks were discovered in time by the moving company "searchers." We averted disaster. As the months went by and we slowly regained our equilibrium, we began to appreciate the fact that we were living in a home that could not be duplicated by a builder today. If you are prepared for the constant hassles and nerve-racking days that you are liable to encounter in house remodeling, the end result should be worthwhile and creatively most satisfying.

WHAT TO DO UNTIL THE MOVER COMES

Selecting a mover ⌂ Tips for getting organized ⌂ Severing the ties in your old community ⌂ How to say goodbye to your friends.

When the agonies and the ecstasies of the out-of-town tryouts have been overcome, the production is about ready to take to the boards, and you will have what seems like five minutes to relax and catch your breath before the "really big show," moving, begins. Don't get too relaxed, though! Like any great performer most of us are at our best when we are a bit "psyched up" before curtain-up, so keep your juices flowing and you may find you have a four-star hit on your hands.

The major financial problems are out of the way, and now it's time to get down to the nitty-gritty. If you have sold your house and located a new home, you will have narrowed down your time of departure to a specific month. Your next step should be to select a moving company. In a company-sponsored move, the selection may have been made for you. It is a common corporate practice to use one particular moving firm. The personnel department of your husband's company will have the necessary information.

A representative from the moving company will make an appointment to come and look over the situation in your home. He will estimate the size of your load, the packing date, the moving-out date, the moving-in date at your new home, and the unpacking date. There are several well-known, reputable moving companies from which to choose. Get cost estimates or bids from at least two or three companies, and compare prices and services. Shop around and get the best deal for you. It's possible that your choice may be limited by the time element. When you sold your home, you gave the new owners a date of occupancy with which you must comply, and you in turn expect to occupy your new home on a particular date: the domino theory in action. Moving companies tend to be the busiest in the spring and late summer thanks to school calendars, so it's important that you be in touch with movers as soon as you are aware of your own schedule. Another factor in the timing of your move may be the size of your load. If your furnishings won't fill an entire van, you may find your goods sharing the trip with the belongings of another family or families. Geography will dictate which load will be delivered first.

I have never yet met a moving company representative I

didn't like. Of course, they are salesmen, and their job is to make you feel as comfortable as possible. This is especially true if they are responsible for all of your company's moves. They have a good thing going and a reputation to uphold, which means business to them in the future. The general spiel seems to be, "Just relax and don't worry about a thing, lady. We will make this move the most pleasant you ever had." The words may vary, but the meaning is the same, and I'm sure that they fully intend to live up to them. Life being the way it is, however, a foul-up may just occur somewhere along the line, and you had best be alerted to a few basic facts.

Often the moving van is owned by an individual driver on a franchise basis. The representative of the moving company becomes a dispatcher or liaison between you and the van driver. For this reason, it's a good idea to keep the representative's phone number with you at all times in the event of an emergency or setback in the normal chain of events. At the time of the representative's visit, be sure to show him everything you intend to move. Trot him through your attic, basement, garage, and other storage areas, pointing out all the items that you intend to take with you. This will help him make an accurate estimate of the cost of your move and the size of truck needed to transport your worldly goods. This estimate is an educated guess of the weight of your shipment, so if you fail to mention that the sundial in the garden and the stone statue of Venus on the patio are family treasures that go with you, your estimate could be way off. As you are expected to pay for your move in cash or with a certified check or money order before the furniture is unloaded, you could be caught short if your estimate was low. If your actual costs exceed the estimate, you are required by law to pay up to 110 percent of the estimated cost of your shipment at the time of delivery. If the bill is even higher, you have fifteen days to round up the rest of the cash. Some people like to accompany the van to the weigh-in after it has been loaded or to have the driver call them so they will know what their exact bill will be. (Large corporations often have special arrangements for the payment of the hauler.)

Under federal regulations, the mover's liability for your goods is limited to a maximum of sixty cents per pound per article. This isn't much protection for small vauables that could be broken. Your mover's representative should give you an opportunity to purchase additional coverage at the rate of fifty cents per $100 worth of goods. (If you estimate the worth of your goods at $10,000, the additional charge to you will be $50.) You may be surprised at the dollar value of all that old stuff when you stop to add it up.

Be sure to make special mention of your fears and worries over the shipping of your valuables and the sentimental objects that you treasure. I have two lovely crystal hurricane lamps that are family heirlooms. Rather than send the lamps in the van, I have had the packers securely crate them for me with special padding, and we take them in the car with us. If they are broken, better to be responsible ourselves. On the other hand, we have an enormous antique grandfather's clock that will never fit in the car, responsibility or no! The mover will make arrangements for a clock man to come in to disassemble the beautiful monster and meticulously crate all the pieces. Upon arrival at the new locale, another expert puts it all back together again and makes sure it's working properly. Many times it will run better than before.

Moving companies have access to specialists for everything imaginable. I have had moving companies send over tuners for pianos that become out of sorts what with the jostling they receive, upholstery cleaners for a soiled sofa, and rug shampooers. There are appliance men who will come in and disconnect the washer and dryer for you and prepare their innards for moving. These fellows are a fund of information. For instance, one told me that if you put a few charcoal briquets or used coffee grounds in your refrigerator after it has been cleaned out, thoroughly defrosted and allowed to dry, odor and mildew will not appear. If you have ever opened the door of an untreated refrigerator to find that smelly purply-blue mold, you can appreciate this tip.

These premoving weeks are the time to get busy with those lists. I cannot emphasize this too strongly. Unless you have nerves of steel you're bound to have sleepless nights and worrisome days. Your head will swim with a myriad of things to take care of before the big day. Make lists and notes to which you can refer, and check them off as you complete them. It's not a bad idea to have

other family members make their own lists. I know there are some women who are so terribly efficient that they can whiz through moving details with no concern, but they are usually in the minority, and more than likely they have a staff of servants to do the running for them. In my wildest musings I am unable to picture Happy Rockefeller or Jackie Onassis grabbing the cleanser from an over zealous moving man and holding onto it for dear life in order to give the bathtub one last scouring before the new owners arrive!

Then there is the helpless wife who has been clever enough to con her adoring husband into believing that she is just too sensitive to deal with all of these taxing details, and he will just have to take care of everything. This type of wife no doubt established the rules early in her game of marriage, but for most of us it is too late to start. Learning to be helpless is a very subtle art. Whenever I have attempted it my husband calls me "good old flaky," pats me on the head and disappears for a half hour until I am back to normal. The majority of us do need a program or guide to get us going in the morning, and for this reason lists are important. While it's a short-run inconvenience, it's so much easier in the long run to have your problems and chores down in black and white.

Let me illustrate some things you will have to take care of before moving day. In most instances these tasks will fall to you:

1. Close out your checking and savings accounts at your local bank. Arrangements can be made to transfer your funds to your new bank. If you have already opened a checking account and ordered checks from a bank in your new town, you can avoid the hassle of trying to cash out-of-town checks in the first days following your move. Don't forget to collect the valuables from your safe deposit box. These will accompany you in a locked strongbox.
2. Close out all charge accounts at department stores, boutiques, flower shops, and your favorite butcher and bookie.
3. Obtain change-of-address cards from the local post office. Send these along to book clubs, newspapers, (*The Wall Street Journal*—you never know when you may need it again!), and any periodicals you receive. If you wish to continue your

subscription to your old hometown daily paper, be sure to give them a call. If you are superefficient, you might even send change-of-address cards to long-distance friends. Naturally, *you must leave your new address and zip code with the post office so that all of your first-class mail can be forwarded.* If you hold national credit cards such as Master Charge or American Express, notify them of your change of address. If you expect social security checks, dividend checks, or money from any other source, for heaven's sake, be sure the sender knows your new address!

4. Send out garments for cleaning, but don't forget to pick them up before moving day. Include any rugs or draperies that could do with a lift. Keep these items in the cleaner's wrappers for packing. It gives you a great boost to have them fresh and clean when you are settling in your new home.

5. Inform the schools of your pending move, and review your children's records in advance of their transfer. Often the old school will have to wait for notification from the new one before they will send the records; they should however, be organized and ready to go. Try to obtain current standardized test scores and your children's workbooks in order to facilitate their proper placement in the new school.

6. Have your doctors and dentists compile your family medical records. These should be sent on when you locate a new doctor or dentist. You should keep an updated inoculation record of your own for your children. *Usually a new school will want these important dates along with the birth certificate when registering your child.* This will expedite matters for all concerned. You will also impress everyone with your efficiency and capability. If you move frequently, and the records are repeatedly recopied by doctors from L.A. to Bangor, important dates are sometimes lost in the shuffle. In our area there has been an increase in cases of "hard" measles lately, and our physician needed to know the exact date of my twelve-year-old's inoculation to determine whether it was still effective. My own records had long since been handed over to some doctor, somewhere, so I had to make a long distance call across the country to our former pediatrician, thrice-removed, to get the necessary information. Keep these records with your birth certificates and other vital documents. They are important.

Perhaps your old doctor can recommend a physician in your new city. Generally, there are nationwide directories to which he can refer, and he can give you a list of names. Sometimes your family doctor just happens to have an old med school buddy in the new town and will be happy to contact him for you. If you or a member of your family has a specific medical problem, your doctor will usually give you a list of specialists to consult.

Be sure to have all your prescriptions filled and current. The drug laws today are so stringent that you will be unable to have prescriptions refilled unless they are from a local doctor known to the pharmacist.

7. If you are affiliated with a church, ask your clergyman to write a letter of introduction for your family. He too may know of a counterpart in your new town.
8. Get in touch with your utility companies, phone company, etc. Tell them when you are leaving, when you want meters read, power turned off, and phones disconnected, and where the final bills are to be sent. Ask the phone company to discontinue service as late on moving day as possible or even the next day. When you are cut off from the outside world of family and friends, there is a feeling of terrible finality. It is inevitable, of course, but put it off as long as you can. As far as utility readings and bills are concerned, it is discouraging and expensive to receive a bill that rightfully belongs to the new occupants only because you have neglected to make a few quick phone calls. Notify your milkman and diaper service, and stop all deliveries.
9. Clean out the freezer. This is not too tough an undertaking if you have only a small freezer section in your refrigerator, but if you have one of the models that would easily serve all of Fort Dix, your procrastination is understandable. Set aside an entire day for the project, and try to summon whatever assistance you can from the ranks. If you have a sentimental streak, cleaning out the freezer can be a nostalgic trip. Try not to listen to the "yucks" and "icks" of your helpers, as it can spoil the mood. The dove breasts from last fall's hunting trip that you were saving for your anniversary dinner would make a

lovely gift for, perhaps, the orthodontist? It may even help with his final bill. Next come plastic containers in every shape and size containing zucchini and all its derivatives, enough to sustain you for weeks in the event of enemy attack. Zucchini spaghetti sauce, zucchini *parmesano en casserole en multitudo*, zucchini *hors d'oeuvres*, stewed, boiled, baked, sautéed, and deep-fried, loaves upon loaves of zucchini bread and, at the very bottom, some very dead lima beans, a partridge once in a pear tree, and some best-forgotten hamburger patties of Stone Age origin. Most of these goodies can be relegated to the garbage pail or into the dog's dish. The zucchini bread can be rewrapped in foil and tied with bright woolen ribbons and given to neighbors early to beat the Christmas rush. The handfuls of assorted vegetables tied up in the bottoms of those voluminous plastic bags can go into the soup pot. The spaghetti sauce and parmesano can be used up in two weeks by the family, whether they like it or not. What you decide to do with the partridge is your own business.

If you have invested in a side or a quarter of beef shortly before the move, the problem is serious and demands a practical solution. If you can afford the expense, your mover will arrange to take the meat to a frozen food locker for storage until word is received that you are settled in your new home. The meat will then be carefully packed in containers of dry ice and sent to you by air freight. However, the cost can be exorbitant—as much as $250 to $300. You might try to sell the meat back to the butcher at cost, or donate it to the Salvation Army and take the tax deduction. If you decide against these alternatives you can send your husband out in the backyard to dig a large hole, line it with taro leaves and hot coals, and throw a luau for the neighbors.

DELEGATE AND DESIGNATE   Ask your husband or son to be in charge of the garage and lawn equipment. Hopefully, most of the lawn paraphernalia was sorted out when you had your garage sale. Have your men collect the lawn chairs and pile them in one central spot. The movers are not familiar with your property and may inadvertently forget that lovely hammock that you gave Dad last Father's Day. We have a strange and motley assortment of rocks, large and small, that we have collected on trips around the country. They are loaded with fun memories and we use them as garden decorations. I have the kids get a large box, gather the rocks together, and stow them near the other outdoor items.

When you're involved with the sorting and selecting business that precedes packing, you're probably going to come across a few items that don't belong to you—the Pyrex casserole that you borrowed from your mother-in-law two Thanksgivings ago, your best friend's fluted pie pan sent over with her special dessert when the last baby was born—four years ago. And good grief!—a gorgeous silver chafing dish that someone left behind when you were hostess at the garden club luncheon six months ago. You may also notice that a few of your favorite things are missing. The back-to-nature cultist down the street still has your ten-year-old's Cub Scout pup tent in his backyard, and your maternal grandmother's embroidered tablecloth is probably still down at the church where it has been since the last Sunday morning coffee that you "poured" at in September. I always find it hard to ask for something that hasn't been brought back in the accepted Amy Vanderbilt time span. And I hate to be the culprit who has kept a borrowed item too long. Save yourself this embarrassment while keeping the kids busy and making them feel a part of the move. Send the darlings out to return and retrieve the items in question.

It's so much easier to have these details taken care of before you are actually in the throes of moving day. Invariably, something will be missed, and you will hate yourself forever for leaving it behind. On the other hand, haven't you always despised that ugly stone gargoyle that your husband swiped as a fraternity prank umpteen years ago? Now is the time to lug it under a bush way out in the yard. If the movers find it, you're no worse off then before. But you may luck out!

My clever mother has her own sorting technique. She belongs to various ladies' clubs and a couple of months before the moving day, she magnanimously volunteers to hostess the scheduled luncheon or meeting. Throughout the living room she scatters haphazardly on the tables small piles of miscellaneous items that appear to be in the process of being sorted. When the curious ladies ask what she is up to, she says, "I'm busy sorting out those things for our garage sale, but I just can't decide whether or not to get rid of them, and I have no idea what prices to ask. What do you all think I should do?" The trap is carefully set, the bait always taken. By the end of the meeting, the tables are empty, and her pin money cache has grown quite a bit. The ladies are thrilled because they have gotten a private advance showing and lots of bargains to boot!

Decide exactly what is to be packed, and dispose of the rest. On packing day you will be greeted by a crew who will sweep through your house like an army of packing ants. If you're not watchful, you may discover when unpacking later that Junior's half-eaten peanut butter-and-jelly sandwich has been carefully wrapped and placed in a carton.

If you are leaving many friends of long standing or even just a few fond neighbors, you'll be caught up in some very emotional farewells. It isn't pleasant to say goodbye, but it is something you must endure. Your friends will want to have one last dinner or lunch or whatever, and you will want to be with them as often as you possibly can. But how do you manage it all in these last hectic days that are flying by? You will be tired out from just thinking about all the picky little details that you must manage at home. There just aren't enough hours in the day, and saying goodbye to everyone with a dinner here, a last bridge game there, lunch with the bowling team, is obviously impractical. One of the nicest and most thoughtful ways to handle this, and surely the most practical for us, we experienced, was before a major long distance move several years ago. Two weeks before we were to leave, three or four neighborhood couples got together and invited just about everyone we knew in our small town to an open house. We were still relatively relaxed before the final onslaught and were able to enjoy everyone who came to see us off. We were given a lovely gift to remember everyone by and pleasant memories we shall always treasure. It was a pretty weepy evening towards the end, but we all enjoyed every wet minute of it.

If no one else volunteers, plan your own farewell party. Many people do, and it's a lovely idea. Arrange to have your party even as much as a month or two before you leave, when your house is still in order and time is not yet pressing. It can be as casual as you like and a nice way to say "thanks for everything."

If possible, try to say goodbye to each of your very good friends individually—whether it be with a tuna sandwich at the kitchen table, a glass of iced tea under the oak tree, a gabfest at the back fence, or a long telephone conversation on a rainy day. Each friend feels the importance of a personalized visit—and a large cocktail party sometimes won't do. New houses you can always buy—but good friends are hard to come by; they deserve special treatment.

Friends want to help in the final days. They also want to be with you. I find it very tough to pull myself together on a packing day, spruce myself up, put on a smile, and go out to an elegant dinner at a restaurant or friend's home attempting to be my witty, charming self. No way! But I did love it when a great neighbor arrived with an old-fashioned chicken dinner for the family the night before moving day. We all sat amid the packing crates on the living room floor and had a picnic. Another savvy friend took care of the breakfast honors on moving day morning. She said, "Come over for breakfast whenever you have the time." One by one we slipped across the street for hot coffee, sweet rolls, cereal and even eggs and bacon, if we wished.

"Keep cool" is the motto for this busy time. Make things as easy as possible on yourself and your family. And do keep in mind, moving is a beginning as well as an end.

LIGHTS, CAMERA, ACTION!

Packing tips⌂Color-coding⌂ The Forbidden Closet⌂Care and feeding of the family⌂Dealing with disasters.

With all that activity at such an ungodly hour, moving day can be likened to Christmas morning, except that instead of opening up you are packing up. Hopefully, but most unlikely, you've had a good night's sleep. The total experience is a bit like opening night on Broadway. You are desperately trying to remember all your lines and cues. The house lights are dimmed and the atmosphere is electric.

This is probably the time when you will take a good hard look at the man you live with and wonder to yourself, "What in the world did I ever see in *him*?" You may be hard pressed to find the answer to that question. After all, isn't he the one responsible for the holocaust that has descended upon you and your little troupe? Maybe you should have married that mortician after all. At least he stays in the same place! Don't worry. Your feelings are perfectly normal.

Consider the mover who will now arrive to pack your things. As Sitting Bull once said, "You never know-um another brave's burden until you walk a mile in his moccasins." A friend of ours left corporate life a few years ago and joined his brother-in-law in partnership in the moving business. Poetic justice. Having been transferred many times, Muldoon was now on the other side of the packing barrel. There he encountered an aspect of moving he had never considered.

How would you like to be confronted with the task of packing the contents of the cabinet under the kitchen sink at this very moment? Or the drawer in your kitchen stuffed with Green Stamps, bits of string and ribbon, birthday candles, keys to Lord-knows-what, crumpled kindergarten drawings and slips of paper with miscellaneous phone numbers, assorted coins, and a handful of broken Crayolas? Muldoon packed houses so filthy they should have been condemned by the sanitation inspector—dishes of spoiled cat food, pots with the coffee still in them covered with a thick layer of gray mold, dirty dishes in the sink, hampers of smelly laundry, and closets that made Fibber McGee's look tidy.

Customers are naturally tense when they are about to uproot their families and move the sum total of their earthy possessions to an alien environment. They are inclined to be snappish and demanding and somewhat less than understanding when things occasionally go awry. One family, moving temporarily to a beach house and putting most of its things in storage, was quite sarcastic upon receiving the box containing the children's snowsuits instead of the one with the bathing suits. They called Muldoon to tell him that their kids were the hit of the beach in their unusual attire.

Another man who expected to move his family into their new home in Michigan in time for Christmas was upset when his van driver elected to spend the holiday with his own family—in Tennessee. The customer found himself in a motel in Detroit with his wife and six kids on Christmas Eve and called Muldoon, his liaison, every hour to remind him of that fact. As the evening wore on, he consoled himself with a bit of the grape, and the calls became increasingly abusive. After a year as a mover, Muldoon went back to the corporate rat race.

Moving a household is a big job, and if you, the householder, are not organized, things are bound to go wrong. By having your goods sorted and weeded out, you not only aid the packers in their work, but you expedite the reorganization of your new household when you unpack. Some of the following ideas have worked for me:

COLOR-CODING   After years of experience moving my large family in and out of large houses, I have devised what I call my color-coding system. Since each one of my children has his own bedroom and is concerned about having all of his most private possessions misplaced, I go to the local five-and-dime store and buy several rolls of sticky tape in four or five colors. I place a different colored tape on the door of each child's room before the packers arrive. As the cartons are packed, each child, armed with his own roll of tape, places a strip on the set of cartons from his room. This system has proved to have a twofold purpose. Not only does it keep the little dears out of your hair, but when the carton is carried into the new house, you know exactly where it belongs. Don't forget to put the proper colored tape on the doors in the new house when you arrive, so that everyone knows the code.

PACKING   If you have not moved before, you should understand that packing and moving occur on separate days. Depending on the contents of your house, packing can take as long as two or three days. It is a time-consuming and wearying process. In comparison, the actual moving-out is relatively quick and easy.

On *The Tonight Show* one evening, Johnny Carson was commiserating with a guest who had just moved. Johnny said his packers had once meticulously wrapped up a cord of firewood, crated it, and moved it coast to coast. Since the weight of the truckload plus the mileage to your new home determines the cost, the extra weight of the firewood was an expensive mistake for the payer. This is an extreme example, but if you are paying for the move yourself, you should mentally weigh the value of the item against its poundage.

You should specify to your packers when they arrive just what, if anything, is to remain in each room. Items such as draperies or lighting fixtures that stay with the house should be so designated. By doing this at the outset, you eliminate much confusion.

You must assert yourself at the time of packing. Make sure that the movers keep the contents of the various rooms separated. It's terribly frustrating when the unpacking is going on to find a box containing bed linens topped off with "fillers" from the kitchen cabinets. In the past, before I learned to be assertive, I have missed for months items that would finally turn up in a box marked "Xmas decorations." Again, bear in mind that *you* are in charge and you want things done *your* way.

Be sure to pack the phone book. You will want it come Christmas for the addresses of people you want to send cards to and the children will refer to it often in the days following your move when they want to write to good ole Bobby Whatshisname from the first grade. Don't succumb to the temptation to throw out the directories from two moves ago when you are sorting through your things. We have a shelf full of dog-eared phone books from old hometowns, and they are used more often than you might imagine.

THE FORBIDDEN CLOSET   It sounds mysterious, but this plan is really quite simple and is *mandatory* for a successful move. Among the many things you have probably had sleepless nights over, and have hopefully jotted down on one of those all-important lists, are the articles that are to be left *out* of the packing: the clothes you'll require on the trip, loaded in suitcases all set to go; the food you'll want for the final meals; a pot and instant coffee; paper plates and plastic utensils; the dog's leash; your purse; the strongbox with vital documents; and whatever else goes in your survival kit. You will also need to set aside the cleaning materials that you will need for the last cleanup before you depart: cleanser, cloths, sponges, a broom and dustpan, and maybe even a vacuum cleaner. *Set aside one closet and place these items in it. Armed once again with your roll of colored tape, place a "Keep Out" sign on the door!* (The temptation will also be to lock yourself in this sanctuary, but it will probably be too small and cluttered! And not at all sporting of you, lady!) Show this closet to each one of the packers, the movers, and all the members of your family, and make a few dire threats about the consequences if they dare to open it.

I think it's probably impossible to overemphasize those instructions. Consider the plight of my friend Judy. Along with her purse and assorted other essentials, her toddler's security blanket was carefully stashed in the front hall closet. When the packers had finished their work and left and the family was settling down for their last night in the house, the little one started whining for her "bankie." Efficiently, Judy bustled to the closet, pulled open the door, and fished around in the darkened recesses for the blanket. Nothing! Horrified, she switched on the hall light. Sure enough, the closet was as empty as a pauper's pockets. Several large boxes stood in the living room with their contents carefully described in grease pencil on the top of each one. Nowhere did it say "hall closet." The movers had evidently packed the contents of the closet toward the end of the job, and they had topped off several boxes with those things. With wails of "I want my bankie." ringing in her ears, Judy had to open and rifle through every box before she finally uncovered the tattered blanket. Unfortunately, she didn't find her little kit containing medications—including The Pill. When she moved again twenty months later, she had another toddler and his "bankie," to contend with.

Here's my standard list of items to be put under padlock in the Forbidden Closet:

1. Plastic scrub bucket containing a can of bathroom cleanser, clean rags or Handi-wipes, and an all-purpose liquid cleaner
2. Vacuum cleaner
3. Broom and dustpan
4. Strongbox containing your important papers and valuables
5. Suitcases for the trip, consolidated as much as possible so you don't have to carry too much into a motel
6. Cosmetics (Vital!)
7. Medications
8. Nerve medicine (This can also be used in case of snakebite while cleaning the kitchen cupboards.)
9. Pet supplies, including leashes, dishes, packets of moist food, pet tranquilizers
10. Birth-control devices or The Pill. (There's no accounting for the vagaries of the human animal.)
11. Sack of goodies for the trip, including candy, games, comic books
12. Maps
13. Baby needs, such as diapers, bottles, food, spoon, pacifier, fitted crib sheets
14. Purse, containing sunglasses, tissues, cash or traveler's checks, lots of change for rest stops and soda machines
15. Instant coffee, foam cups, "hot pot" or small pan for heating water
16. Thermos bottle for coffee or lemonade
17. Keys to house, car, strongbox
18. A couple of pillows for napping in the car
19. Coats, sweaters, or jackets, depending on the season
20. Packets of moist towelettes
21. Name of your van driver
22. Phone numbers, including moving agents on both ends, realtor, psychiatrists, Dial-A-Prayer or Suicide Prevention, whichever seems most pertinent

The movers will leave one or two empty cartons to be used for your last night's bedding. On moving morning, quickly strip the beds and pack up the boxes yourself. With a marking pencil, label the cartons clearly so you will be able to find the bedding quickly when you arrive at your new home.

If you have been dreading clearing out all your bureau drawers, forget it. Today, the movers will take the entire dresser, filled drawers and all. It does make sense, however, to remove any breakables and have them packed separately. It won't do to have Eau de Lily of the Valley scenting your husband's underwear. That's no way to start a new job!

SPECIAL PEOPLE Moving with babies or very young toddlers, can be trying for all concerned. You can't afford to ignore your little ones at this time, as in most cases they sense the confusion and the disruption of the household. Their schedules may become way out of kilter. There are, however, some positive solutions.

Whenever possible take advantage of a kind neighbor's offer to care for the little one at her home for the day. If you are really lucky, you may have a grandmother or an aunt living in the vicinity who will help you out. If you are not so lucky, call your baby-sitter or an agency and arrange to have someone come in all day to watch the smaller children for you. It is even more desirable to have them out of the house completely. It's nigh unto impossible to be in all places at once, and you and your husband will be needed to supervise the movers. You'll find yourself barraged with questions from all sides, and you should keep yourself as available as possible in order to have things run smoothly on both ends of the move. Aside from the general confusion, there is potential danger to little children. With all the hustle-bustle, a child can easily be stepped on or misplaced! An open door is a great temptation to a curious, investigative tot. And how exciting it is for a small child to play hide and seek among all those great big opened boxes! Honestly, you don't need the extra aggravation and worry at this busy time, so see to it that your *most* precious possessions are well cared for and safe. Just don't forget to pick them up before you leave town!

The day has arrived, and the movers are expected any moment—but where are they? It's time now to point out some of the things that can and unfortunately do go awry, just so you won't be caught unawares. You have all been up and ready and waiting since the crack of dawn. Everyone's been fed, the animals are confined somewhere in the backyard or perhaps even a kennel. Everyone is peering out the windows and doors awaiting the arrival of the van. The expected time has come and gone. You are sure you agreed on eight o'clock. The phone rings and a voice says, "Gee, lady, I'm sorry, but we seem to be lost. We took a wrong turn in Columbus." Now Columbus is still an hour's drive from where you are. Oh well, don't be too upset. Pour yourself a cup of coffee (the instant's in the Forbidden Closet, remember?), and take a break. There's nothing else that you can do, so just relax! If you are into Yoga or TM, there will be a few hundred reasons to practice it today.

A friend of mine had a really wild experience the last time she moved. Sybil is an exceedingly organized, calm, on-top-of-the-situation sort of person. Things were so well organized that her family hardly knew they were moving. The van arrived early on the appointed day—on time, of course. It was large enough to hold all their goods, and the movers were a clean-shaven, businesslike lot. An auspicious start. But when I arrived on the scene a couple of hours later, like a good neighbor, with a pot of coffee and a package of foam cups under my arm, confusion reigned.

It seems that a second van had driven up shortly after the first. It contained the household goods of the new owners, and their driver fully expected to unload . . . that morning! Somebody had goofed, and he was a day early. Generous and open-minded as she is, Sybil had suggested that it would save everyone time and money if both crews proceeded with their work simultaneously.

Her furniture was speedily carried out of the house and set on the lawn. Now the new owner's furniture was being carried in, and neighborhood kids and dogs were arriving in droves to investigate the intriguing spectacle. (You don't often get the chance to inspect all of a neighbor's worldly goods in the harsh light of day.) Kids were trying out the tables and chairs, and Sybil was leaping around the yard with a dish towel, shooing the canine population away from her upholstered pieces. Well, it wasn't as bad as it might have been. She ended up with just three cardboard boxes of stuff that didn't belong to her, and the only things that turned up missing were her bedding and her great-aunt's wedding china, which had a couple of chipped pieces, anyway. But it didn't rain! When I asked her how she could possibly have suggested such a ridiculous plan, Sybil said, "Well, it sounded reasonable. That's how they do it at the White House, isn't it?"

A myth has been perpetrated on the American people. I mean, another one. Who knows how many millions of women have been given inferiority complexes by the charade played out every four years or so when we have a change of occupants in the White House. We have always been led to believe that a magical switch of the two families' goods takes place while they drink a ceremonial cup of coffee and drive over to the Capitol for a fairly brief service marking the change of administrations. Veteran movers have always found this feat mind-boggling!

How did the movers keep Jerry Ford's ski boots from getting mixed up with Jimmy Carter's farm boots? Who kept Susan Ford's posters from ending up on the walls of Chip Carter's bedroom? And who kept Amy's lemonade mix out of Betty Ford's truth serum? It sounds like a job for a crew of hyperactive fairy godmothers. I realize that these families have access to lots of help, but still, in the final analysis, certain decisions can be made only by the owners of the goods to be moved . . . and they have a few other matters to attend to on Inauguration Day.

Now, in this era of Truth In Washington, that myth has finally been exploded. Thanks to Barbara Walters and Morley Safer and their colleagues, the sleeping arrangements of First Families have been revealed to the waiting world. There was much to-do about the fact that the Fords have slept in the same double bed for years and continued to do so in the White House. This led to the observation by sharp-eyed reporters that on Inauguration Day last, all the Ford's possessions had been moved out of the house before the actual day of transfer of power except for their double bed which was spotted being loaded on a van backed up to a side door that morning.

With typical candor Jerry Ford admitted to the press that he was having difficulty putting his hands on his favorite turtleneck in that last week, and Betty was heard to remark that she could have used a few more days to get it all together. Thank God! Now we can all feel a little more adequate. Still, you have to wonder how Pat Nixon managed to get out on such short notice. Her husband was bounced out of a job, the family was bounced out of their house, and every hair on Pat's head was still in place.

Finally the truck is fully loaded and the last little "grafti" have been stowed. (Grafti, by the way, are the last of the small articles that the movers use to fill in spaces or empty pockets in the van. As an example, the vacuum cleaner and the broom and dustpan that you carefully guarded in the Forbidden Closet may now become grafti, as will the almost forgotten laundry basket from the basement, or an old basketball discovered under the front porch.) As you wish your driver Godspeed, give him the names of the motels where he can reach you en route and the time when you will be arriving in your new town. He may have to contact you in the event of an emergency or a change of plans. You will also want to set up a time to rendezvous for the unloading at your new home.

Your car has been packed with the suitcases, the hamsters, and your favorite Swedish ivy. The last spit and polish cleanup has been done, and the house looks so absolutely gorgeous that you hate to leave. Say a prayer that the lady of the house you are heading for has been as considerate. You have tidied up your face and hair and the kids and said your final private goodbyes to each room; you've shed a few tears and tried to smile for your husband, the rat, and have cheered everyone up as you pull out of the driveway for the last time. You're on your way! You begin to relax and let fatigue take hold of your aching body. But it's hard to dispel the nagging feeling that you've forgotten something. "Oh my God! Did somebody pack the baby?!!"

PLANTS, PETS, AND SPECIAL PEOPLE

What to do about your plants when you move⌂How to move horses, dogs, cats, fish and others⌂Caring for an infant during a move.

Special members of your household need special consideration and handling when you move. For instance, most movers won't touch plants with a ten-foot pole. Moving vans are neither heated nor air-conditioned, so plants could freeze or suffer heat prostration. No water and no light and little air for several days may result in a slower death. I prefer to present my plants to my friends as a farewell gift, something green and growing to remind them of me after I've ridden off into the sunset. This goes, by the way, only for plants that are in good shape. Nobody will be thrilled with a long, scrawny, starved philodendron even if it was a gift from Mary Tyler Moore! Pitch the poor specimens in the trash after taking some cuttings if you know someone who would appreciate them. Tidy up the good ones, trim them if they need it, and bestow them on your friends. Make sure they aren't harboring a family of bugs, though. You don't want to start an epidemic in your friend's collection—not if you want to be fondly remembered. On the other hand, if you have a rotten neighbor. . . .

If there are one or two favorites that you can't bear to part with, take them along in the car *if you have room*. Don't try to travel across the country with a Sprengeri in your lap tickling your nose, or a dwarf orange tree blocking the view in the rearview mirror. If the weather is cold, you'll have to haul the plants into the motel at night. The kids will strongly object to making a spectacle of themselves, so you'll have to do it yourself, Mom. If it's hot, don't leave plants in a closed car in the sun. Remember that these are living things, and your objective is to keep them in that condition. This is going to some extra trouble, but sometimes it's worth it for sentiment's sake. I have a Schefflera that has moved cross-country with us three times, all done up in a plastic dry cleaner's bag (with a few holes punched in it) to conserve moisture and protect it from drafts. It has flourished and may be too big to make another move, in which case it will make a noble gift for a deserving friend. If you are traveling with an empty back seat, sans children and animals, you can put up one of those telescoping clothes poles and hook your hanging plants over it. Secure the hangers with sticky tape so they don't slide into each other.

It's important to recognize that replacement of your plants will be an expense in settling your new home. Be sure to figure it in with your other moving expenses. This is one that husbands often overlook. There's nothing like some flourishing greenery to make a house a home, and you're going to need all the help you can get! Besides, it gives you an excuse to locate a good greenhouse in your new town right off the bat. On one move I brought some cuttings with me, all done up in Sphagnum moss in a plastic bag. They moved beautifully, keeping quiet and taking up little space, but I was too busy getting settled to rustle up the necessary peat moss and vermiculite and pots to get them rooted, and eventually they were thrown out. Plants that root easily in water are possible to handle, though. You can put them in a jar on a window sill when you get to your new house. By the time they are rooted, you will be unpacked and ready to deal with them. Be sure to take enough cuttings from each specimen so that you'll have several to plant in each new pot. This gives you a nice bushy-looking plant. Many years ago we were given a cutting that would purportedly someday be a banana tree. "You must be kidding," we said. "Bananas only grow in the tropics, not in Massachusetts."

"You'll see," said our friends. "With tender loving care, it will be beautiful, and in seven years you may even have a banana or two. Just follow the instructions and it will be O.K.!" That same humble banana shoot has lived a life its forefathers back in Puerto Rico would not believe. It has become part of the family, moving throughout the country with us. It has endured wind and rain, an earthquake (the news called it a "tremor" but it was an earthquake, nevertheless, and a hurricane; it has been moved hither and yon in the trunks of cars and the back of a U-Haul, and squashed in the back seat of the car underneath the cat cage. It has been dug up and replanted in unfamiliar territory, never allowed really to put roots down for any length of time; it has been trampled by the neighborhood dogs and has withstood other indignities by various and sundry animals; rabbits have nibbled at its leaves; still it has continued to survive. Not only has it made it through all these travails, but it has managed to reproduce itself over and over again. Every fall when the weather begins to grow cold, our noble friend and her children must withstand one destructive frost which turns her lovely leaves to brown. Somehow they survive it all, and after a winter of hibernation cuddled in peat moss and plastic in the basement, they are replanted on the first warm day of spring, in the sunniest spot in the yard. They grow taller and taller and within a short time, more sprouts are poking their heads up. Survival seems to be their motto.

In the years since we were given our feisty banana, she and I have been moved four times. I have given offshoots of the original to family and friends throughout the country, and they too, are doing well. All the banana has ever wanted is a secure resting place in the sun and to be left alone to raise her little ones and grow big and fat and leafy and admired, and maybe some day to produce a real banana. This parallels my own desires remarkably, but as long as Blaze continues to move, I guess the plant and I will just keep on moving right along with him.

Then there are the animals. Most eight-year-olds won't turn a hair when Mother gives away the grape ivy, but just try to get rid of the family cat! Almost all pets can and should be moved. The only exception I can think of is fish. It might be possible to move an aquarium across town, but a long-distance move is difficult, considering the requirements of fish—a tank of water weighing ten pounds per gallon (that's a hundred pounds for the average-size ten-gallon tank!), a constant temperature, and an electric air pump to keep the water oxygenated. Forget it! Give the fish away to a neighbor who will take care of them, and promise a new, more interesting collection when you are settled in your new house. Clean up the tank and equipment and have it packed for moving. If you or your hobbyist are insistent on trying to move the fish, or if the collection is a very valuable one, you can *try* this method: Put the fish into a plastic bag containing water from the aquarium. Tie the top of the bag tightly with a Twist-em, and put the bag into one of those foam coolers that you use to carry beer to a picnic. This will maintain the constant temperature that fish need. Once every day open the bag and allow it to stand open a few minutes so the carbon dioxide can escape and the oxygen supply can be replenished. Good luck!

Most pets will be happiest and healthiest if they can travel in the car with you. In the case of cats and dogs, I order new name tags for their collars several weeks before the move. Have *your name* and your *new address* printed on the disk, and attach it firmly to the pet's collar. If your cat has no collar, get one. Usually animals don't care for long trips, and they may escape from the car while you are getting gas or making a rest stop. Don't let an animal out of the car *at any time* unless you have him firmly on a leash. A dog will have to make a rest stop when you do, but make sure that someone who can control him holds his leash while he inspects the roadside shrubbery. Also have his water dish handy. All that panting he's been doing in your ear for the last two hundred miles has made him thirsty. You can fill his dish in the rest room and give him a drink whenever you have one. Bring along a supply of his favorite food, but don't feed him too heavily, and feed him at night. Animals can get carsick too, you know, and this can place a distinct damper on the mood of the trip. Your vet can provide medication to quiet your dog's stomach if Rover has this problem.

Sometimes a move can be too much for an older pet, as in this sad instance: Some friends of ours started out for their new home halfway across the country with their three small children and their old family retainer, a large black Newfoundland. They were on the Pennsylvania Turnpike on a muggy, overcast, mid-summer afternoon when they noticed that the dog was lolling about on the children in a rather careless fashion. She was panting heavily and drooling unsanitarily on the baby when they decided she was in trouble. They pulled over onto the shoulder where the sign said "Emergency Stopping Only" and wrestled the dog out of the car. Whether from the heat, the excitement, or what, she was in bad shape. She breathed her last in my friend's lap in the gravel at the side of the road with the cars whistling past and the children wailing. Shortly after the husband took the kids and went to get help, the skies opened up. The wife dragged the old friend under a tree and crouched there praying that the rain would deter any rapists happening by. After what seemed an interminable time, the husband returned with a farmer and a shovel and the crying children. They buried the dog beside the turnpike and climbed back into the car. I don't know if this incident had anything to do with it, but that marriage lasted only a month after they moved into their new home. I like to think they were already in trouble.

On our last long-distance move, we started out with the

flourishing schefflera mentioned earlier, two cats, an Irish Setter, and five kids in a station wagon. Talk about Project Hope! We had scheduled the move over a weekend so that we could spend a couple of days sightseeing in Washington D.C. on our way to St. Louis. We checked into a local motel the first night, after a long day of getting the van loaded and scrubbing up for the new homeowners. One night in a motel with that menagerie was enough! My husband and I settled the children in the room with their burgers from McDonald's while we went down to the dining room for a nice quiet dinner. We were enjoying a couple of steaks when we became aware of a commotion in the lobby. The waiters and busboys were buzzing among themselves and glancing out the door. When we asked our waiter what was going on, he said, "There's a big red dog tearing around the lobby with a bunch of kids chasing him." My husband said, "Oh," and calmly spread butter on a roll. We furtively glanced at each other and, in one of those unspoken meetings of the minds, decided to remain anonymous.

As if that weren't enough, the dog promptly forgot his toilet training and lifted his leg against the doors, walls, and furniture of the brand new Holiday Inn. It was apparent that not only did he take up too much room in the car, stepping on kids and wagging his tail in our faces, but an Irish Setter was not a congenial hotel guest. Since we were still close to home, the next morning we got a certificate from our vet showing that his shots were up-to-date. Then we drove to Kennedy Airport in nearby New York City, where the SPCA operates a kennel.

We took man's ex-best friend to air cargo, left an old pair of the kids' jeans to comfort him (we're still hearing about that!), and paid for his flight to St. Louis. His fare included a charge for constructing a large wooden crate to hold him. An agent delivered him to the kennel where he stayed for a week before being put on a flight to our new home. Be advised that air cargo flights do not run on as strict a timetable as passenger flights do. We failed to check with the airport before we left our new home to pick him up, and after an exhausting day of moving in, we had a two-hour wait at the airport. Then we were told that they had no invoice showing a dog on the flight, but when they made radio contact with the plane, the pilot said yes, he did have a dog aboard. I shudder to think how he knew!

At last the plane landed and our setter was delivered, crate and all. We had planned to keep the box for another time, until we caught a whiff of the aroma wafting from it! We pried it open and took one shaken, airsick, but overjoyed dog to his new home and left the crate on the loading dock. New York's Kennedy is one of the few airports in the country that has a kennel operating on its premises. In other towns look for a kennel that will deliver your pet to the airport for his flight. *Remember that you must provide a health certificate from your vet.*

For several years now a controversy has raged on the safety of flying pets on cargo flights. Some airlines refuse to do it during the hot summer months because air cargo holds are not air-conditioned. Generally speaking, it's safer for a pet to travel in the baggage compartment of a passenger flight, where the air conditioning from the passenger compartment seeps in to help keep things cool. In order to be eligible, however, he must be accompanying a passenger on that flight. Many airlines are now making an effort to ban cargo containing dry ice when animals are aboard. In the past, carbon dioxide fumes given off by the dry ice have caused the death of some pets. It would be wise to investigate the accommodations provided by the airline you have chosen, for the sake of your own peace of mind.

You may think that the cat can travel very nicely in the car, riding in little Susie's lap. Wrong! As soon as you put the car into gear, little Susie is going to be stabbed by Kitty's claws, and the cat will be under the seat yowling. This is not really safe, because she could leap to the dashboard or to the top of the driver's head at any moment. Besides that, she will streak for daylight as soon as anyone opens the car door.

Actually, our cats were very little trouble. At the pet store I bought a metal cage large enough for the two of them. It collapses when not in use, and is much roomier and airier than the ordinary cat carrying case. It has a handle on each side for toting and a removable tray on the bottom for cleaning. We put in a bath towel to make it comfy, put the two cats in it, and put it in the back of the station wagon. Because it was the dead of winter, we tucked a light blanket around the cage. This not only kept out the drafts but made the cats feel more secure. There was a little meowing at first, but they soon settled in for a long nap.

We packed a shopping bag containing kitty litter, a small plastic litter box, some plastic liners for the box, dry cat food, and their dishes. When we checked into a motel, one child set up the litter box and the food and water in the bathroom and then, making sure that the doors leading to the hall were closed, we let the cats out to explore the room. In the morning the plastic liner containing the used litter was neatly tied up with a Twist-em and dropped in the wastebasket. The dishes were emptied and put back into the shopping bag, and we were on our way.

The only hang-up is making sure the cats don't escape from the room when the kids are going in and out on their many trips to the Coke machine. Cats, being naturally curious, like to have a look around. When we were staying several days in the same motel in Washington, we put the cats back into the cage during the day when we were out. This kept them from making a dash for freedom while the maid was doing up the room. On moving days we kept them in the cage, too. Cats don't like noise and confusion, and they are very likely to go away and hide until it's over. For the first few days in the new house, we kept them confined to quarters until they realized that this was where we were going to stay. They soon made themselves at home and found all the good warm places to sleep.

No matter what animals are traveling with you, *do not leave them in a closed car in hot weather*. If you are going into the Colonel's for lunch, park the car in the shade, and leave all the windows partially open—enough to allow the passage of air but not enough to allow the passage of the pet. Heat can build up in a closed car very quickly.

Monkeys, rabbits, and guinea pigs can travel in much the same manner as cats. Birds, gerbils, and hamsters can go along right in their cages, but be especially careful not to expose them to drafts. Cover the cage in the car, and in and out of motels. See your vet well before moving day for your animal's medical records and a possible prescription for tranquilizers—for the animals, I mean. Medication will really quiet down nervous or very active pets, and make the trip more pleasant for everyone in the car.

If you must travel with a horse, you must, and you probably know all about trailers and hitches already. Just be sure that your equipment is in good shape and that your pet has had a practice ride in the trailer, so you don't wind up as my sister did, with a horse loose on an interstate highway.

Susie was moving from Duluth to Milwaukee to start a new job, and her horse was going with her. Cheyenne was a big powerful bay who was having his first excursion in a horse trailer. He didn't like it very much. He was restless and nervous when they started out, but when Susie noticed that his faint rumblings back in the trailer had grown to thunderings, and she began having trouble keeping the car on the road, she thought she had better stop and see what all the commotion was about.

She pulled the car over to the side of the road, and walked back to the rear of the trailer to investigate. When she opened the door, she saw that Cheyenne had gotten his foreleg caught up in the feedbox, and this was causing him quite a bit of distress. In order to release his leg, she had to back him out of the trailer, and when Cheyenne got a look at the cars whizzing by next to him, he was terrified. He stood there, wild-eyed, nostrils flaring, and refused to budge.

After several minutes of trying to urge him back in, Susie's own fears mounted as she stood there hanging on to his halter. Then she noticed a rest area up ahead and decided to walk him there where she could calm him down. Just as they reached the parking lot, a state trooper pulled up and got out of his car. "What's the matter, lady?" he asked as he approached from the rear. Wham! Cheyenne let him have it with a hoof in the solar plexus. As the officer struggled to his feet, a school bus pulled up for a rest stop, and forty kids on a field trip poured from the bus, yelling, "Wow! Look at the horse!"

"Can we have a ride?"

"Can I pet him?"

The children crowded around while the officer, one hand massaging his stomach, shouted at them to get away. Cheyenne rolled his eyes, flattened his ears, and trembled. Suddenly he bolted and made for the adjacent alfalfa field. Another trooper pulled up, and to the delight of the children, Susie and the officers chased Cheyenne around the field until they had rounded him up. One of the men offered to drive the car and trailer up to the rest area so they could put Cheyenne back in. As he pulled the car into the parking lot, the bus backed up and smashed into the rear of the trailer, tearing the door from its hinges.

Susie and Cheyenne spent the night at a nearby farm while the trailer was repaired by a local smithy and Cheyenne recovered from nervous exhaustion. It took Susie a little longer. Fortunately they were traveling through farm country. Imagine being stranded on the New Jersey Turnpike in those circumstances.

If you are traveling with a horse, you will have to arrange in advance for accommodations for him on overnight stops. Some parts of the country have "horse motels" along the major interstate highways where both you and your animal can spend the night—under separate cover, of course. Elsewhere, horses can be accommodated at local stables, but do make reservations. Your local saddle club can help you with this.

In these days of disposable diapers and ready-mixed formulas, babies are easier to travel with than pets *or* plants, and *much* easier than horses! An infant will need a comfortable, roomy car bed that can be securely attached to the seat. It should have handles if the baby is very young, so that you can tote a sleeping infant into restaurants and motels without disturbing him. Of course, it goes without saying that you never leave a baby in the car alone.

Babies are soothed by the motion of the moving car, and they usually travel well. See that your crib gets loaded on the moving van last, so that it can come off first at the new house and be assembled immediately. It will be a relief to you and the baby to have him back in his own bed as soon as possible. Be sure to let motels know that you will need a crib when you make your reservations. Their supply is limited, and sometimes all the cribs are in use. I like to bring my own fitted crib sheets along in my suitcase, because some motels just fold a regular bed sheet over the crib mattress, and if the baby is able to stand up in the crib, the sheet is soon in a tangle around his feet. Besides, I always feel that my laundry is more germ-free than the hotel's, although that may be a fantasy.

Have a good supply of disposable diapers and a small box

of plastic bags (with those Twist-ems again!) in which to deposit the used ones. That will help keep the air in the car tolerable. If the aroma gets too bad and there's nowhere in sight to get rid of the bag, stop and put it in the trunk! You can put it in the trash can at a gas station or a roadside rest area.

Be sure to bring an adequate supply of formula and baby food and whatever utensils you will need. There wil be stores along the way, of course, but usually they are off the interstate highways and take time to find—no fun when you have a hungry baby. Stash all this stuff in the car early on moving day, or store it in the Forbidden Closet until you are ready to leave. If you are a nursing mother, your feeding problems are simplified, but not eliminated. Try not to become overtired, and be sure to eat regular meals and drink your fluids to keep the milk supply plentiful. Easier said than done. If you are going to be in a public place at nursing time, you will have to decide in advance if you want to use a formula for that feeding. For airplane travel I always bring a bottle along, because I'm not the exhibitionist type and there's no place to be alone. Those johns are too small, and there's always someone else waiting to get in. In the privacy of your car, nursing is convenient . . . but not always private. On one trip I was nursing the baby in the front seat of the car as we were riding along the Massachusetts Turnpike when we were overtaken by a convoy of Army trucks loaded with troops, all of whom gazed with intense interest as they passed.

As I've said before, if you can get a friend to take care of your infant on moving day, do it! All the confusion does not make for a contented baby or a contented mother. The movers prop the doors open, and the house becomes drafty and cold in the winter and hot and humid in the summer. When my youngest son was a baby, we were moving out of a house in Wisconsin on a dazzling winter day with the temperature a crackling 17° below zero. That's minus 27.2° Celsius, baby, and that's cold on any scale. I kept the baby in his room with the door closed for awhile, but soon I could see his breath freezing in an icy cloud as he slept. We reluctantly decided to leave the movers to finish loading the van, called a service to clean up when they were through, and got started on the trip to Connecticut.

Toddlers are more difficult to handle on a move than infants. They don't sleep as much, and they don't stay where you put them. They are as curious as the cats and want to be in on everything that's going on. Get *someone* else to watch a toddler, perferably *somewhere* else!

The National Safety Council reports that most children's accidents occur when Mother is distracted or tired. I can't think of any experience more distracting or tiring to Mother than moving—except possibly Daddy running off with a twenty-year-old go-go dancer, or catching a glimpse of yourself in the nude in a full length mirror and realizing that it's not only your arches that have fallen.

Be that as it may, a couple of years ago I found a brown-eyed, curly-headed four-year-old crying his heart out in my back yard. His family was moving into the neighborhood that day, and his older brothers had teased their mother to distraction until she gave in and allowed them to go over to look at their new school. It was just a couple of blocks away, so she told them to take Mikey along.

They agreed, but as older brothers will, they ditched the four-year-old when he couldn't keep up. Now Mikey was lost and terrified even though he was only a few doors from home. I had noticed the moving van earlier in the day, so I had a good idea of where Mikey belonged—even if he didn't.

It's important to be sure that young children know their new phone number and address. You can make a game of teaching it to them, with lots of praise when they master it. When our children were small, they loved playing "school" at the dinner table or in the car, with me asking a question geared to the level of each child in turn. The youngest always got the address and phone number question until he knew the answer backwards and forwards, and the others were as tickled as he was when he finally knew it.

A friend of mine recently moved her family to a suburban Connecticut town, hopefully the last in a series of moves from Georgia to Wisconsin to Connecticut. Her happy and gregarious kindergartner came home from school the first day in tears. "Why, Colleen," said her mother, "What's wrong?"

"My teacher yelled at me," sobbed Colleen.

Finding it difficult to believe that any teacher would raise her voice in anger to an obedient, eager-to-please little girl on her first day in a new school, her mother incredulously asked why.

"Because I didn't know what state this is." sobbed Colleen. "Mommy, is this Wisconsin or what?"

Most teachers are more humane, but if we consider it important to tag our pets with their new address, it is equally important to teach our youngsters their phone number and address as a safety precaution, and to give them a sense of security and of belonging somewhere. Young children are awfully disoriented when you move, so keep a close eye on them even if they *are* wearing dog tags.

ONE-NIGHT STANDS

The importance of advance planning⌂Psychological care of the family⌂How to keep from going crazy in the car⌂Traveling in two cars without getting separated⌂The last resorts.

As you pull away from your old home for the last time, with friends and neighbors waving on the curb and you and your children sobbing, or at least sniffling, with the pain of the farewells, you may wonder how you can possibly *survive* the trip to your new home, let alone enjoy it!

You've put in an exhausting day seeing your beloved home stripped bare and looking suddenly forlorn and dirty. There were base boards to be wiped, bathrooms to be scoured (even though you knew the new owner would do it over again), and floors to be mopped up after the movers. Now you are physically decimated and emotionally wrung out, and that grim look on your husband's face means he feels the same way. Besides, he has to bear the burden of guilt for this whole fiasco—it was he, after all, who was promoted!

This is when you need the pampering of a little luxury, and the best thing you can do now is to put into the nicest motel in the *next* town. The reason I say the *next* town is that it's best to put a little distance between yourselves and your old home, not only symbolically but physically. (Otherwise your children will spend the evening on the phone with their friends prolonging the good-byes and the tears. In the case of teens—even worse. They will want to take off for the evening to spend yet another "one last night" with their friends. At a time when you need your rest, you shouldn't be walking the floor wondering where your children are.) Don't try to drive any more than twenty or thirty miles though. You're too tired and nothing but trouble can result, like fighting among the children over who is suffering the most—or worse, between you and your husband, over just about anything!

You will feel pretty tacky walking into a nice motel in your filthy clothes and bedraggled hairdo, but you'll feel a lot better after a hot bath. Packing a small bottle of firewater in your suitcase isn't a bad idea either. After a bath and a drink (which can be simultaneous), you'll begin to feel human again. What could be more luxurious than ordering your dinner from room service? By all means, if you are traveling with children, even only one or two, have adjoining rooms. Put the kids in front of the TV in the other room with their hamburgers and fries while you and your husband share a steak and a little bottle of red wine or whatever your heart desires—even if it's a poached egg and tea. And then get some rest.

As for the trip to the new house, do plan it well in advance. If you arrange your move over a weekend you'll get a couple of extra days for some leisurely sightseeing. Get some up-to-date road maps to follow. If you belong to an auto club you can obtain very detailed ones showing points of interest along the way and describing the countryside through which you'll be passing. Let the children see where they're going on the maps—it's a good practical geography lesson. Make reservations at motels well ahead of time. Again, the AAA furnishes excellent guidebooks listing all the motels in each city along your route, what facilities they offer, and their ratings. If you're traveling with children, try to stop at motels with indoor pools unless, of course, it's summer, when an outdoor pool will suffice. After hours of riding, the kids need to work off some energy, and it's much nicer for everyone if they can do it in a pool instead of running up and down the halls. Incidentally, these guidebooks are a fund of interesting information, including the history of the regions through which you will be passing and descriptions of the products and resources of the area. (Did you know that one of Topeka's principal exports is soap?)

Stop early, before everyone gets too tired and cranky. If you are married to a "keep-on-truckin" type, as I am, be sure that your husband understands this ahead of time. If you need to stop when Blaze is driving, you have to throw yourself from the moving car. If you have reservations, this will be less of a problem. Six or seven hours of traveling is enough in your condition. Remember, you still have some harrowing days ahead of you, so don't overdo.

Once in the dear dim days, practically beyond recall, when we didn't have any children, we made a move shepherding only a mongrel dog known as Ole, The Black Swede. He was an endearing little fellow whom we managed to spoil so badly that when children eventually did arrive on the scene his nose was permanently out of joint. In his halcyon days, however, he was the apple of our eye and traveled first class, so to speak.

En route to our new home, we had stopped to spend the

night at a carefully chosen motel, the only requirement being that it have television. Younger readers may find this hard to believe, but there was a time when some of us had no TV in our homes, so the prospect of having a set all to ourselves for a whole night, or at least until the test patterns appeared, was fascinating to say the least. We settled the dog and our suitcases in the room, and then went out for a hasty supper and a quick stop to load up on snacks to see us through the evening. We planned to turn on the TV, get into bed, and lounge there happily munching pretzels, swigging colas and watching Sid Caesar and *The $64,000 Question* to our heart's content. That was the plan, and a good one it was too! All this luxury, and the company picking up the tab—it was worth moving!

Old Bobby Burns surely put his finger on it with that line about "the best laid plans of mice and men." While we were out, Ole became upset at being left alone in the room and vented his feelings by chewing on the fat black cord hanging from the back of the TV set. The one that led to the outlet on the wall. Until it was severed. Don't talk to *me* about dumb animals.

We came back to the room with our goodies, hurried into our pajamas, switched on the set and hopped into bed. Nothing. "It'll take·a minute to warm up," said Blaze, who was knowledgeable in these matters. We waited expectantly. Ole snuggled up to me for his share of the pretzels. Still nothing. Blaze climbed out of bed and padded across the room to fiddle with the dials.

"Maybe it's not plugged in," I said.

The next few minutes will have to censored, but when he calmed down Blaze showed a flash of real American ingenuity. With a penknife and a piece of electrical tape, scavenged from a floor lamp in the room, he spliced the cord and we had our evening of TV. For weeks after that, though, I watched the papers with guilty apprehension for news of a big motel fire in that city. Blaze is *no* electrician.

Speaking of stopping—when you do, whether it's for gas or food or whatever, be sure to count noses before you resume your trip. More than one family has left a member in the washroom along an interstate highway thinking he was still snoozing in the back seat. You can imagine how disconcerting this can be!

By the second day of your trip, the tears should be drying up. Every turn of the wheels lessens the pain, and your group will begin to sit up and take notice again. This is the time when a little entertainment will be needed. For young children, bring crayons and coloring books, large connect-the-dot picture books, sewing cards, and a pillow for a nap. Older kids like books of riddles and jokes. We've had a lot of laughs with the booklets of "Mad-Libs" that are available at most variety stores. "Mad-libs" players are asked to supply words at random which the moderator writes into the blanks of an incomplete one-page story. The resulting silliness is then read aloud to the group.

License Plate Bingo is another favorite of our family. Sometimes I can find pads of Auto-Bingo cards already made up, but when I can't we make our own. Give everyone an ordinary Bingo card with the names of states written in the squares. As you sight a car with a license plate from each state, you color in that square. It can take the better part of the day to get a row to make Bingo. Be sure to have prizes, as kids are very interested in that aspect of the game. Candy bars satisfy my group. This game can be played with younger children by filling the squares with little cutouts of things like a red barn, a black horse, an orange VW, etc.

Then there is the alphabet game, good for everyone with 20/20 vision who knows his ABC's. Players here must spot the letters of the alphabet in sequence beginning with "A" from signs along the road. You can kill miles trying to find a "J" or a "Q". The first one to complete the alphabet wins the M&M's.

If things are really getting out of hand, and you feel that your iron grip on your nerves might snap, you might try a breath-holding contest. The only equipment required is a watch with a second hand. This game has a twofold advantage. First, the players, must, by the very nature of the game, be silent while play is in progress. Second, if the action is intense, one or more of the contestants just might pass out for a few minutes of blessed peace and quiet. Drivers, of course, are excused from this competition.

When spirits are flagging, tempers fraying, and the trip begins to seem endless, I bring out my secret cache of movie magazines, comic books, and other such ordinarily forbidden reading material. These are pounced upon with cries of delight and usually get us to our next stop without further snarling and bickering. A few rolls of Life Savers and a couple of packs of gum can help to relieve the tedium, too, so be sure to have a generous supply on hand.

If any of your kids or pets are prone to car sickness be sure to see your doctor in advance for medication, and don't forget to give it to the little darlings. Nothing can spoil a trip quicker than someone whimpering, "I think I'm going to be sick." If he should actually carry out this threat, his brothers and sisters can be counted on to offer such words of sympathy as:

"Oh, it's gross!"

"He got it on my sweater!"

"Why did *he* have to come?"

They would willingly drop him off at the next gas station, such is their compassion for the white-faced, green-gilled victim. To be on the safe side, keep a few plastic bags in the glove compartment for such emergencies. A package of Wash 'n Dri's can't hurt either.

Keep the food simple when you're traveling. My kids go berserk when confronted with a breakfast menu, and if I don't monitor their orders they'll have pancakes and syrup, donuts, and hot chocolate, not my idea of a breakfast to travel on unless you happen to be going by dogsled. Incidentally, I make it a rule not to leave the motel without breakfast under our belts. As I mentioned before, Blaze doesn't like to stop, and if I fall for his line that we'll get a bite at the next diner, it's likely to be a long morning.

One of the worst misfortunes that can befall a family on the move is the illness of one of its members far from the comforts of that old familiar friend, the family doctor—or in this day and age, your favorite consortium of internists. One night I found myself in a motel waiting for the furniture to catch up with us, with a three-week-old baby who was still practically a stranger to me, wheezing and blowing bubbles with his nose and sounding as if each breath were going to be his last.

Ordinarily I am inclined to take the approach to family illnesses that if you ignore them, they'll go away. But put me on the road and all my subconscious insecurities take over. I avert my eyes if a hearse is sighted, mumble incantations over loaded haywagons, and knock on wood at the sight of a sign stating that there is a hospital at the next exit. In fact, one dawn as we hit the road loaded to the gunwales, I was horrified to see the sun rising in a blood-red sky, and I could hardly be pursuaded to continue the trip. I know a bad omen when I see one!

In this case I was convinced the baby had nothing less than pneumonia, and maybe worse. At the first ray of daylight my husband called a man he had just met in his new office and asked him to recommend a doctor. After getting the doctor out of bed and begging him to come to the motel, Blaze set out for a diner down the road to get some donuts and milk for the two-year-old, who was awake and hungry. He was no sooner out of sight when the conscientious young physician rushed in, no doubt expecting to find a terminal case. He carefully examined the baby and dryly pronounced that he had—a cold. After prescribing nose drops and a vaporizer, he was ready to be paid for the call. I turned around to get my purse. It wasn't on the dresser. It wasn't in the closet. It wasn't even in the bathroom. It was in the car with Blaze! I weakly explained that I had no money, and the doctor and I exchanged addresses. He promised to send me a bill, and off he went on his appointed rounds. Later when we became almost intimate, thanks to multiple cases of ear infection, rubella, and the croup, he confessed that he had gone to his office that morning and told his partner to chalk that call up to charity. "A bunch of gypsies in a motel, for God's sake!"

In the event that one of the family comes down with a real emergency, and Dramamine won't solve the problem, keep your eyes peeled for one of the signs along the highway that will direct you to the closest hospital. Drive directly to the emergency room or the outpatient clinic, and you will be taken care of. If you are in the boondocks when something goes wrong, stop at a service station and ask where you can locate the nearest doctor. It's gratifying to learn just how helpful people can be when you're in trouble. Motels always have the phone number of a doctor they can call for you.

Try to see that everyone is healthy before you set foot out of your old home. Fill up on vitamins and get current on your booster shots. Tie gauze masks over the noses and mouths of the entire family, and then cross your fingers when you set out. If you see any ambulances on the way, stop, take three umbrella steps backward and say, "Captain, may I?" before you continue on your way.

If you are traveling in two cars, have check points occasionally along the day's route where you can get together and see that everything is OK. Also have the phone number of some friend or relative that each of you can call if you do become separated. My mother spent a sleepless night in a motel room once, wondering where my sister was when they were driving two cars cross-country. It's hard to stay together on an interstate highway, and when my sister had to stop for repairs to that horse trailer she was hauling, my mother didn't notice it. If they had both thought to phone me, I could have put them in touch with each other. Make sure both drivers know in advance where you are planning to spend the night so if you can't make the rendezvous you can at least notify the other.

Above all, be sure that both drivers have a map and at least a general knowledge of where you are heading. Trying to keep two cars together in heavy traffic is not only impractical but unsafe. If one car gets through a traffic light and the second one doesn't, it's difficult to catch up without speeding or taking unnecessary chances. Plan ahead where you will stop for lunch or a breather. Walky-talkies or the popular CB radios are a good way to keep in touch en route, and they also help to pass the time.

Some years ago a friend of mine was making a move from Long Island to Philadelphia. Not a very long trip, you will say, but to a young girl from Slippery Rock, Tennessee it seemed as fraught with danger as Lewis and Clark's trek through the wilderness.

Pat's firstborn was only six weeks old, and her executive-type husband insisted that the baby would be safer traveling with him. When they were ready to leave, he put the car bed into his blue Ford and said casually, "Just follow me." As he pulled away in a cloud of exhaust fumes, Pat realized that she didn't know how to get to Philadelphia. Her husband was a block away before she even got the key in the ignition.

The next couple of hours were a nightmare. Pat drove white-knuckled through the labyrinth of congested roads that wind like a maze around New York City and Philadelphia, straining to keep her eyes on the blue car in the distance. Her whole life was in that car, and she was convinced that if she lost sight of it, that was the end. Meanwhile her husband cruised blithely along, humming to the baby, never thinking to look for Pat in the rearview mirror. When she finally pulled up behind him in front of their new home, suffering from eyestrain and apoplexy, he grinned and said, "Now, that wasn't a bad trip, was it?"

When we took two cars on a recent trip to Colorado, we let the teens travel together in one car. Their idea of sweet listening music is my idea of Halloween night in a fright house. The rest of the family rode peacefully tuned in to the golden oldies. The radio was no problem, but the speeding ticket they got in Kansas was. By their own admission, they beat us to every checkpoint by at least twenty minutes. You will have to weigh the appeal of sweet harmony against the hazards of reckless rock, but at least be sure that both drivers have money enough for gas and emergencies.

If it's impossible for your family to drive your two cars, there is a solution: For a fee you can hire an auto transport service to drive your second car to the destination. In the case of a long-distance move, this option makes a lot of sense. If none of these options grab you, go Greyhound!

READY
ON THE SET

Moving-in day⌂Directing the operation⌂Making room layouts⌂The Forbidden Closet reappears⌂What to do with teens and toddlers⌂Paying up⌂ Refueling the family.

Pre-moving day jitters should attack you about midnight on the eve of the big day. You're committed to this venture, and there's no way out. You are ensconced in a motel in an area convenient to your new house, hubby's snoring has taken on its usual comforting rhythm and the kids are sound asleep in a swirl of sheets and blankets. Even old dog Tray is deep in slumber curled at the foot of your bed. Mom, however, is wide-eyed, her mind whirling with questions in anticipation of the big day ahead. Did the movers lose the map to your new home? When you said that you would see them at the new house at 8:30 did they know you meant Central, not Eastern time? Will the utilities be turned on as requested? Did someone remember to call the telephone company to install your new line? And oh, please, let Mrs. Oldowner be conscientious about leaving her home as spic and span as you left yours. Perversely, the day dawns just as you have drifted off into a deep sleep.

Fortunately, nature is kind to our exhausted bodies, and the adrenalin begins to flow even as your feet hit the floor. Up and at 'em—into the coffee shop for a good hearty breakfast. You will be eating nothing but on-the-run hamburgers and pizza for the next forty-eight hours, so make this meal nourishing and substantial. Pack up the suitcases, count noses—don't forget the dog and the gerbil cage—load up the car again, and once more you are on the way. Your new home is awaiting its new family and maybe, just maybe, the moving van will be parked in the driveway as you pull up.

I have always felt like a bride when I walk into my new home, whether it be the first move or the fifteenth. I am usually a little the worse for wear but still excited and nervous at the prospects that are ahead. This house will protect and comfort me and my family, those that I love. It will be our haven during the good and bad times that life holds in store for all of us. There will be laughter and tears within its walls. The most important history in the world—that of my family—will be enacted right here in these still barren and empty rooms. I am filled with a sense of well-being and optimism—this is our home. Sentimental fool that I am, I feel that a house takes on its owner's personality. For this reason I once hid a small family group picture in a crack in a closet of our very first home when we moved out. Silly, I know, but I had to leave something of us behind.

On one occasion, as we unlocked the front door of our new house, we were greeted by a lovely bouquet of flowers thoughtfully delivered by our real estate agent before our arrival. This gesture was so kind and welcoming that I have often wondered why more real estate people don't do that little extra something for their clients. Flowers bring so much happiness and can make an empty house so much brighter.

The children have bounded from the car and are busily investigating every nook and cranny in the yard, the basement, and the attic. They are excitedly staking out their own territory like homesteaders of old, finding their personal and secret hiding places, coolly and casually surveying the equally curious neighborhood kids—sizing one another up from a distance, watching and hoping for a small gesture of friendship. If this is their first view of the new house, they will rush to find their rooms and immediately begin to take possession.

By now the van has arrived with shouts of delight and greeting. This moment becomes a reunion of sorts. The moving men, virtual strangers to you a short time ago, have suddenly become your long-lost buddies and practically an extension of the family. If you consider this sudden camaraderie, you realize that these men know a great deal about you and your family, both good and bad. It has always unnerved me to have my deepest housekeeping secrets on display to the world, yet these men have discovered the balls of dust behind the beds, the hidden ant traps in the kitchen cabinets, and the confused disarray of the linen closet and I feel no guilt. Because of these shared intimacies, your greetings to one another may be somewhat emotional. You will compare notes on the trip route, the amount of traffic, the weather conditions, the hours spent in driving. Movers are generally very kind in complimenting you on your new home. This must be one of the lessons in the *Movers' Manual.* Their praise helps to make you feel that you have made a good choice and starts you out on the right foot as you begin to settle in.

On to the business at hand. Unless your move is charged to the company, you will have to pay up before your goods can be unloaded. This is the law. Personal checks will not be accepted, so be sure you have obtained a certified check or cash in the proper amount. Now the van doors have been opened and the house doors are thrown wide, awaiting all your worldly goods. You spy the neighbors peering out of their windows, trying to catch a glimpse of you and your furniture, too, no doubt! It's time for you to take center stage again! The production is in full swing, and all your well-laid plans will be put into operation—hopefully without too many hitches. If the weather is fair, have your husband or one of the movers find something for you to sit on outside the door. If it's rainy or snowy, station yourself directly inside the front door so that you can direct the unloading operation. Remember the color-coding system that you used on the packing end of the move? Now is the time to put this plan to work for you. Have the children scurry around and place the colored tapes on the doors of the rooms before the unloading actually begins. Then, when a carton comes off the truck marked "Susy's room" with a piece of blue tape under her name, you will be able to tell the movers quickly, "The blue room, top of the stairs and to the left." The unloaders will quickly catch on to the coding. Believe me, this system really does work well and will eliminate much confusion. Movers have told me how much easier unloading was when we used this technique.

Another good idea that you may want to try is what I refer to as the "layout" plan. Many hardware and decorating stores carry furniture layout kits. These kits are similar to children's "Willy the Weatherman" color-form toys. They come equipped with different furniture shapes that can be moved around at will like the boots and raincoats for Willy. You can determine beforehand and at your leisure just where you want to place the grandfather clock or the baby grand piano or the loveseat and sofa. Note: Even the sweetest of movers tends to become a bit testy if he is expected to try various furniture arrangements to satisfy your aesthetic whims. Grandfather clocks are heavy, and time is money.

On the offchance that Mrs. Oldowner didn't own a vacuum cleaner or a broom and didn't shape up as the immaculate housekeeper you'd hoped she would be, don't get yourself in a snit. You will have a little time, after the truck has been unloaded and before the cartons are unpacked, to wipe out the crumby kitchen cabinets and the greasy oven. If you are the superefficient type, you may have planned far enough ahead to have brought shelf-lining paper which you carefully kept in the Forbidden Closet. You are now ready to prepare your kitchen shelves to receive your pots and pans and dishes.

It is helpful if your husband has been able to reconnoiter the neighborhood a bit and has spotted a hardware store nearby. There are always some items to be purchased almost at once. Example: The old owners were skinflints and took every last light bulb out of its socket, and it's a dark, dreary day. Or you discover a colony of evil-looking crawly things under the kitchen sink— quick, the Raid! Or the john is making strange jungle noises and you need help fast from the Liquid Plumber! You can't have put *everything* in the F.C.!

Speaking of the Forbidden Closet, those items that you protected there with dire threats to life and limb and that were the last items packed on the truck or in your car will now be the very first things to reappear. Grab them quickly and put them into a good safe place, out-of-bounds to all comers once again. Find the instant coffee and the pot, and the foam cups, and you are ready for anything that may come your way.

It's a good idea to have definite chores for the more capable members of the family. "Capable" in this particular instance means anyone who can wield a broom and dustpan, wipe a shelf, stuff trash and litter into boxes to be carried out to the back, and sponge out a sink. (I am compulsive about dirty sinks, and therefore this is always my first order of business. I have been known to scour sinks in filling stations, motels, and airline terminals, to the consternation of my children and the bewilderment of those who might be watching. The tips aren't bad either.) From among the Forbidden Closet items, you will now dig out your supply of clean rags or Handi-wipes for your cleaning chores.

My children, as they grew older, have relished the thought of unpacking their own belongings and settling themselves into their own rooms. I do realize, however, that allowing a four-year-old to have this responsibility is courting catastrophe. For anyone under five, better to take care of the settling-in process yourself.

Our teenagers spend hours poring over cartons, discovering precious possessions that have special meaning known only to themselves. They may have seen these items a mere forty-eight hours ago, but the element of excitement and surprise is akin to a joyous Christmas morning. Were they perhaps fearful that they would never see their things intact again, or could it be that these treasures represent security blankets recognizable as such only to them? With most teenagers, the stereo or the eight-track is the first thing to be put back into operation. In a short time, much shorter than you had hoped perhaps, the house will be reverberating to the sounds of *Chicago* and *Led Zeppelin*. Nothing serious may be undertaken until this is accomplished. The next order of business will be the unfurling of the posters that boldly proclaim, "Hang in there, baby," "Peace," "Keep on truckin'," and "Right On." As I take a breather from my chores and climb the stairs to check on the progress above, I am struck with the thought that perhaps after all the talk of generation gaps, these colorful, curious posters have some messages for me too. I certainly am hanging in there, I have kept on truckin', everything is pretty much right-on, and soon, hopefully, there will be peace!

Babies and toddlers, adorable as they are, can indeed be a pack of trouble at this hectic time. As you did before, get some outside help. Before your arrival, ask your husband to make some inquiries and phone calls to the local churches, the local high school (which may have its own job bureau), or a well-recommended baby-sitting service in the area. Secure an understanding and competent sitter willing to give you the hand you need—i.e., chasing, feeding, changing, napping, changing, and chasing again and again. You will be needed elsewhere today. Baby will survive without Mommy for these busy hours, and you will be a lot less frazzled if you devote yourself to one job at a time.

Keep your pets confined somewhere on moving day so that they too won't be underfoot or lost in the shuffle. Choose the area of confinement carefully. It should be escape-proof, of course, or the pet may take one look at the pandemonium in progress and head for the hills. It should be equipped with all the necessary amenities, such as rest room facilities and fresh water, and it should be protected from the interference of other curious animals and human beings. If you can think of such a spot, let me know.

We were once the owners of a very classy Dalmatian, a real lady named Roadstar's Daisy of Dover. (She had come to fill the shoes of Ole, The Black Swede who had gone on to that great smorgasbord in the sky.) As is often the case with creatures whose breeding is very good, her temperament was not as fine as her looks. In short, Daisy was a little nervous. (After a few months of living with us, during which we were now moving for the second time, who wouldn't be?) So here it was moving day again, and looking around for a safe place I decided to chain her up in the garage. Now I ask you, is that any way to treat a lady? But she was out of the sun, was supplied with a pan of water, and her chain was long enough to allow her to use a square of lawn for her "necessaries." Satisfied that all her needs had been met, I turned my attention to the more pressing affairs of the day.

The movers were almost through, and I was upstairs putting sheets on the beds when I heard the screams. A mother's ear—any mother's—has a fine-tuning device that automatically screens out superfluous crying and zeros in on the real thing. This was the real thing. A neighbor's preschooler had wandered over to see what was going on and had stopped to pet the nice doggy. The nice doggy had promptly bitten him on the hand, badly enough to require stitches. This is not a recommended method to meet the new neighbors. It's quick, to be sure, but somehow it doesn't present you or your family in the best possible light. Poor Daisy had to serve a ten days' quarantine in solitary confinement, but I got ten months.

There are a lot of decisions to be made on moving day, but one of the biggest has to be what to wear. It must be something suitable for breakfasting out, scrubbing toilets, meeting the neighbors, and lining the kitchen shelves. I personally strive for a sophisticated yet casual look—something that Rhoda might wear—perhaps a peasanty shirt with a bright scarf wrapped around my head, accented by a pair of large hoop earrings. Unfortunately, the look I usually achieve is more like Ma Kettle. If the weather is cold and the doors are propped open, you will have to cover your costume with a coat, but which coat? Again, it must be one that is good enough to be introduced to a neighbor but not too good for floor mopping. You can see that costuming is a knotty problem.

From your station at the doorway, you now spot a cheerful-looking creature dressed in a well-tailored tennis outfit and exuding sparkling cleanliness and sunshine, with every hair in place and looking terribly chic. This lovely apparition seems to be coming up your walk bearing a luscious-looking, goody-laden tray. Your first instinct will be to run and hide. You can't possibly meet anyone now, looking the way you do! What to do? You might hide in one of the open cartons, or you might pretend you're the hired help. Don't! Just be gutsy, smile, and enjoy! You are being welcomed into the neighborhood, by a pleasant soul who could very possibly become your friend. Perhaps this is the neighbor to join you in a quiet cup of coffee when the children are off to school, to help you chase down a good bargain, to be the friend you can turn to when you're feeling alone and blue. I have learned that it only takes one friendly face and one thoughtful gesture of good will to make you feel more comfortable and at home. We wives and mothers, mature, ultraefficient, and worldly-wise, we who must cope with sniffles, emergency appendectomies, and yes, even major moves across the country and sometimes across the world, we all sometimes desperately need a friend to talk things over with. This thoughtful neighbor may not be your true soul mate and best friend for life, but her initial gesture of kindness should always be remembered and appreciated. I would make one plea to any woman who has gone through the turmoils of a move, whether once or twenty times, and even to the women who have never left town: try to be kind and do something to make a new neighbor feel welcome. It may take the form of a plate of brownies for the kids, or a casserole for the first night's meal, or maybe just a phone call or an invitation to share a quiet cup of tea. No matter what it is, your gesture will be something special to a tired and lonesome lady, who will remember it. Keep in mind that in the transient society we live in today, though you may have lived in the same town all your life, your day may come, and you too may be the new person on the block who needs a comforting welcome from a friendly face.

There's no accounting for the little surprises you may find awaiting you in your new home on moving day. I'm referring to the presents the former occupants leave you—the yards of shag carpeting scraps in the attic or the defunct refrigerator in the garage. Usually it's the things they couldn't cart to the dump in the station wagon. When it comes down to a choice of paying to have something hauled away or leaving it for the next owners, you've got it! Take, for example, the huge cast-iron plate of an old upright piano that is leaning against my basement wall at this very minute. Some former owner evidently took a sledge hammer to the rest of the piano and burned the pieces in the fireplace. It would take six men and a water buffalo to budge the piece that remains, so he left it. As will we.

One girl I know found quite a number of discards in her new garage, and her first order of business was to send her husband to the dump to get rid of them so they'd have room for their own junk. A day or two later the wind shifted and the weather turned cold. In a blinding flash she realized what those pieces of heavy vinyl with the zippers were—the covers for the airconditioners! She and her children tore to the dump to retrieve them. They spent several hours sorting through the rubbish and found some really nice stuff—a lamp that just needed rewiring, a tricycle with a little more life in it, and a plastic laundry basket that was like new. But no covers for the airconditioners. Moral: If you don't know what something is, hang onto it awhile.

The hustle and bustle of this interminable day are drawing to a close. Everything is beginning to shape up. True, each room still contains unopened cartons stacked in corners, all to be waded through in good time. If you or your company has contracted for packing service, you are also entitled to *un*packing service. You may have this done on moving day, if time permits, or later at your convenience. You should schedule your unpacking date with the local moving company representatives.

If you are planning to spend that first night in your new home, be sure to have the movers assemble the beds as soon as possible so that you can make them up before total exhaustion sets in.

The driver will ask you to sign releases stating that your

goods were accepted in satisfactory condition. You should sign them, but be sure to underscore or insert the words "pending further inspection." You are given nine months in which to submit a claim for any damages you may uncover. The sooner you settle, however, the better for all concerned.

But for now the sofa fits perfectly on the wall opposite the fireplace, the animals have found their favorite chairs and contentedly snooze, oblivious to the confusion around them; and while you may not be prepared to serve up Julia Child's *Coq au Vin*, you can at least boil water. This is a moment when the postpartum moving blues may strike. Someday soon this house will be a lovely home, a secure and comforting shelter, but right now the vibes are definitely hostile. The same lamps that once cast a cozy glow now glare harshly, exaggerating the starkness of the unlived-in rooms. Get thee to a motel if it's all too much for you. The whole family is probably in need of some tender treatment; a good hot meal, a steamy shower, and some cheering up with Laverne and Shirley. Life will look much rosier after a good night's sleep and a change of atmosphere. The extra expense will be worth it in terms of family morale. As a well-known Southern heroine once said, "Tomorrow is another day."

It's good to know how well you made out or where you went wrong for the inevitable next time you move, so once you're in bed prop yourself up on your pillows and take this little self-test to evaluate your moving performance. Keep a running score.

+ 2 If you found an item that's been missing since the last move.
+ 2 If you scrubbed down the bathroom tile before you left your old house.
+ 3 If you have already scrubbed down the tile in your new home.
- 2 If you have lost a pet in transit.
- 3 If you have lost a child in transit.
+ 2 If you removed all your old junk from the house you left.
+ 6 If your family feels closer at this moment than they did before you moved.
- 6 If any family member has physically assaulted another in the last five days.
+ 3 If you know where you can put your hands on a hammer at this moment.

0   If your new house is cleaner than the one you left.
- 2   If any family member is sick.
- 7   If you are sick.
- 1   If you failed to wear mascara on moving day.
- 2   If you failed to wear lipstick on moving day.
- 4   If you failed to wear a girdle on moving day.
+ 2   If you combed your hair.
+ 3   If you have met a new neighbor.
+ 5   If the neighbor offered you a drink—even if you took a rain check.
0   If you left plumbing or any appliance in need of repair.
+20   If you paid all your local bills before you left your old town.
-20   If the sheriff will soon be after you.
+ 2   If you can lay your hands on the key to the strongbox.
- 8   If you can't find the strongbox.
+ 3   If no member of your family has to wear dirty underwear tomorrow.
- 9   If you removed the light bulbs from the ceiling fixtures in your old house. Unless the people were hateful. In that case, you may give yourself +2.
+ 5   If your old neighbors gave you a party before you left town.
- 1   If no one cried.
+ 6   If you wouldn't mind bumping into the people who bought your old house at a cocktail party.
+ 5   If you understood everything that was going on at the closing.
- 1   If you have discovered a key to the old house in your purse.
+ 3   If all your utilities are operational by the first night.
+ 6   If you are operational by the first night.
+15   If you and your husband have had sex in the last two weeks.
+ 7   If you have had a tender moment.
- 2   If you wish you had never laid eyes on him.

A perfect score is 100. If you scored over 50, you qualify for Wonder Woman!

20–49, Very efficient.
 5–19, Eh!

Less than 5, go directly back to where you started; do not pass Go; do not collect $200.

THE LOW-BUDGET PRODUCTION

How to cut costs when you move locally ⌂ Things you can do ahead of time ⌂ Persuading your friends to help ⌂ Settling in easily.

Moving is a lot of work, make no mistake about that. Most large companies that transfer their employees plan to pay to have as much of the labor done for the family as possible to make the transfer more palatable. Often a company filling a job with an outsider will also pick up the tab for his moving expenses to sweeten the pot. A transfer can easily cost a company as much as $12,000 or even more, but most firms feel the expense is justified in keeping employee morale up and getting the right man in the right spot. It could be much more expensive to hire a new man who may not have the knowledge and expertise of an employee who has been with the firm for years.

There are times in the lives of many, however, when liberal company moving benefits are not available, and you will have to foot the bill yourselves. If you decide to change your address locally, if you are retiring, if you are dropping out of the rat race, or if you are among the young and the restless trying out a few spots in this vast land before deciding where to put down your roots, your move won't be company-sponsored. You may find yourselves holding the moving bill also if you are changing jobs when you don't happen to be in a good bargaining position. Whatever the reason, you will want to cut corners on the costs of the move. Though less so than in the 60's, the young are on the road today in large numbers looking for their own particular Utopias. The West still holds a strong lure for Americans, with the South running a close second, according to the Census Bureau. Small cities are growing, while people are fleeing the large metropolitan areas. Young college grads often seek a simpler life in rural areas, but jobs are often scarce there and they may move on. Generally the young are unencumbered with wordly goods and are well-endowed with youthful optimism, so moving is no big deal. Their biggest concern is usually the proper packing of the stereo equipment. Sometimes it's just a matter of rolling up the sleeping bags and stashing a few pots and pans in the psychedelic van and hitting the road.

Many times youth and adventure go hand in hand with naiveté, and in some cases, what could very well pass for stupidity! Our friends Charlie and Clothilde met with a hairy experience while making their very first do-it-yourselfer. The couple were newly married and on their way from Chicago to a tiny three-room flat in upper Michigan. Their possessions were almost nil, except for a few nice wedding gifts, some hand-me-downs and castoffs from family, a three-piece sectional, a rug, and three tables from a garage sale. Charlie rented an open trailer, and we carefully helped pack all the worldly goods with which they had endowed each other. Over the top we tied a huge tarpaulin, secured on all corners with rope. Family and friends alike stood in the driveway waving and shouting, "Good luck" as the couple took off on their new life.

It was just about an hour later when the sky darkened, the winds mounted, and the little coupé began to sway from side to side on the road, bucking the heavy turbulence of an unexpected summer storm. Charlie drove white-knuckled as he tried to control the car and trailer and keep all his new responsibilities from harm—including Clothilde! Clothilde kept watch out the back window as the tarp flapped and snapped in the gales. The tightly secured ropes had the strength of wet noodles. The headlights of the little car pointed skyward as the weight of the overpacked trailer pulled the car back on its haunches. Rain reduced visibility almost to zero, and the greetings from passing cars were as friendly as might be expected from drivers who'd been waiting to pass them for the last 20 minutes!

The trip, scary and seemingly endless was a trial by fire for the young couple, but their marriage survived the ordeal. Their wordly goods did not fare as well. Blaze and I visited Charlie and Clothilde in their apartment a few months after the adventure and were dismayed to see their carpet, so carefully chosen, reduced to little more than a dreary 9' × 12' piece of gray pressed felt. The three-piece sectional looked as if it had been covered with fabric spray paint by the previous owners—it was now a muddy-looking, badly-streaked mishmash of ugly color—but Charlie and Clothilde were blissfully content, so it wasn't a total loss.

Blaze and I learned a lesson too. If you rent a trailer for a move, and if you must drive some distance with it, try to order a closed model, similar to a horse van in appearance. Be prepared for any weather you might encounter. Have your car checked thoroughly before you leave on the trip, and be sure that you have heavy-duty shock absorbers installed for the extra weight you'll be towing. Have the headlights adjusted to the proper height. You'll eliminate a lot of hazard to you and your fellow travelers by taking a few extra precautions.

With the job market tight, more and more young people are continuing on to graduate school, and marrying and starting families along the way. When the time comes to move on, they are often faced with a do-it-yourself project. Sometimes the furniture has been makeshift and is expendable. Perhaps it can be sold and replaced at the new destination. When Blaze and I were married we started housekeeping with the furnishings of some friends who were moving to California to make a fresh start. They figured it would cost them more to move their things than to buy new furniture when they got there. So for $135 we became the owners of a davenport, two chairs, some rugs, a used refrigerator, some dishes and kitchen utensils, and an ironing board. We moved our new belongings ourselves from their third-floor apartment to our Quonset hut, and there they served us nicely while Blaze finished school. When he graduated we were the beneficiaries of a company-sponsored move, so the furniture went with us—several times. After twenty-some years, all of the furniture has fallen by the wayside, but I'm still using the ironing board. Well, to be truthful, I'm not using it much, but it's still the ironing-board-in-residence.

On the other hand, if you have quality furniture that you have lived with for years and loved, don't be too quick to dispose of it. When some friends were readying themselves for retirement in Florida, they were inundated with advice on the havoc that would be wrought on their furniture when moving it from the extreme cold of Chicago to the warm and humid tropics. In a nutshell, the advice most widely offered was "get rid of everything you own and start all over again!" Upholstered furniture of any kind would die an unglorious death from dry rot, and the antiques . . . well, they just would not survive! The popularity of this opinion is obvious when you visit the condominiums and residences of the recently retired new Floridians. You can feast your eyes on a plethora of wicker, rattan, and plastic furniture covered with patterns in vivid oranges, lemon yellows and bright lime green. A veritable fruit market! For a few months, the émigrés are delighted with their new start, but the brilliance begins to fade and a longing for the deep mellow maples and mahogany of past years returns. Disregarding the advice of well-meaning friends. Gladdy and Bill took their furniture with them and have never been sorry. Oh, sure, they added some bright throw pillows that look great with the dark woods of the tables and chairs. Airconditioners and dehumidifiers have reached the sunny tropics, and your favorite furniture is as safe as it would be on Park Avenue, New York, New York. Gladdy and Bill are comfortable with familiar possessions surrounding them, and their home is charming. In their case, the expense of moving their furniture was justified.

Almost all of the dos and don'ts for embarking on a long-distance transfer apply to any resettling you may do, whether it be up the street, around the corner, or to the opposite end of town. It will still be necessary to put your current home on the market, organize your furniture and possessions, and decide just what you will need and what things you want to toss out via the garage sale route and, of course, to alert your friends and correspondents with change-of-address cards. To illustrate the types of things you should be aware of when you are making a local move, let's talk about a family that has happily decided to resettle into a newer, larger home to accommodate their ever-increasing brood. They have worked and saved for years and looked forward to the day when they would be able to afford their "dream house." What a wonderful, exhilarating time this can be! Sure, there will be lots of work involved, and there will be exhausting days as they prepare, but the happiness that the family shares in anticipation will make it all worthwhile.

You have "discovered" your perfect new home. This may even happen by accident on a leisurely Sunday drive. Now, with the frenzy of having to locate a place to live within a specified time eliminated, you can proceed in a more relaxed manner. The business part of the move has been taken care of. This, ladies, pertains to finances, and in this local situation, where your spouse is on the scene to take care of the bartering, if you play your cards right, these mundane details are lifted from your shoulders.

Allow yourself as much time as you need to vacate your old home and move into the new. Remember, the accent is on happiness, so don't allow yourself to get into a bind or a pace that will wear you down.

It's repetitive to keep reminding you, but this is a good time to make one of those famous lists that I refer to so often. At the head of this particular list should be finding a moving company and deciding on a mutually satisfactory and convenient moving date. As I mentioned before, shop around and compare prices on the overall cost and services rendered. Generally, with a local move the expenses are yours and not the company's, so do be sure to obtain estimates and bids. I.C.C. rates do not apply to moves within the state, so you may find a wide variance in the estimates that you receive. Be aware of and consider what *your* budget will allow.

In many cases it's possible to handle the moving yourself. If you are a young couple and your furniture consists mainly of early Goodwill and orange crate tables, it's fun to gather some of your stronger—both emotionally and physically—friends together to help out on moving day. There are many good, reasonably-priced vans available to rent for moving your larger pieces, such as couches, refrigerators, pianos, and television sets. If, on the other hand, your friends are all busy going to dentists, family weddings, or the big anniversary sale at the local department store, you may want to hire one of the independent local movers for those things too heavy and cumbersome for you and your husband to handle. But again, do be sure to get written cost estimates.

A friend of mine went into the real estate business a few months ago. She hadn't been on the job very long when she succumbed to an occupational hazard of that industry. She spotted her dream house. Her first sale was her old house, and she and her family prepared to move the few blocks to the new one. They did the packing themselves and hired a local trucker to transfer the appliances and the heavy stuff. The rest they would take themselves in their station wagon.

"How did it work out?" I asked.

"Well," she said, "it was more expensive than we'd planned."

It seems that when the movers arrived to load the heavy items, her husband kept saying, "Oh, why don't you take this too?" "and that," "and maybe that," until there was hardly anything left to go in the station wagon.

This gal came up with a moving variation on Murphy's Law: If anything gets broken, it will be something you love. The family had all helped with the packing, and the results were somewhat less than professional. Two pieces of her crystal, which is no longer available, and her favorite bowl for flower arrangements bit the dust.

There are a few tricks of the trade in packing and moving yourselves and effective ways to cut the costs without sacrificing your treasures. Go to the local supermarket or liquor stores, and ask them to save you some of their strong cardboard boxes. These boxes generally end up on the rubbish heap, so the markets are usually willing to part with them. Incidentally, the boxes that you obtain from the liquor stores are so sturdy that they can be safely used for your heavy books and your most delicate glassware and china.

Movers advise against using newspapers for wrapping and packing your belongings as was commonly done in the good old days. Newsprint can leave permanent marks on certain goods. A phone call to one of the local moving companies to obtain wrapping paper, and/or boxes, and some of that heavy-duty plastic bubble wrapping (the kind you love to pop), is very worthwhile and a good safety precaution for your more valuable possessions. Building supply houses carry rolls of heavy "resin" paper which can be used for runners in the walkways and traffic lanes on moving day to protect your floors and carpets.

Never pack boxes that will be too heavy for you to handle. One slip or loss of balance can be a catastrophe, so do be careful. Resist the urge to pile everything into a few boxes unless the Jolly Green Giant has offered his services.

Arm yourself with a good marking pencil, and write the contents on the outside of each carton. A beautiful friendship could well be ruined by having your husband's best buddy toss Aunt Edith's crystal hurricane lamps on the truck with gusto because he thought the carton contained nonbreakable books.

Have your appliances serviced so they won't be damaged in transit. Rent a "dolly," one of those slantboards on wheels that movers use, for the heavy things. And once again, be sure small children are out of the way so they won't be injured.

Don't plan to have your husband and his friends do more than they can really handle. Once Blaze helped some friends move out of a house perched high over Long Island Sound. There was a long flight of winding stone stairs leading from the street up to the house, and by the time they were finished carrying out all the furnishings, he needed mouth-to-mouth resuscitation and a chiropractor.

If you have a grand piano, don't expect your husband and your teenage sons to lower it out of a second-story window. Assess the job realistically and get professional help for the things that are too heavy or too cumbersome to handle. The heaviest thing we own is a fairly delicate-looking hide-a-bed. Moving it upstairs once, we almost lost Blaze for good. (Canny designers managed to make sofa beds look slim, but I can testify that that is an optical illusion. They are unwieldy to move, and the springs in those things weigh a ton.) We had been in one new house only a few days when we had second thoughts about our furniture arrangement. We decided to move the hide-a-bed to an upstairs room, where guests could use it and we could have a sitting area as well. It was evening when we had this brainstorm, and I was in my pajamas and Blaze in his trusty boxer shorts as we wrestled the thing to the foot of the stairs. We had grossly underestimated its weight, but now it was at the foot of the stairs in the tiny entry hall blocking passage from any direction, so with some misgivings we decided to continue. We wedged it into the stairwell, and with me pulling and Blaze pushing we managed to slide it up the stairs. We stopped close to the top for a breather, and that was where we made our mistake. As we lost momentum, the sofa started to slide backwards just a little.

"Hold on to it!" yelled Blaze.

"I can't" I screeched.

Blaze couldn't hold it either. Deciding that discretion was the better part of valor, he turned and ran down the stairs trying to beat the careening sofa to the turn at the bottom. The sofa almost won. It came to rest against the front door with a sickening thud and missed pinning Blaze by an eyelash. I wonder how psychologists explain the unaccountable impulse to laugh that comes over some people in such times of tension.

The very first home we bought was no more than a shell and, naturally, it was inexpensive. Thanks to a slim bankroll and the house's proximity to our apartment, we moved in gradual stages. We purchased the house in May and intended to move in the weekend of July 4th, a three-day holiday. We busily and creatively spent evenings and weekends before the big day, painting and papering walls, sanding and varnishing floors, hanging curtains and draperies, laying rugs and carpeting. We were on a very tight budget, as are so many young couples, and we couldn't even consider hiring anyone to help. Once the major decorating and the messy jobs were out of the way, I was ready to add some of the finishing touches. After Blaze left for the office in the mornings, I would load up the car with whatever I could carry—clothing and linens were toted in large plastic bags, and nonperishable things and canned goods were piled in cartons, driven the short distance, unpacked, and carefully placed on flower-bright, newly-installed shelving paper in the cupboards. I was playing house and loving every minute of it. Blaze discovered that he had the makings of a true do-it yourselfer, first class. After work he papered and painted, installed shelves and doors and hardware. We worked hard putting in many long hours together preparing the house for the big day. Our pride in ourselves and our handiwork as we labored to turn this house into a cherished home was enormous.

We had arranged to hire a small trailer to be towed by the car on moving day and since it was a holiday weekend we prevailed upon two or three other young couples to help us. A bit of bribery was used in the form of a couple of cases of cold beer and sandwich fixings and invitations to a "Moving Day Beer Blast." Our friends enthusiastically arrived early that Saturday morning raring to go. The women were stationed at the new house and did the unpacking and sorting as each box was carried inside. The men, all young and still in good shape, made the trips back and forth with the trailer, loading and unloading. Once the apartment was cleared and cleaned out, we had our picnic lunch and relaxed. Stage one had been successfully completed with very little trouble. Stage two began by setting up the beds with the box springs and mattresses, hooking up the appliances—it's more helpful when issuing invitations to a "Moving Day Beer Blast" to include a friend who is familiar with electrical workings—and the proper placing of what little furniture we had in just the right aesthetic spots. At the conclusion of that long day we were all exhausted but very proud of our combined efforts. Our good friends dragged themselves home with promises from us to help them whenever they needed it, and Blaze and I were finally alone in our very first home. A good time was had by all, the cost had been nominal, and our happiness knew no bounds. Ah, youth!

Incidentally, if friends are helping you make a local move and you are not up to the beer and sandwich route on moving day, you may want to throw a party for them later on—as soon as you find the cocktail glasses and potato chip bowls.

Probably the nicest single factor in the local move is in being able to accomplish all that you must do in a relatively relaxed and leisurely fashion. By having your closets outfitted with your clothing ahead of time and linens neatly placed on closet shelves just the way you want them, by hanging your draperies and curtains, and by stocking your kitchen cupboards before the actual moving day, you have eliminated most of the frantic on-the-spot decision making that you normally encounter on a long-distance move. To be sure, it takes thought and organization beforehand, but the benefits to you both mentally and physically are great and will most assuredly result in a very happy local move.

THE ELIZABETH TAYLOR MOVE

Overseas transfers ⌂ What to do about housing, schools, furniture, and toilet paper ⌂ How to handle the language barrier ⌂ Your attitude ⌂ Reaping the benefits.

If your husband is associated with an industry or corporation that maintains international offices to serve a worldwide market, you may be aware of the possibility that some personnel will receive one of those much-coveted overseas assignments. Now let's suppose that yours is one such chosen family.

How glamorous and bon vivant of you to embark upon an overseas move! The rugged Alps of Switzerland, the hustle and bustle of continental Paris and swinging London, the mysteries of Mozambique and Hong Kong beckon you. The small-town girl from a little mining town in the west is finally going to see the world, and best of all, to have the world see her, the new darling of the international jet set! Never mind that you are also bringing a motley pack of typical American kids whose main joy in life seems to be watching *Happy Days* and *Welcome Back, Kotter*. Never mind that you flunked second-year French in high school. Forget the fact that your swinging husband's idea of a big night out on the town is a Little League baseball game, topped off with a stop for pizza with everything—hold the anchovies—at the local pizzeria! Get ready, fascinating world—you're being transferred to Europe for three years! Long-ago dreams of Dior dresses, skiing in the Alps, travels on the Orient Express, visits to the Louvre, dinner for two at Maxim's, luncheon at the Savoy, strolls on the Left Bank, cultured offspring with fluency in two or three languages override any fears you may have—that is, for the first fifteen minutes!

The initial announcement of your impending transfer to exotic new lands will, in most cases, be greeted by delighted screams and squeals, great anticipation, and much speculation. Your friends, though sad at the prospect of your leaving, will be happy for your good fortune. On the other hand closest relatives—sisters and brothers, mothers and fathers—will no doubt shed a few tears and moan, "But you'll be so far away for such a long time." All of these reactions from the people you care most about will bring a lump to the throat and a tear to the eye, of course. Swallow the lump and brush away the tear. The prospect is exciting, and the point is for you to *keep* it exciting—a wonderful educational adventure that your entire family will benefit from in a myriad of ways, an experience that will last a lifetime. (Incidentally, the happenings that lie ahead of you will make for great party conversation on your next assignment in Keokuk, Iowa.)

But whether it be to Keokuk or to Zurich your family is unique and so, therefore, is your move. In all moves, though it be just around the corner or just around the world, plans must be made, details and instructions followed to a T—lists composed to live by! Perhaps boring to keep repeating, but indeed a necessity, especially in the case of the overseas transfer.

Depending on the size of your family, whether a tribe of kids or the fashionable and *au courant* 1.5 children per couple, you will have to decide, within a limited choice, just what kind of housing facilities will suit your needs and requirements. Naturally, in an overseas move, unless you or your spouse happen to be the president of a large and very successful corporation, you are not going to be able to embark on weekend househunting jaunts to Istanbul or Luxembourg. This is just not practical. Your company's personnel department, however, working with your husband on the moving details, will find out about the housing situation and advise you as to what is available. In most instances American families opt for apartment living when abroad. Even dyed-in-the-wool homeowners, do-it-yourselfers, and garden putterers seem to jump at the chance to be rid of domestic chores and responsibilities in exchange for a nifty apartment on the Rue de Rivoli! The obvious and reasonable explanation for this radical change seems to be the desire of the transferees to be free and unencumbered by a house and all of its demands. People tend to look upon their two- or three-year sojourn as a once-in-a-lifetime experience, a holiday to be enjoyed to the utmost. They plan to travel, to see all that is to be seen without having to worry about the leak in the basement (or the wine in the cellar) or questioning whether or not to use plastic or aluminum mesh to mend the hole in the screen door. Might as well rent and pay the concierge (the building super, if you haven't gotten to the c's in Berlitz yet) to fix all that demands repair. You will be too busy watching the running of the bulls at Pamplona!

There is, of course, another reason to rent, and a sound one at that. Real estate prices in a foreign country can be exorbitant. Even though corporations provide generous housing allowances to those transferred abroad, unless you are on an unlimited budget, which very few of us are, or if you happen to be related to or on intimate terms with Lord and Lady Gotrocks who know of a quaint villa that would be just perfect for you and the kiddies, you might as well discard all thoughts of being a homeowner in Europe. It is just not practical. Another factor to be considered is housing availability. There are very few Levittowns in Italy or France. Remember at all times that this experience is to be a stimulating adventure, and forget about your creature comforts. Most of your creatures will be comforted in ways you weren't aware of back in Pawtucket, Rhode Island, U.S.A.! So enjoy. Be loose and relaxed. Be satisfied with an adequate apartment—double or even triple up the kids, if necessary. Share a bathroom again. Perhaps the plumbing is not as efficient and as up-to-date as what you are used to back home, but keep in mind that you are lucky it has hot running water.

Another creature comfort that you may have to do without in some countries across the "pond" is central heating, which we have come to know and love and take for granted. If you're going to a country that experiences seasonal changes in weather, you had best bring along enough long johns for the entire clan. One very chic and cosmopolitan lady friend told me that when she lived in Australia, it was quite normal to wear "longies" all winter long. She even got used to sitting through elegant dinner parties wearing her winter coat as she tackled a seven-course meal. Drycleaning bills got to be rather large, but better that than suffering frostbite while coping with the jellied madrilène.

Conversely, central air conditioning is sorely lacking in the summer in many countries with a tropical climate. Most people there adopt the siesta habit: they draw the blinds and shutters, plug in the fan, and strip! This might be a bit unorthodox in Salina, Kansas, but when in Rome. . . .

All the women I have ever talked to who have lived overseas remark about the ready availability of household help—and the price is always right. A charwoman in London will do everything from sewing on loose buttons to serving morning tea and biscuits at eleven. She will do windows too, and at less than half the wages you would pay in the States.

One American friend who moved her household into a high-rise apartment in Hong Kong found it difficult to adapt to having help. She was accustomed to taking care of a suburban house and yard and family herself, and with all the chores taken off her hands, she found herself feeling pretty useless. It took a little while to shift gears and get involved in other activities to fill her time, but then she loved it.

The only drawback to this pampered living, which is so easy to get used to, is the painful withdrawal you must endure when you return once again to reality and bathtub ring in the States. As I contemplate the hours I will again have to spend watering the plants every day during the summer drought, and the leaking tubs and broken air conditioners and balky furnaces that will surely demand time and attention when we are back home again, I would be delighted to tear up those tickets to Kennedy Airport and renew our lease on the apartment on the Seine and leave all the domestic worries to someone else for three more years.

Not long ago, close friends of ours were transferred on a three-year assignment to Switzerland, the wife lovingly referred to by all of us who knew her as our own personal Mrs. America. She was always on top of all that needed to be done to run a home smoothly. She was the first to try new products on the market and would extol the virtues of a new cake mix or fabric softener to those of us who waited on her every word. Whenever a question arose as to the best way to whip up a pair of drapes or how to handle a belligerent child, dear Peg was the first one to call. She always knew. Now Peg and her family were going abroad!

The family decided after much thought and investigation and with their financial situation in mind to rent their home in the States with a three-year lease, store their furniture for the duration, and rent an apartment in Zurich. (In view of the rapidly escalating real estate market, it may be wiser to rent your home in the States and cash in on the boom when you return.) They were advised by those in the know that furniture could be rented in Europe from an American organization in Switzerland set up to accommodate transferees. At the same time, our friends acquired a list of hard-to-come-by products to take with them on their journey. I will never forget Peg busily packing up cartons of soft double-ply toilet paper, a scarce commodity overseas at that time. She later discovered to her delight that she was able to shop at United States commissary-type stores in Switzerland, loaded with premium American goods. I often wonder whatever happened to all that toilet paper! For those of you who are sure that you cannot possibly survive without Betty Crocker in the kitchen, chances are, if you are going to one of the major European cities with an American sector or populace, you will be delighted to find that Betty C. moved to Europe long ago—along with Ronald McDonald and the Colonel. Peg tells me that one of the biggest after-school treats that she could give to her children was a trip to the American Deli! What do you think they craved the most? Oreo cookies!

Transferees with growing children have passed the word around to incoming families that it would be wise to stock up on a supply of your favorite Buster Brown or Stride-Rites in graduated sizes. In spite of the huge number of imported shoes found in our department stores, it is an almost impossible task to find shoes overseas that fit our longer, narrower feet. The expensive shoes that we regard as status symbols are, in the main, made especially for the American market. Therefore, forget toilet paper and concentrate on the feet as you prepare to leave home sweet home. American-made jeans are coveted in Europe, so if your kids are interested in picking up a little pin money, they might pack a few extra pairs of Levis!

Shopping is always fun for most women, but shopping in Europe is widely regarded as the closest earthly thing to heaven. Just imagine buying a complete set of Royal Doulton china for about 30 percent of our price! If you live abroad and own your purchases for a period of one year, you can ship them back home along with your other goods as household belongings and eliminate paying duty. Silver from England and antiques are perhaps the best buys. Once again, you can bring them back to the States duty-free if you've had them for at least one year.

It is wise, as in any move, for you to be current with medical and dental checkups for all of your family members. Of course, you will all have to go through a battery of inoculations before leaving this country anyway, so you might as well take care of the repairs that you have been delaying—Dad's root canal job, Junior's retainer, Mom's bunion removal—with your family doctors and dentists before you leave. But keep in mind that European civilization has been around for a good many years, and medicine there has advanced considerably since the days when leeching and cupping were the physician's main stock in trade.

Most Americans who live overseas find that the physicians and medical facilities are quite good and, to top if off, housecalling Dr. Welbys can be found. Some countries have a socialized system of medicine, and the patient pays nothing. In England and Australia for instance, many doctors are affiliated with the National Health Association. Americans use these doctors for the normal everyday "kid stuff"—sniffles, flu, stitches. The doctors are capable, but the individuality is missing. You will have to go to a clinic, wait your turn, and take whichever doctor you are assigned. These clinics are readily accessible and certainly worth the wait and the impersonal atmosphere if you are not trying to soothe little Clyde who is running a temp of 104 and erupting in strange red blotches. The alternative is to see a specialist of your own choosing. They, too, are available, but in many instances the cost is high, as these doctors are not affiliated with the government. Most Americans feel that it is well worth the cost to pay one of the independent physicians to diagnose a possibly serious ailment.

In non-English-speaking countries it is pretty important to be able to interpret the instructions of the doctor. If your husband is suffering through the miseries of a kidney stone, this is no time to be translating from Berlitz. By all means, find the specialist who speaks English, and pay the piper!

Government-operated dental clinics also abound in England and Australia, and you can use their services at no cost. When you need a cleaning or a simple cavity filled, you may go to a National Dental Health Clinic, but when teenage Jenny has impacted wisdom teeth, you may want to find yourself a dental specialist and pamper the poor thing.

Schools will be an important consideration to any transplanted American. If you are to be located in a country or city which has a large international population, there will probably be an American school staffed by American teachers, and excellent ones at that, with a curriculum coordinated to stateside schools. While these schools are termed American, the student body will in fact be multinational—children of diplomats, foreign businessmen, as well as local residents. If there is no secondary school in your village in Zaïre, it may be necessary to consider a boarding school either in the United States or one of the excellent private English-speaking "public schools" in Europe. Though I hesitate to recommend family separations, it may be a good idea to allow your child to spend his or her remaining school career with a good family friend or close relative in Hometown, U.S.A. This is a question that you and your family must resolve.

If your children are in the elementary grades and you are not located in a major foreign city, it may be worth considering enrollment in a local school. Children, especially younger ones, are quite adept at picking up new languages, and learning about another culture from their peer group can be an experience that will profit them for a lifetime. Many European schools are multilingual, and you'll be surprised and delighted to see how quickly little Johnny will answer to "Jean" when Mére and Pére parle.

Occasionally every family is faced with what appears to be an insurmountable problem. One of the ticklish problems you may have to solve if you are going overseas to live is whether to take the family pet along. After all, Fido is a loyal and faithful member of the family. Who rushes to the door to greet you when you return home at the end of the day? Fido! Who curls up at your feet on cold winter nights? Not your kids or your husband. Yup! Good old Fido! Whose greatest joy is having his stomach rubbed? *That* could be your husband, but usually it's Fido again! What are you going to do about your devoted friend?

In many countries, your pet will not be welcome. I know that this is a hard pill to swallow. It's incomprehensible to believe that entire governments will not adore your cuddly, warm companion, but the facts of life are sometimes cruel.

England and Australia are two countries that are fortunate in not having had any rabies—and that's the way they intend to keep it. American pooches are immediately placed in strict quarantine when they arrive in these countries. They are incarcerated for six long months, living like four-footed monks, prevented from engaging in the normal activities of dogdom. Nary a woof or a sniff is allowed between any two of man's best friends. (A few years ago, Liz and Dick Burton, on one of their honeymoons, couldn't bear to place their pampered pets in quarantined quarters and put them up instead in their yacht anchored on the Thames for a lovely six months basking in the lap of luxury until the designated time of quarantine had been served. Not many two-legged animals ever had it so good!)

All costs for Fido's six months' sentence are paid by his owners to the visited government. If Fido were allowed to mingle with his unhappy inmates, he would discover that they all barked in his native tongue. In most cases, we Americans are the only pet-loving people who are willing to go to such expense and trouble for our animals. But we're talking about one of our best friends and a member of the family who just happens to have a moist, cold nose, and who loves us in spite of our faults.

One couple living in London paid regular Sunday afternoon visits to their pet "so he wouldn't feel that we had forgotten him." But one Sunday they were unable to make the trip. The kennel keeper called early Monday morning to see if something was amiss. Barney was devastated and wouldn't eat a thing. They dropped everything and quickly went to reassure him that he was still number one. Some dumb animal! When the quarantine was up, the entire family went to pick him up. "It was as if we were bringing a new baby home from the hospital!" they said.

If your tenure in another country is for a relatively short time, you might be able to have your dog visit with relatives or friends for the duration. If yours has not been the deepest of relationships (Fido growls at your husband and would seemingly savor a morsel of leg, and has still not learned the difference between grass and carpeting), you might try to find him a new owner through the want ads in the newspapers or through your vet. Try to make sure that he'll be going to a good home, though. You owe him something, after all.

If you are that gal who flunked French in high school, or

one who has merely lost the knack after spending years changing diapers and mixing formula, hie yourself off to the local night school or adult education program and take a language brushup course, if time allows. Your local bookstore probably has foreign language dictionaries on hand. Your library can supply language records. Play them while doing the housework or fixing dinner, rather than watching the daily soaps. (They will probably be telling the same story when you return in two years, anyway.) Memorize the most-used phrases from the dictionaries and records if your time is short—"Please," "Thank you," and "Which way to McDonald's?" Upon your arrival, carry the pocket-sized dictionary with you everywhere. These measures won't make you fluent in the language—nothing but daily practice can do that—but they will give you a sense of security and add a touch of exotica to your departure preparations. Acquaint yourself with the currency of the country to which you will be going and also with the metric system which is in use everywhere overseas.

Another good idea is to get hold of an English map of the locale. Embassies and automobile clubs furnish these for the convenience of Americans. Househunting without a knowledge of the geography or the language can be harrowing. My friend June is married to a man who has made his career in international business. Their family has probably made more moves internationally than most of us will ever make in our own country. June says that locating living quarters in any new area can be difficult, but when you are coping with a language barrier too, the problems can seem insurmountable.

When she and her husband and their two young daughters moved to Rio de Janiero, they were temporarily billeted in a beautiful hotel on the beach. Sounds terrific, so far. Not so terrific when it was time to start househunting! June spoke no Portuguese, and the only English-speaking person she came in contact with during those first few days was the front-desk clerk at the hotel. Engaging him in conversation, she described her problem. Desk clerks usually have a good knowledge of their cities and always seem to know just where to turn for help in a crisis. He told June he would see what he could do, and within a day or two he had some leads on housing for the Americano family.

The plan worked this way. Early in the morning, June would arrive at the front desk, ready for a day of househunting. The clerk hired a taxi for the whole day. Since the driver spoke no English, the clerk gave him a list of addresses of properties for rent. June carried another note, also in Portuguese, describing the needs of the family—the number of rooms desired, location preferences, and price range. The driver took her to the addresses on his list, June presented her note to the managers of apartments for rent, they showed her the property, and she took notes on their suitability—in English. At the end of the day she met with the desk clerk to decipher the notes and pertinent information. The negotiations began between the hotel clerk and the manager of the apartment they settled on. In this roundabout way, she eventually found a place to live. A nerveracking process but I daresay the clerk loved it, and he no doubt profited handsomely from the arrangement.

The language barrier can also present problems in day-to-day living in a foreign country. Shopping for food and clothing, and such necessary chores as getting your hair set or having your shoes resoled can grow all out of proportion. For this reason, one of the first orders of business in settling down in a non-English-speaking country is learning the language.

There are bound to be cultural differences as well. Sure, it is unnerving to pass those cute little stalls on the sidewalks of Paris, with only a pair of shoes visible from the bottom. Maybe the populace of your new home away from home isn't aware of the advantages of Right Guard, and your hair dryer becomes temperamental when you plug it into the local voltage, but try to take it all with a spirit of adventure and smile. You are a representative of your country and a guest in theirs. Nobody loves the proverbial Ugly American and besides you are sopping up CULTURE! Consider this an educational experience for the whole family.

June and her family have lived just about everywhere. Not only have they resided in some of the exotic places that most of us have only read about, but they have managed to visit and see as much as they possibly could. When they were planning a holiday trip or even a long weekend while living in Milan, Italy, family members made the decisions of where to go by drawing straws because there were so many options available to them. Would it be a one-hour drive to Switzerland? A two-hour drive into the Alps with the lure of fabulous skiing? Three hours to the Italian Riviera and sunshine and a chance to mingle with the Beautiful People? Weekends in Venice and Florence, or a quiet stay at home in Milan with perhaps a visit to museums and La Scala? June says that Milan is a fabulous city and has much to offer, but it is so close to so many other fabulous places that they found themselves always taking off. Someday, she hopes to go back and see more of the sights of Milano!

Holidays in other parts of the world are a time of excitement and enlightenment. Since Americans tend to stick together when they are a long way from home and all that's familiar, they cling to their own particular customs and share all of the holidays that are just our own—Thanksgiving, the Fourth of July, Memorial Day, and even Groundhog Day.

My nomadic friend June says that Christmas in other lands can be quite an experience. In Australia the children's summer vacation is just beginning. Temperatures are very warm—sometimes 100° plus. The first Christmas June and her family spent in Australia, they attempted to simulate Christmas at home by preparing a turkey and all the fixins for the family and the American friends they had invited for the day. Someone brought cranberries, another mince pie and hard sauce. They decorated a tree and sang carols around the table, and they all but expired from the heat. The second year they joined the natives on the beach for a picnic, loaded down with pails and shovels and surfboards, while newly arrived American émigrés tended the blazing Yule log.

American women—even without benefit of ERA—enjoy more freedom than their sisters in most other countries. Another friend who spent several years living in an American oil company compound in one of the Arab countries reports that life within the compound was much like that of any small American town, complete with schools, stores, hospitals and bridge clubs. If she wanted to leave the limits of the compound, however, she found her freedom quite restricted. It was even illegal for her to drive her own car, and she had to find a man to play chauffeur.

By and large, unless you already own a foreign car, it is best to forget shipping your automobile overseas. When you arrive at your destination, you can make arrangements to rent or buy a local minicar, if you need one. If something goes wrong, you'll be able to get the car repaired. Your Chevy Impala could spend the better part of its time in the garage awaiting parts from home.

We Americans think the price of gasoline here is steep, and we are advised by government and the media to get rid of our gas guzzlers and join car pools. We complain bitterly about the rising cost of gasoline, but in Europe it is even higher. For some reason, in spite of high gas prices, taxis in London are a cheap means of transportation, and bus service is the best deal in town. They charge by the block. For example, if you hop a bus for a three-block ride, you pay only a few cents. On a beautiful spring day it's possible to ride atop a red double-decker all over London town for less than a dollar. Americans who have lived in London tell me that no matter how many years they have spent in that lovely city, the thrill of riding on top of those bright red beauties has never worn off.

Subways may not be as scenic, but many European countries have underground systems far superior to our own. They are sparkling clean, graffiti-free, quiet, and safe. Rickshaws are an adventure unto themselves. If you *must* drive while you are abroad, however, you can apply for an international driver's license before you leave this country. This can be arranged quickly and easily at your local American Automobile Association office.

You are bound to encounter some unpleasant aspects of living abroad, but you have probably run into lots of things that you were unhappy with in your own hometown. You will have homesick days when you yearn for a coffee klatch with the girls back home.

Take heart. Living in a foreign country is no different from the situation you may find yourself in if you are blessed with a summer home directly on the ocean or high in the Colorado Rockies. Your popularity soars when word of your residency gets around to friends, relatives, distant cousins, and even remote acquaintances, and this phenomenon occurs overseas as well. The Man Who Came To Dinner is not pure fiction. When you live abroad you will also be the recipient of many "just passing through on the Grand Tour" phone calls and letters. Friends, and friends of friends, Aunt Millie's second cousin, twice removed, and your butcher from Saginaw will all want to look you up. Strange as it seems, you'll more than likely be delighted to see them all. Someone straight from home will look awfully good to you. You will probably find yourself hanging on his every word as he answers your questions about current hemlines in New York, and what's happening on *As The World Turns*. If he happens to have a late copy of an American newspaper or magazine with him, he will be set upon by every reading member of the family.

Always remember my friend, Peg, who on her return home attended a neighborhood cocktail party looking sensational and soignée in a simple black St. Laurent, her hair styled in the latest fashion from Paris. The admiring men of the neighborhood fairly danced attendance on her—hanging on her every word, lighting her cigarettes, and checking the status of her wineglass. Our own personal Mrs. America had become Mrs. World, and the results were terrific!

DECORATING FOR TRANSIENTS

What kind of furniture to buy and what to avoid⌂Where you should economize and where you can splurge⌂Decorating kids' rooms⌂Some portable tricks of the trade.

Moving can precipitate a variety of family crises, but one of the most predictable is that of How-To-Fix-Up-The-New-House. Husbands can be quite impatient when it comes to decisions about draperies, rugs, wallpaper, and the like. Most of them want instant decoration, no doubt feeling responsible for the discordant surroundings in which you now find yourselves. Like you, they know everyone will feel better about the move when the house starts to look homey.

"Why don't you just go out and get a couple of chairs and some curtains, and hang some wallpaper?" they say. Little do they realize that you don't know where there is a furniture store, let alone a furniture store where a bargain could be had. It takes even the most experienced mover a little time to find out where she can have slipcovers made by a little jewel of a woman for half the price the upholstery shop quoted. And as for wallpaper, well! First you have to know what the print on the chairs will be, what you're going to hang at the window, etc., etc.

In a moment of false prosperity and hoping to get the ball rolling, Old Blaze suggested after one move that I go to see a decorator. It was true that I needed help. The house was one of those with "a lot of potential," but at the moment it was looking very dreary. The wallpaper in the entry hall was strictly "early hotel," that kind of textured stuff in a color best described as dirty. I think decorators call it greige, but that's like calling World War II an international incident. Our furniture was spread through the house at a rate of three and a half pieces per room, and the bare windows were a peeping Tom's delight. It brought tears to my eyes to think of the price we had paid to entitle us to live in this desolation!

Our realtor very kindly came to the rescue with the name and number of his friend Spumoni the Decorator. I had an introductory interview with him on the phone. (Actually, *he* was interviewing *me* as to my willingness to put down a retainer.) When I inquired about his "style," which *House Beautiful* said you must always ask a decorator, he assured me that he and his staff—one girl who handled the phone and the billing (the latter the bigger job of the two, by the way)—were trained to come up with a design in whatever style the client preferred. Oh, boy! He suggested that he come by the house for a look-see some day the following week, thereby putting me a week behind, according to Blaze's timetable. He did arrive as scheduled, however, tape measure in hand, and happily remarked that there was *so* much to be done.

Despite the fact that I owned only two outfits suitable for wearing to a decorator's studio, I spent most of the next month at his studio going through furniture catalogs, fabric swatches, and wallpaper books. I thought I would go blind before the moment of decision arrived, but finally somehow, it did. Spumoni invited me to bring Blaze down after work that evening to approve the final choices—and, of course, to write the check.

Now (finally) we see artistry in action. The studio empties of other people, lights are dimmed, and we are seated on an enormously comfortable divan in a luxurious model room setup. The samples are handy, but perhaps first, a drink? Spumoni opens a beautiful little inlaid cupboard revealing a complete bar, where he proceeds to pour Blaze a double Scotch. You get the picture?

The goods we ordered from distant suppliers trickled in over the next eight months. Workmen came and hung draperies and shutters, and we spent a bundle. *House Beautiful* had led me to believe that the decorator would come in afterwards to see what he hath wrought and say a benediction. Not Spumoni. Whether he was guiding another hapless client through decorator catalogs or had gone on vacation to the Riviera, he didn't even call to see how I liked the "look." Two years later, though, we got a bill from him saying that his auditors had been in and that we still owed him $75. The doctor said Blaze would be himself again with rest and proper medication.

Our own experience notwithstanding, a decorator has a source for everything right at his fingertips, and this can be convenient when you are new in town and don't know where to shop. You can order everything through him, with the decorator functioning much as a building contractor does. Naturally, you pay for that service. In many cases you will have to order your furniture from pictures in catalogs, which may not be the best way to operate if you are one who likes to see the real thing before you buy.

I know I would have liked the results much better if I had

taken my time and gotten used to the house first. It takes a little knowing of a house to really make it *your* home. The way the sunlight falls in certain rooms and doesn't in others, the rooms you find yourselves living in, and where the plants and cats have chosen to take over, all will influence how you decorate.

It is a fact of life that new begets new. A new dress begets new shoes, new shoes beget a new purse, and so on. Thus it follows that a new house begets new furnishings! Most of us, however, have to move into our brand-new house with furniture and fixtures collected over a lifetime—couches containing permanent impressions of familiar family rumps, chairs that only the cat and Archie Bunker could love, rugs that have been turned so many times that the worn spots have become the pattern, and assorted tables with the rings and scratches to prove that you have thrown some great parties in your time. Wouldn't it be lovely if the Good Witch of the North would suddenly appear, command us to click the heels of our red sequined shoes three times, and voila!—transport the *Let's Make a Deal* showcase into our new living room!

Sometimes the miracle of new furniture does happen. For years my Mom and Dad had thought about building their "dream house," but like most of us they had long since filed the idea in the back of their minds. One morning over breakfast, though, they looked each other in the eye and suddenly decided to place their home on the market and take the plunge. The very marketable house was sold the next day to a lady who adored the place and who not only met the asking price with no questions but also inquired as to the additional cost of everything in it. Playing the scene coolly with the aplomb of Lunt and Fontanne, Mom and Dad agreed to assign prices to those items with which they would reluctantly part. To say that they made out like bandits would be overstating the case, but they sold a lamp for $150 that Mom had bought for a pittance at a rummage sale years before and had rewired and antiqued herself for a total of $25.57. An old living-room couch that had a terminal case of swayback also garnered an astronomical fee. When I heard about their coup I seriously advised them to consider going into the furniture-scavenging business and to heck with retirement! But anyway, much of their easily- (if not ill-) gotten gains immediately went back into new furniture.

One of the toughest things about moving every couple of years or so is that just when you get the house looking the way you want it to look you have to move on and start from scratch again. There are always some things that looked great in the last house that just don't "go" in the new one. The decorating atmosphere also changes from one section of the country to another. That's why I think it's a good idea to try for an eclectic look—a mixture of styles and periods. Decorating magazines extol the virtues of an international blend—in our case, a transcontinental mix ranging from a weathervane from New England to ginger jars from San Francisco's Chinatown. It is common for members or our mobile society to be stuck with a houseful of Early American furniture that looked great in Vermont but just doesn't make it in the Western-Spanish atmosphere of Gila Bend, Arizona.

Most young couples start out on a limited budget. It is almost impossible for them to afford to furnish completely an entire house or even a small apartment all at once. They are usually unsure of just what adjustments are in store for them as far as careers are concerned. Will the first job that the young husband secures be a lifelong position? If he has entered the corporate world, most likely not. Since finances must be limited and transfer may be in the offing, I would wholeheartedly advise young couples to select their furniture slowly and conservatively. It is wise to invest in a traditional motif which will look appropriate anywhere and will fit in with almost any decor you later choose.

Danish Modern was the "in" thing during the middle fifties. As a new bride, I had difficulty remembering whose home I was visiting because of the similarity in style. Blaze and I couldn't afford a Danish suite, so we frequented local house sales and furnished our small apartment with the bare necessities. Twenty years later we are still pleased with an often reupholstered hide-a-bed sofa of simple, traditional lines. Our erstwhile secondhand bedroom set in a traditional style has been attractively antiqued and is now used by our oldest daughter in her career girl apartment.

You can't go wrong with a good overstuffed chair and sofa of no particular period. If you want to change the look at a later date, this can be accomplished easily with slipcovers. Try to restrain yourself from buying fad pieces you will quickly grow tired of. Invest in the best construction you can afford. Good furniture will last many years, and you can spend your decorating dollars on atmosphere instead of expensive furniture replacements when you move.

End tables and coffee tables of classic design or even clean-lined Parsons tables blend easily with almost all styles. Glass-topped tables look great with everything today, but beware of these if you have a brood of toddlers and an accident-prone husband. Your nerves, as well as the shiny glass surfaces, may shatter when the mischiefmakers pound their blocks and metal trucks on the table tops. Those shiny surfaces may also become a headache with all the tiny fingerprints and smudges you will constantly be wiping up.

It isn't necessary to buy all matching tables for your living room. In fact, in decorating circles today, it is considered very chic to have a variety. You don't want your living room to look like a furniture store display! Or maybe you do! That's what makes horse races! Eclectic decorating is much more economical for the mobile family. If you start out in sunny California by the sea and have surrounded yourself with heavy Mediterranean tables, you are apt to find that these same tables look pretty gauche in old colonial Charleston! It's much easier on the pocketbook to have furniture that can go anywhere than to start all over again to fit the new surroundings.

I do feel, however, that you should buy those pieces that you really love. During a long-ago visit to a Goodwill store, I discovered a lovely old breakfront with beautiful leaded glass panels. In a fit of practicality, I hesitated and decided to think it over. A few days later, after inveigling Blaze to come along with me to take a look, I was *very* distressed to find that "my" breakfront had been sold. Funny, whenever I move into a new house, I can always find the perfect spot for that breakfront, and I still eat my heart out.

I don't remember just how or when I was bitten by the

antique bug. I guess it happened because I neglected to get my shots before we moved to New England, where the bug is pandemic. There is no known antidote, but the disease can be held in check by occasional purchases of warped, battle-scarred furniture, dented copper boilers, or genuine steeple clocks with the works missing. I dragged a carload of whining, squabbling kids from one broken-down barn to another seeking relief, but unfortunately I never could afford to effect a real cure—or even a remission. Then one glorious weekend Blaze invited me to accompany him on a business trip to Cape Cod, and promised that if I could manage to be decorative but unobtrusive, he would gladly stop at any antique place I wanted to investigate on the way back to Boston. No one has ever lined up a baby-sitter so fast!

The weekend passed pleasantly enough, and as we said our goodbyes on the steps of the hotel I was busily plotting the route home that would take us past the most antique shops. We stopped at any number along the way, but we hit the jackpot on the outskirts of East Bridgewater, Massachusetts, where a weathered old salt sat in front of an equally weathered old barn housing the usual assortment of broken picture frames, old whiskey bottles and mildewed quilts. There is something intoxicating about the smell of a place like that!

There—standing right out in front of the barn in full view of every passerby—was the most beautiful old blanket chest I had ever seen. It was made of pine boards three feet wide and mellowed to the color of honey, and it sat on round, fat, very old bun feet. It had one wide drawer along the bottom and the rest of it was simplicity itself. I had a compelling urge to throw a rug over it—quick!—before anyone else could see it, but in antiquing the name of the game is *cool*—you must never let the dealer know how interested you are. Playing out this little charade, I wandered around picking up and pricing some pieces of rusty hardware and a chipped stoneware crock. Then, as Blaze moved restlessly toward the car, I casually asked the price of the blanket chest. "$80," allowed the old man.

Once you have asked the price of an antique you are free to look it over carefully, snorting over its condition and haggling about its probable age and ancestry—which is hard to do when you are breathing and salivating heavily. (I have never mastered the art of haggling. I guess that's why Blaze doesn't take me to foreign countries. He knows I'd never be able to handle those exotic marketplaces.) But $80 was out of the question, not because the piece wasn't worth it but because I didn't have the $80. And so I told the old salt.

"Whatdya got to trade?" said the old man. Trade! What a wonderful idea. I had all kinds of things to trade! We stood in the driveway, tracing circles in the sand as we negotiated a deal: The blanket chest for our broken rocking chair, Blaze's old portable radio-phonograph, his school desk which had lately seen service as a changing table for babies, his shotgun which he used only once a year, his chest of drawers, and a washing machine with a broken water pump, plus $40 cash. It took three trips back and forth from house to barn, but I had my blanket chest. It has since served us beautifully in various homes in a hall, a bedroom, a living room, a family room, and two dining rooms. Its simple lines and warm patina make it one of the most versatile and beautiful pieces of furniture we own. Besides, the last one I saw went at auction for $550.

Antiques are usually good anywhere. An antique chest of drawers is an extremely versatile piece. It can go in a foyer or vestibule with a mirror over it, in a living room with a lamp on it, or in a bedroom with your undies in it. A long narrow table may be perfect behind your sofa in one house, and might look terrific in the entry of the next house with a lamp and a painting, or it could make a wonderful serving table in the dining room.

A collection of furniture to which you add as you move around has an interesting look that you can't achieve in a single spree at the local furniture store. Once you get over the idea that everything has to match, your rooms will have pizzazz instead of that sterile model-home look. Versatility is the key. Think of your furnishings as you would a wardrobe—mix and match. The accents can be changed from house to house with the addition of new cushions or pillows colorfully worked in crewel or needlepoint, new lamps or fresh lampshades, artworks and prints, and lots of attractive house plants. Incidentally, in many cities you can rent oil paintings and prints for a small fee from the local

library or art galleries. These touches keep your decor from looking dated, which can very easily happen if you stay in one house
for a long time. Seen in this light, moving can be a big plus for the
home decorator. We have all been in homes that have been inhabited by the same people for years and years. Many times the
families have become so comfortable and used to things as they
are that the home tends to become outdated and just plain dull.
Going into new surroundings we are inspired to freshen and
brighten up our old possessions. You should also take into consideration that tastes change over the years. I often wonder what all
those young couples from the fifties did with their Danish Modern suites! I haven't seen any in years! The best advice in buying
and decorating is to try to avoid both extremes of style and of
color. If you do, your furniture and decor should blend beautifully for many years to come.

For the sake of practicality and economy, here are a few
rules of thumb for the transient decorator:

No wall-to-wall carpeting unless it's already in the house!
Invest your carpeting money in good wool area rugs. There are
many beautiful styles and designs available in everything from
real Orientals to colorful ryas, depending on your taste. Even a
piece of good carpeting, cut into an oval or rectangle with fringe
sewn on, can travel anywhere with you. Rugs last longer because
they can be turned around occasionally for even wear. Try to stick
to the conventional sizes that will fit most rooms. If you do move
into a carpeted house, you can lay the rugs over the carpeting or,
after having them professionally cleaned and wrapped, store
them in the attic or a dry basement until your next move.

As I have said it is a good idea before making any move to
have your area rugs cleaned and wrapped. It's a joy to start life in
a new home with everything spic and span from top to bottom.
The lifetime of your rugs will be many years longer if you take
this extra precaution. A good cleaning by a professional will
eliminate the threat of moth eggs and their subsequent damage.
It's not a good idea, however, to take up your old wall-to-wall
carpeting with the thought of installing it in your new house. It
would be most unusual for it to fit correctly without a great deal of
cutting and splicing, which is an expensive proposition. Generally,

carpeting aids in the sale of your home, so unless the carpet is in excellent condition but is of a color the new owners hate and they plan to tear it out, better to leave it for them. If the buyers are adamant about getting rid of it, have it cut into room-size rugs to be used by you at a later date. So they don't care for puce!

Don't spend a lot of money on custom-made draperies. Good department stores in every city and town carry a nice selection of ready-made drapes in a great variety of colors and fabrics. You can trim them yourself, if you like, to suit your decor, with any number of ready-made trims. For one house I sewed yards of grosgrain ribbon to make a border on some ready-made drapes. I used a long running stitch on my sewing machine, and they looked elegant and attractive. I was able to dress seven windows for the price of one pair of custom-mades.

Cornices are an attractive finish to any window. If you have a handy husband or know an inexpensive carpenter, have him make cornices out of 1 × 8 or 1 × 12 boards. We covered our cornices in one house with matching material left over from a slipcovered sofa. With a jig-saw, Blaze shaped the wood into wide curves. He used a padding of cotton batting (foam rubber is also good) to soften the lines. Then he carefully stretched the fabric over the padding and tacked it down on the underside with a staple gun. The results were professional and good-looking. The draperies and cornices were included with the house when we sold it, and the buyers thought that they got a real bargain. We knew *we* did! Before I got wise, I used to cart boxes of drapes and curtains around the country, thinking I could use them again, but all they were ever good for was covering the patio furniture in the winter or making Halloween costumes for the kids.

Try to steer clear of buying enormous, oversized pieces of furniture unless you are a chronic buyer of large old houses. It's heartbreaking when a favorite piece just doesn't fit, and you have to sell or store it. Furniture arrangements are much more flexible with average-size pieces. Of course, if your grandmother's grand piano is your favorite thing in the whole world, you are going to have to buy your houses accordingly. Our prized grandfather clock spent three years vaingloriously resting on its side in the attic when we moved into a rambling ranch with low ceilings.

Slipcovers can do a lot to help coordinate your furniture with its new habitat. I'm not talking about wrinkly ready-mades, but good, well-fitted slipcovers. These aren't cheap, I know, but if you shop for your fabric at one of the many "seconds" shops springing up all over the country you will not only save a bundle on the material, but they can often provide you with the name of a fairly inexpensive seamstress to do the job.

Blaze always favors sturdy fabrics—the kinds that remind you of the seats on a Greyhound bus—in the hope that the material will hold up for the rest of our natural lives. I have found, however, that we get reasonable wear from the pretty cotton prints I love if I have the fabric quilted and have an extra set of covers made for the seat cushions, and then switch them frequently so they wear evenly. Of course, those little extra covers you pin on the arms are *de rigueur*. If the fabric has not been pretreated, buy a can of Scotchgard and thoroughly spray the material yourself. For longer wear, send slipcovers to the dry cleaners instead of sudsing (and invariably shrinking) them yourself.

Don't spend a lot of money on outfitting a child's room. A good bed with a sturdy box spring and firm mattress and some kind of chest of drawers is all a kid really needs or wants. The chest can be a used one, painted or antiqued to suit. A student may need a desk, but then he may prefer lying on his stomach on the rug. If you feel obliged to buy a desk, a used one will do nicely. Unpainted furniture is also a great investment for teens and young children. The styling and designs today are great and will blend with any decor. This furniture can be stained, painted, or antiqued. We once bought a beautiful maple bedroom set for one of our children. After the next move a big argument ensued over whether or not he had to have "that square stuff" in his room again. You can't win, so it's best to let the kids do their own thing with the least possible expense to you. Then you won't have to wonder what to do with all that expensive furniture when they finally leave the nest for good. Most kids will provide their own "atmosphere" with a clutter of toys, sports equipment, records, posters, and a scattering of clothes casually draped over everything, giving the room that "lived-in" look. A colorful bedspread is about all you will have to provide, and it should be durable as well as attractive. Don't spend too much on it, either, as kids like lots of change. Be sure that spreads are machine washable. If you invest a lot of time and money on furnishing a child's room you will be forever frustrated, because it somehow never looks like the rooms pictured in the magazines. Those slick pictures don't show potato chips crushed on the rug, empty soda cans, last week's gym socks rotting in the corner, and the soggy towel that has mildewed on the closet doorknob! I advise you to spend the money you'll save on your own sanctuary, the better to preserve your sanity. If you feel compelled to buy good furniture for your children's rooms, consider the units that fit snugly together to arrange in different combinations. They save a lot of space and can be changed around to fit the next room.

In your son's room, hang the tennis rackets and hockey sticks on the wall along with the baseball pennants and football posters. Treat fish tanks and gerbil cages, stereo sets, and guitars and drums as decorating components. They will look less like useless clutter and more as if they belong in the room. Incidentally, rugs and draperies do help to keep the stereo noise level down, and are therefore worth spending some money on. This may be the place where your old wall-to-wall carpeting which was cut and bound into room size rugs may once again be utilized.

Girls of all ages love plastic Parsons tables, and those big squooshy bean-bag chairs, and collections of candles, stuffed animals, and old bottles with straw flowers stuck in them. Shelves are a good addition to any child's room. These can be bought reasonably in any large hardware store. They are easy to install and can be used in a multitude of ways by kids of all ages. They will help organize some of the clutter that children surround themselves with. Cork squares with adhesive backing applied to the wall over a desk make a great bulletin board for teens. These same squares may be used in the phone area as a pin-board for family messages. They also serve as sound mufflers, so you may want to "paper" the entire room with them!

Since funds for decorating are usually limited, put your money into the rooms where you spend the most time—the kitchen, the family room, and the master bedroom. It's nice to have a living room right out of *House and Garden*, but unless you are obliged to do a lot of entertaining, how often do you and the family really sit there? The living room is often used only when the minister, insurance salesmen, and the Welcome Wagon hostess come to call, and most of us end up decorating for company instead of ourselves. Usually we throw the odds and ends into the family room, where we spend the most time with our nearest and dearest, and there we sit in the mishmash.

Nothing is more comforting than having a serene, lovely bedroom to retire to when the world is getting to you, but that is usually the last room to be decorated. Often you don't get to it until it's time to put the house on the market once again. Put it first next time! On our last move we did just that. The master bedroom was very large, which enabled us to have a wall erected dividing the area into a good-sized bedroom and a small sitting room. This is my own private haven where I can do my needlework, letter writing, and reading with relatively few interruptions. In my heart of hearts, I know that this retreat was one of Blaze's subconscious bribes to induce me to accept yet another move happily. And it worked!

Wives of traveling men enjoy the security of a phone beside the bed, but this can lead to some humdinger battles when the teens invade your territory for those endless telephone conversations. They will sit on the bed and wear out your prized Nettle Creek spread, drink soda and leave rings on the night table, and there goes your serenity. A telephone, as well as a television set in the bedroom, can lead to problems, so lay down the law early in the game—they are X-rated and off limits to anyone under thirty!

Wallpaper is the biggest bargain in decorating. It gives the greatest effect for the least amount of money. Paint is cheap too, and does a good job of cleaning things up, but wallpaper really decorates! Unless you can afford a professional paperhanger, anyone who moves often should learn to hang wallpaper. Volunteer to help someone who knows how, so you can pick up the basics by watching and assisting. Then go ahead and hang some! Many people choose the bathroom for their first papering project because it's usually a small room. It's not always the easiest though, unless you have lots of tile. Fitting paper around a toilet is no snap. For starters, pick a room where there's not a lot of fitting to do. Better yet, practice in some room you don't really need, one that can be boarded up in case the paperhanging doesn't work out.

In most activities dealing with home improvement, I recommend the involvement of the man of the house. After all, his name is on the mortgage, too. Wallpapering is the one exception to this rule. DO NOT make your first stab at hanging paper with the help of your husband. I can think of no situation so likely to end up as a major battle. (Unless, of course, he is already an expert and will take charge of the operation, and your role is no more complicated than holding the ladder.)

The first and only time that Blaze and I hung paper together the fight started with the mixing of the paste: We couldn't agree on how thick it should be. The man at the wallpaper store had said it should be "about the consistency of cream." The problem was one of semantics. Did he mean coffee cream? Heavy cream? Whipped cream? Blaze thought it should be thin. I thought it should be thick. He added more water. I added more paste. Finally we reluctantly agreed to go with the thick and to hang a strip to see how it worked out. A beautiful compromise, you might say, but already there was suppressed hostility in the air.

Do as I say, and not as I do, and choose inexpensive paper for your first experiment. Cutting that first strip is scary enough, but if you have paid more than ten dollars a roll, it can be a disaster. Blaze and I measured the wall from floor to ceiling, and cut a strip of paper exactly that length. We slathered it with paste—the thick version—and applied it to the wall, carefully lining up the edge with the plumb line we had created by hanging a pair of pliers with a piece of long string from the ceiling. Perfect! Then we went to work with the long narrow brush to smooth out the bubbles and wrinkles. Not so good! The paper lay on the wall in lumps and ridges. We were horrified. Blaze said, rather meanly, I thought, "I told you the paste was too thick!"

We were operating under the misapprehension that once the paper was affixed to the wall, it was a permanent arrangement, and not realizing there was any alternative, we turned to the next strip. Again we carefully measured the strip and cut it exactly the same length as the first, but this time we thinned the paste and used less. We rushed the strip to the wall, and with Blaze on the stepladder and me trying to hold the end of the paper off the floor, we quickly hung it next to the first one before the paste could dry. Oh oh. Trouble in River City! The pattern didn't match. We hadn't heard of allowing for the "repeat." Neither had we allowed any extra paper on either end for matching. This time Blaze had the wit to pull the strip off. He crumpled it up and threw it on the floor, and we started with another one. By now he was muttering that he knew why Hitler had given up paperhanging and gone into politics.

This time we did a little better. Allowing extra on the top and the bottom of the strip and working rapidly, we managed to line the pattern up but there again were the lumps and wrinkles! Brushing feverishly, trying to smooth them out, I managed to rip the paper with a fingernail. Wisely, I didn't mention this to Blaze but surreptitiously patched it with my finger. He was busy cutting the next strip which was to go around the window.

This is where, if you will pardon the pun, the going really got sticky. Shortly after we started hanging that strip, the woman from the neighboring apartment came in to see what all the yelling was about. The pliers at the end of the plumb line had crashed through the window, and the strip of paper ripped in half when Blaze was trying to fit it around the window frame, and once more, those damn wrinkles!

We had wisely waited until the children were in bed before we started, and by midnight, when we ran out of paper, two-and-a-half walls were papered and we were no longer speaking except in hisses. It would be nice to say that the walls we had done looked great, but actually they looked as if we were trying to create a stucco effect with papier-mâché. Wrinkles everywhere! Bits of paper were pasted to the linoleum, and ruined strips lay about in crumpled testimony to our mistakes. There were shards of broken glass we'd swept into a corner and paste everywhere, even in blotches on the ceiling. Blaze staggered off to bed, leaving me to clean up the mess. That was the last straw.

Sleeping on the davenport always gives me a backache, and

when I got up with the baby at the first light I was stiff and sore. I changed him and carried him into the kitchen for his breakfast. As I put him into his high chair, I glanced out of the corner of my eye at the wall behind him and did a double-take. Smooth! Beautiful! I looked again, closer. The wrinkles were gone! I couldn't believe it. During the night, the paste had dried, or the paper had shrunk, or the good fairy had come to take care of the problem, but in any case it now looked great.

I ordered more paper to finish the job and hung it myself when Blaze was on the road. I learned that the paste won't dry for several hours, that you can pull a strip off and rehang it, and that you should save the bits and pieces for patching. I also learned that the paste should be neither too thick nor too thin, how to fit the paper around windows, and that Blaze would never hang paper again.

There are lots of little tricks to decorating that you pick up if you move often enough. For instance, any kind of old table, fitted with a round plywood top, can be skirted with a few yards of fabric to fill a bare spot and brighten a room. A group of plants is a great space filler too, if the proper light can be provided. If good natural light isn't available, buy a plant-lamp. These are available in spotlights and floor lamp models that can go with you when you move.

Incidentally, round tables take up less space than rectangular ones, so they are a good bet for kitchen eating areas or anywhere space is likely to be tight. A round table with leaves for extension is an extremely versatile piece. There are still a few old ones around at used furniture shops and antique sales and you can find them if you are willing to hunt. If you find a source for these tables, buy two. You can shorten the base of one, and use it as a coffee table in the living room or family room.

In many cities and towns stores are opening that sell well-constructed unpainted furniture. This furniture is more expensive than what we find in the discount stores, but the selections are much more interesting and unique, and the price is still nominal, compared to the cost of a finished product. If you have yearned for a lovely tester bed with pineapple finials, a Boston rocker, or an elegant French armoire, you might buy the unfinished model.

The antiquing kits on the market are a cinch to use and allow you to be your own artisan. If you really want to be creative and daring, try using a glossy enamel on your unpainted pieces. This creates an interesting effect; the bed or armoire can become the focal point of the room. I recently saw a large four-poster bed right out of *Gone With The Wind,* painted in a luscious shade of periwinkle blue. Almost everything else in the room was done in white, except for the throw pillows piled high on the bed in varying shades of blue. The room was a sensation and the cost was minimal. The owner told me that she had originally stained the bed in a wood finish and had then decided to brighten it with paint when she moved to a house with a northern exposure. She said she intended to repaint it whenever her mood or place of residency changed, whichever came first!

A collection of framed family photos can be arranged to fit any empty wall space and is especially interesting if you can scare up some oldies of your worthy ancestors in their period costumes. Old baby pictures are fun, too. These can be used very effectively in halls, stairwells, a den, or wherever you need wall fillers. The frames can be an interesting mix.

A great adjustable, portable wine rack can be made from ordinary drain tiles that come in that terrific terra-cotta shade. They can be stacked like blocks to fit any size space, and they're just the right size to hold a bottle of wine. When you move, just take them along.

If your new house is short on closet space, consider having two clothes poles in some of your closets, one hung high and the other one low. In this way you can accommodate twice as many blouses and shirts, pants and skirts. The separates in our wardrobes take up a lot of space in an ordinary closet.

For kids' rooms you can make beautiful, practical comforters to use as spreads from two sheets and a couple of layers of fiberfill batting. Just make a big pillowcase of two of the most dazzling sheets you can find—permanent press, of course. Insert the batting and sew up the fourth side, and then tuft it with little knots of washable yarn. Voila! Warm, washable, colorful, and cheap—all prerequisites for kids' furnishings.

It is every woman's natural instinct to feather her nest. We all love to have homes that are beautiful and reflect our tastes, but let's face it! Most of us can't go around the country creating *House Beautiful* every time we land somewhere for a couple of years. The wife of a career army officer once told me that she sets up housekeeping on each assignment as though she is going to be there permanently. I admire the sentiment, but my pocketbook tells me that it isn't practical. After many moves I've learned to put the big decorating money into things that can go with us, and fake it on the rest.

MISERY IS A KID WHO JUST MOVED

Thwarting the cafeteria complex  Establishing lines of communication with the schools  The senior syndrome  Keeping tabs on your teenager  A bit of educational philosophy  And practices  Constructive ways to help your child.

American teenagers are extremely bright, articulate, and idealistic. They are constantly on the go, and after-school activities and socializing are as vital to them as breathing. But take one out of his natural habitat and you may have a disaster on your hands, because teens are extremely clannish and conformist. This generation, despite its vaunted independence, is perhaps the most conforming of all. I must truthfully admit that when I am attending a school event or picking my kids up at a school function I have difficulty recognizing my own flesh and blood. The hair is generally the same length, the jeans faded to the same well-worn hue, and the shirts—well, if they didn't have bumps in the right places, you could be picking up your son instead of your daughter. Plunk a strange kid down in their midst, and this "love generation" will treat him as though he were a creature from outer space.

Our last move was the most difficult for us. Our children were in their teens and trying desperately to find their place in the new school's pecking order. At home we encouraged them not to give up. We impressed upon them their past achievements and accomplishments; we gave them pep talks on Initiative and Gumption in our best Vince Lombardi style; we even tried ignoring the problem. Maybe we were making too much of it, and things weren't really as bad as they seemed. Each evening at dinner we waited for a happy progress report on the day's events. None was forthcoming. We crossed our fingers whenever the phone rang, but it was always some aggressive insurance man or aluminum siding salesman who had gotten the word—via ultrasonic impulses?—that we were new in town.

The genius who sired this brood decided that something had to be done, and soon. Endowed with a logical mind, he carefully laid out plans to thwart the enemy, all of those kids at school who failed to recognize the gems in their very midst! The best solution was really quite simple. Blaze advised our kids to meet with their counselor and find out just how many new students had enrolled in the high school within the last six months or so. Surely there were others in the crowded hallways and the dreaded cafeteria who were just as miserable and hoping just as anxiously for a smile or a word of acknowledgement from their peers. Others must be driving their worried parents to distraction!

Within a week the counselor had compiled a list of new-comers, both boys and girls, with addresses and phone numbers. Amazingly, there were more than thirty kids who were in the same "new" boat. Our youngsters decided to post notices on the school bulletin boards of a meeting open to all newcomers, to be held after school. The purpose: "to get to know one another." The counselor agreed to help. The first meeting was reasonably well-attended, and all thirty-plus showed up at future meetings as the word spread. It was decided to plan some activities for the members, events that were simple and inexpensive. Perhaps a Friday night movie or bowling on a Saturday, going out for pizza, a cookout, and even slumber parties for the girls. When an activity was planned and the time, date, dress, and drivers were settled— the innumerable details that teens worry about endlessly—each person was to call the name on the list following his, and so on down the line until everyone was alerted.

Within two weeks the phone was ringing again, and it hasn't stopped since. Later that year the Transplants Club, as they became known, planned and manned a successful booth at the yearly high school carnival. Several old-timers at the school even asked if they could join the group because it was so active and they had so much fun together.

As do many others, this high school has an active foreign exchange student program, and these students were immediately included in the club. One of my daughters who is now in college keeps up a running correspondence with a lovely girl from France. They became fast friends through the club. One interesting sidelight was the fact that age and grade level seemed to make no difference in establishing friendships. My senior daughter became close friends with a sophomore from California, and my sophomore daughter's best friend was a year ahead of her in school. In the beginning the theme was "misery loves company," but this quickly changed to good fun and fast friendships.

If you are faced with a glum and unhappy transplanted teenager at mealtimes and don't know what you can do to alleviate the miseries your child is enduring, making a phone call to the school and speaking to a counselor or teacher about starting a similar group may be the answer for you, and your kids, too.

True, there are many days and nights when I long for the peace and quiet of a desert island chopped off from civilization with no phones and motorcycles, but when I remember the awful mind-shattering stillness that we lived with when the kids were so lonely, I'll take the noise and confusion and astronomical grocery bills anytime.

There are some positive steps that you can take to help your junior and senior high kids. The first step is to open the communication lines with school personnel. A guidance counselor is an obvious choice. It is his or her job to help all kids adjust to their school. You must be forthright and honest about your worries when you call for help and assistance. An interested and active teacher is another source of help for you and your child, but these professionals must first be alerted to the fact that there is a problem—that your child is unhappy. Many times, especially in the larger schools, teachers cannot possibly know the difficulties of each and every student. Junior presents a pleasant facade whenever school personnel talk to him about his progress, and if his grades are good, what's the problem? They are not aware of the Gloomy Guses that sit across the table from Mom and Dad at mealtime growing more uncommunicative every day and breaking your heart every night.

In many of the larger schools on opening day the individual teachers have no idea which students are new in town. Some classes meet only two or three times a week, which makes it difficult for a busy teacher to know the backgrounds and problems of each one of his students unless he has been informed beforehand. It would be relatively easy for the office to place a small check mark opposite the new students' names when making out the roll for each class. When the teacher looks over the roll he will be aware that little Stanley and Livingston are new to the school. He can introduce them to the class, and make them feel welcome, and imbue them with a sense of belonging right from the start.

This simple procedure could eliminate a lot of confusion for the teacher as well. Our daughter Barbie received A's in English all through school. Her themes and essays were excellent, and some had even been published in the school paper. She loved creative writing and was seriously considering a journalistic career. In her senior year, after two months in the new high school, a warning report arrived in the mail: "Your daughter will receive a D in English this quarter. Her creative writing abilities are nonconforming and undisciplined." The poor kid was crushed, and I was confused. Under normal situations I am not an interfering mother when it comes to teachers and their grading procedures. I don't for a moment believe that my children are infallible. They have been known to drive me to the very edge of the precipice at least twice a week, so I am well aware that they are at times less than perfect. In this instance, however, I felt the teacher must be wrong. My daughter had developed a style of writing that was successful for her during the preceding eleven years, and now she was expected to change her manner of expressing herself to conform to the criteria of this new teacher.

I made a call to the English teacher and learned that the students in the class had been given an outline form in their junior year that they were to follow when writing papers. She said that Barbie had disregarded the instructions and was not following the outline. I calmly explained that she couldn't possibly follow the outline since she wasn't attending the school when the form was taught. Much consternation from the English teacher! Oh my! She had no idea that Barbie was a new student and couldn't understand why she had not been so advised. Again, a tiny check mark beside a name would have eliminated a lot of anxiety for my daughter and confusion for the teacher.

As a footnote to the story, the English teacher was grateful to be made aware of the situation and pledged to give Barbie as much help and understanding as she possibly could, both scholastically and emotionally. At the end of that year, two poems written by my talented child were published in the senior literary magazine!

Be sure to check on the credits required for graduation from the new school. There are often differences in the courses required and in the credit given from one school to another, so explore this subject early with the counselor to avoid any misunderstanding or possible disappointment later.

Teens who are involved with athletics often have a decided

advantage in gaining a toehold in the new school scene. Camaraderie is quickly developed in team sports, and coaches are always on the lookout for new talent. Unfortunately, advisers in other extracurricular activities are usually not so alert, and new students often fail to participate in the very activities that could help them make the social adjustment because they are reticent to make the effort themselves. Often it takes a special invitation, and it's most effective when it comes from another student. Your child's counselor should be able to help here too.

When making choices in curriculum, the mobile student would be wise to stay away from experimental, innovative courses, and stick with the meat and potatoes. If your family is transferred in the middle of the term, it's hard for the new school to place your youngster in a course it doesn't offer. One of our daughters was not a real whiz in math, so she enrolled in a combination algebra-geometry course that was to hit the high spots of both those subjects. When we were transferred in the middle of the year, she didn't have enough background in either subject to fit into a class already in progress. She had to go back to basic math, and start all over with algebra the following year.

Most schools today have a big brother/big sister setup that could be very helpful to the incoming student. This is a system that is used primarily to help the new freshmen find their lockers and generally orient themselves to the unfamiliar building. Some schools extend this courtesy to other newcomers as well when school opens in the fall. Unfortunately, if you have moved into the new area in midterm, your child may be out of luck. Oh, some student may be pulled from a class to show the new one around. The orientation may consist of showing him his locker and his first classroom, and that's often the end of it. It would be so much more helpful if a student who has a similar schedule to follow were assigned to the new student to show him the ropes and keep him company at lunch. I have learned from my kids that the most horrible time in a new school is lunch hour. One approaches the cafeteria alone and is faced with row upon row of boys and girls laughing, eating, and having a good time together. There don't seem to be any seats, and if a place is found, it is being "saved."

The shy girl or boy will sit out lunch hour in the rest room or library. The more self-assured child, who assumes an elaborately casual air and pretends he is enjoying his lunch and his solitude enormously, will immediately be labeled an antisocial "weirdo." How much nicer it would be if someone were to accompany the newcomer to the lunchroom and introduce him to some of the bunch.

For the big brother/big sister plan to operate effectively, the designated helper should be someone from the new student's class, preferably sharing the same homeroom and lunch hour. Eons ago, when I made a cross-country move in my sophomore year of high school to an enormous school complex, I was escorted around the halls by a popular senior girl. She gave me a whirlwind tour, explained the layout of the school, and then dropped me off at my first class as I clutched my schedule in my hot little hand. I never saw her again! Decades later, I am still apt to wake up from a nightmare that takes me back to that horrible day! Every one of us has endured a similar desolate feeling at some time, and it never becomes easy. Perhaps these *are* the very trials that make better people of us all, but at the time it sure does hurt!

Adolescents can be miserably unhappy when they are transplanted. This is the age when they are most dependent on and influenced by their peers, and most vulnerable to boot, as any parent of a teen will testify—at great length. After a move, a boy may withdraw into himself and speak only in grunts for weeks at a time. A girl may miss her menstrual periods, break out in blemishes, or console herself with overdoses of food. It's difficult for a parent to know how to handle the situation, and the temptation is to nag and push and accuse the teen of not making an effort. Actually, the best (and most difficult) thing a parent can do is keep quiet. Usually the child is old enough to understand the necessity of the move, and there is no need to keep covering that ground. If you can quietly arrange activities that will bring him in contact with others, that's good. Tennis lessons, a swim club, golf or skiing lessons, or a youth group at church may help. As with adults, it's the person with the most interests and activities who makes the quickest adjustment, but the parent for the most part will simply have to be patient and supportive while the teenager works out his social difficulties.

Moving with these adolescents is really one of the biggest challenges a family may be called upon to meet. It's especially difficult if you have a child in his senior year. Some families opt to leave the senior with a family in the former hometown to finish high school with his class. Others decide not to make the move until the school year is over, and Dad must then become a weekend visitor. Each family has to weigh the choices, carefully based on the maturity of the child involved. It is sometimes very difficult for him to fit into someone else's family, and he may be very lonely. In some cases the child may not be mature enough to handle his newfound independence. Many girls tend to form a closer attachment to a boyfriend who serves as a family substitute, and this is not always desirable. Decisions involving separation of family members are difficult to make, and there is certainly no pat answer to the question. The needs of the individuals concerned must be weighed carefully.

If he has remained behind, when the child rejoins the family after graduation it is often tough for him to find friends or establish ties in the new town. This is also true of college-age offspring. They tend to keep their roots in your last town, where their high-school buddies remain. It's a good idea in this situation to scout out some activities that these older offspring might enjoy when they join you in your new home. Some newcomers' clubs and churches sponsor parties and get-togethers for college students during school vacations and holidays. Lining up a job in a place that hires other young people is also a good way for them to make contacts in a new community. But, mothers, restrain yourselves from arranging dates for them with any eligibles you may have unearthed. This is the kiss of death for any possible future relationship. Stifle your natural impulse to accost good-looking young people in the supermarket or at the ballgame. Let your young adults find their own romantic interests.

Another major concern for parents of the mobile family is the kinds of friends their children make in the new community. What are the kids like? Who are their parents? What are their values and life-styles? Naturally we parents are eager for our children to make new friends. We quiz them anxiously when they return home from school, "Did you meet anyone today?" . . . "Who is he?" . . . "What is he like?" Sometimes we overdo in our eagerness to see them settled into a social circle, pushing them into relationships that are not right for them. And sometimes they are so eager to become part of a clique or to have someone to eat lunch with that they glom onto the first person who is friendly to them, regardless of suitability.

For months after our last move, we worried and fretted over our fourteen-year-old son. He came directly home from school every day and plunked himself in front of the television set. The phone never rang for him and he never called anyone. He didn't go out, except to a movie or a ballgame with us. Occasionally a boy who lived nearby would stop over to shoot a few baskets, but our son didn't seem to be encouraging the relationship. One day I overheard him tell the boy, "No, I can't come out. I'm doing my homework," when he was actually watching a *Lucy* rerun he had seen three times before. I was upset, but when I asked him why he wasn't making an effort to be friendly he said, "Mom, you wouldn't want me to be friends with that kid." That was good enough for me! I let him take his own sweet time from there on, and when he finally did start bringing some boys home, we were pleased with the kind of friends he had made.

If you have moved with a teenager in high school, and his adjustment has been somewhat less than spectacular, you might want, when the time comes, to consider a small four-year college where he can establish himself and feel that he belongs, even if, God forbid, you should move again. These schools are more expensive than the state universities, but there are many financial-aid programs available. Too often, resorting to a local commuter college simply extends the problem of left-out-itis that he may have experienced in high school.

If it's financially feasible, mobile parents may also want to consider enrolling a younger child in a private school. Such schools are generally smaller than public secondary schools, and children find it easier to get acquainted and involved in activities. Admission may be difficult to arrange if your student is in the upper grades, but if he is enrolled when he starts junior high school it is often possible to transfer him into a similar private school in the new town.

Growing up in a community where he is known and recognized places restraints upon a child, restraints that are very helpful to the parent in keeping Junior on the straight and narrow. When I was young and growing up in a small town, we thought twice about doing something that was verboten, because it would quickly be reported to our parents by the butcher, the baker, and the town drunk, all of whom knew us and our parents and sometimes even our grandparents. There were watchful eyes and listening ears everywhere, so we toed the line—usually! The mobile family doesn't get that kind of help and guidance and caring. They have to "prove" themselves to their new neighbors. It is only natural for people to be critical of someone they don't know. If your Johnny gets in a fight with the neighbor's little Billy the day you arrive at your new home, Johnny has created a problem for himself in the eyes of Billy *and* Billy's parents. Billy may be a monster, but everyone has known him since he was a babe in arms, so the new kid on the block must be the troublemaker! There are, of course, some positive actions you can take. You can carefully instruct your children to be on their best behavior and to avoid any controversy in the neighborhood and in school. If worse comes to worst you can always con Johnny into a game of cowboys and Indians and tie him to a chair for a few days. First impressions are important, and when you are new to the neighborhood, it's a good idea for the family—including the dog—to put its collective best foot forward.

Even under normal circumstances it can be very difficult to keep tabs on an active teen, but when you are also disoriented by a move things can get out of hand rapidly. My friend Cora, who had moved with her brood to California, soon ran into problems with Amy, her thirteen-year-old. Little discrepancies crept into Amy's accounts of where she was going and what she was doing after school and on weekends. Becoming alarmed, Cora overcame her natural tendency to let the older residents make the first move, and called several of the mothers of Amy's new friends to suggest a morning coffee.

When the mothers started comparing notes, they discovered that they had all been getting the runaround from their kids, who, once they were out of the house, were doing just about as they pleased. Instead of gathering "at Susie's house" or "going swimming at Sara's," they were spending hours at the local shopping center and hanging around the pizza parlor. These mothers made a pact to check with one another on the girls' whereabouts thereafter, and before long they had the situation under control. They were also able to lay to rest complaints that "everyone else's mother lets her" and to agree on suitable curfews. There is strength in numbers!

It is often difficult for the newcomer to make the first move socially. From the outside, it may appear that everyone else knows one another, whereas this is not always the case. Cora made some new friends for herself by taking the initiative, and many of the other mothers told her that they were happy finally to meet the parents of their child's friends. They all felt more secure about the activities of their fledgling teens. And as we all know, parents of teens need all the help and support they can get!

One thing I've learned to my great regret is that it's very easy to fall into the trap of becoming relaxed in matters of discipline after a move. We are so eager for our kids to be happy in their new surroundings and in making the adjustment as pleasant as possible for the family that we sometimes bend the rules a bit. Kids, those astute creatures, sense your vulnerability, and before you know it, you've lost the upper hand. You have spent years instilling values and molding young minds, but within a matter of weeks your darling children may become perfect strangers, and not very nice ones at that! Do not, I repeat, DO NOT lower your standards of behavior. No matter how exhausted you are, no matter how lonely you are, no matter how much pleading and sweet-talking your children try to snow you with, keep repeating to yourself at all times that you are the parent and they are the children. You set the standards and they must follow them. Moving is disruptive enough without allowing your way of life and its values to be changed, too. If your teenagers have had a curfew that they have lived with and respected, don't suddenly allow them complete freedom in the new environment. It's awfully difficult to go back to the old set of rules once you have given them their heads. You, as parents, will suffer for your leniency in the long run, and your kids very well might too.

A child who moves during elementary school will find the academic side of life as deeply disrupted as the secondary student does his social life. Each school system in the country is autonomous, teaching whatever subjects and skills they deem appropriate at whatever level they think best. Historically, school systems have staunchly defended this autonomy, maintaining that the local community knows best what knowledge is required by its future citizens. The local professional educators—teachers and administrators—develop the curriculum and submit it for approval to the board of education, a group elected by the local citizenry. Some states impose mandatory subject areas, but these are often limited to the evils of drugs, of alcohol, and of free love. A few states, notably California, have worked out guidelines for curriculum at each grade level, but the child who moves out of the state has no such assurance of an orderly progression in his education.

Through the years educators have violently opposed any kind of federal regulation, but with millions of children changing schools every year maybe we ought to consider seriously working out some national curriculum guidelines. The good old days are gone. Johnny is not necessarily going to stay in his hometown and follow in his father's footsteps. Today the welder's kid may become a doctor, and the doctor's son may want to be a welder! Television and mass communication and the ease of travel have made us a much more homogeneous society, and maybe we ought to take another look at the wide disparity in the curriculum as well as the quality of our schools.

In the meantime the closest thing we have to national guidelines comes from the textbook publishers who in the absence of such guidelines, become major arbiters of when fractions will be introduced, at what grade level American history will be taught and so on—rather like the tail wagging the dog. In fact, in some school systems each teacher has complete freedom to teach whatever seems appropriate to her as long as she touches on the three R's and doesn't offend parents' sensibilities. There is an unspoken agreement that if one teacher does a unit on Indians, another won't step on her pedagogical toes in that particular area.

Since the advent of the new math and experimental programs of one kind and another in the development of reading skills, there is even more chaos. Some friends of ours moved to the Cleveland area several years ago with a daughter in the first grade. Her school there was experimenting with the British phonetic alphabet consisting of fifty-some symbols representing the sounds in English. They intended to switch over to our twenty-six-letter alphabet later, but unfortunately our friends were transferred again before that was accomplished. The child was so thoroughly confused that she eventually had to repeat two grades, and she still bears the scars.

That fiasco was worse than most, but anyone who has moved with youngsters in school can tell a similar hairy tale. One of our daughters missed multiplication completely when we moved while she was in third grade. Luckily, that's a skill that can easily be taught at home with a set of flash cards and a little perseverance. Then we moved with a son in second grade who had been taught to "write" in manuscript printing, as is common throughout the country, the theory being that it is easier for the child to correlate reading and writing if the letters look the same. Cursive writing, which most adults use, is generally introduced in the third grade. Unfortunately we moved into a school where that theory was being challenged by teaching the cursive style right from kindergarten. The whole family tried to help him learn the skill, but three years later he's still embarrassed because he considers his handwriting poor, and he avoids written work as much as he can.

Our older boy, who attended three different schools in first and second grade, can read well, but about the only thing he can spell correctly is his name, and he never did really get the basics in math. With the current trend toward individualized instruction, many of these problems could be avoided, but few classroom teachers have the time to see to it that each new child is brought up to date in all areas. This could be a function of a resource teacher, but they are generally all booked up with children with other learning difficulties. The child who moves in from a school that is more advanced in some areas also presents a problem. He often becomes bored because "we had that already," and discipline problems can result.

A child moving into a secondary school usually has fewer academic difficulties. The basic skills have presumably been mastered, and subject areas have become more specialized. If he was taking chemistry in his former school, he is plugged in to chemistry again, and while the new class may be ahead of him, there is a fifty-fifty chance that they may be behind, too, and he will pick up a little reinforcement of material he has already covered. With the "tracking" system in use in most high schools the student can more easily be placed in a class at his own level. Many high schools have become miniature colleges with quarter-courses and semester-length courses and "minicourses," and a catalog with enough electives to choke a horse. This does make it easier for a transferring student to choose subject matter that he hasn't covered before. As I have said, his major problem will be in the area of social adjustment, and that can be a doozy!

Another difficulty frequently encountered, especially by children with autumn birthdays, is correct grade placement. Cutoff dates for enrollment in kindergarten for five-year-olds range from September in Missouri to January in Massachusetts. If someone had explained this to me years ago, I would have planned to have all my babies in the spring!

Picture this, if you will. One cold morning in December I arrived at the new school to enroll my children. Mary, whose birthday is in May, was quickly ensconced in the sixth grade, and the principal turned his eye to eight-year-old Hank, who was tightly clutching my hand.

"And this young man is in third grade?" he said. "Yes, he is," I replied proudly. Hank's birthday is in October, but in the Connecticut suburb where he started school, since his birthday came before December 31, he had started kindergarten when he was four. But now we were enrolling in a school in Missouri. Looking him over carefully the principal said, "He seems a little young for third grade."

This took me by surprise. Hank had always been at least as big as his classmates and was a good student besides. We had had no problems with him at all. I pulled out the envelope I was carrying and presented the standardized test scores and Hank's workbooks from his last school. We could take care of this problem in no time.

The principal looked the materials over carefully, and then explained to me that in this system a child had to be five by the end of September in order to enroll in kindergarten. He pointed out that even though Hank could probably handle the academic work in the third grade, he would be the youngest in his class by at least two months. He added that this could be a handicap in many ways, and that it was far more advantageous, especially for a boy, to be one of the older members of his class. On the athletic field, in social relationships, as well as in the classroom, he would be on a much more solid footing.

Sizing up my look of alarm and Hank's brimming blue eyes, he quickly suggested that we give him a try in the second grade for the week that remained before Christmas vacation. He added that if we still felt uncomfortable with that decision at the end of the vacation, he would have a desk waiting for him in the third grade on the first day of the new term. In the meantime, the second-grade teacher would be able to test him and observe his interaction with the other students, and if she felt he was improperly placed she would let us know. He sagely observed, "It's much easier to move a child ahead if we feel that it's necessary, rather than start him in the higher grade, and then have to move him back."

I agreed, and it didn't take long to realize that this was the proper decision. Hank's adjustment was quick, and before long he fit right in. It's a decision that we have never regretted. Once kids are in the secondary grades, juggling grade placement is a tough thing to do. It would be extremely helpful to have a cut-off date for kindergarten enrollment that is the same throughout the country.

One thing a parent can do to aid in a child's proper placement in his new school is to bring, or have sent, complete records and data regarding his education thus far. A few weeks before you move go to the school and ask to see your child's file. The 1974 Federal Right to Privacy of Parents and Students Act guarantees your right to inspect the file of material that will be sent ahead to the new school. Have the counselor make up a packet of all the material that would be helpful in dealing with your youngster, and *ask the new school to request this information two or three weeks before your move*, so it will be available when you arrive to enroll him. You will be required to sign a consent form to release the information. If there is anything in the file that you don't wish to be sent, you have the right to challenge the contents of the records.

There has been a consistent downward trend reported in the SAT scores of high-school seniors in the last fourteen years. These are the Scholastic Aptitude Tests given nationwide to students to measure their ability to apply verbal and math skills, and to aid colleges in selecting students for admission. Educators have been searching for the reason behind these discouraging statistics, but I haven't heard anyone suggest that the mobility of the school population might be a contributing factor. The students who take these tests are the ones who are considering a college education, and it stands to reason that many children from the highly mobile middle-class stratum of our society are heavily represented in these figures. Perhaps it's time that educators gave more thought to the significance of the problems of the mobile child. With one-fifth of the nation's population moving annually, surely this is a matter that needs to be dealt with as a prescribed program, one that deserves equal time at faculty meetings with how to conduct a fire drill or collect lunch money.

What *can* the schools do to help the new student in the elementary grades? There should be greater awareness and understanding of the scope of the problem of the mobile child by teachers and administrators. An effort should be made by the entire staff, right down to the janitor and the cafeteria lady, to help the child reestablish his identity and make the transition. Frequent informal counseling by all school personnel can help smooth the adjustment. Often it is the most troubled youngsters who are the most reticent about discussing their problems in a formal setting.

Administrators should make every effort to place a new

child in a class with low enrollment to ensure the individual attention he will need to bridge the gaps in his education.

There should be greater uniformity from one school district to another, and indeed, from one state to another, in the teaching of basic material—"the three Rs." Educators insist that no two communities are alike and that all require different programs, but surely all children from the ghetto child to the child of the affluent suburbs have the same need of the basic tools of reading, writing, and arithmetic. Tailoring of the curriculum to the community *should* come in the cultural-enrichment areas to fit the character and needs of the particular town. Of course, without experimentation there can be no progress, but perhaps educational experiments should be relegated to the "laboratory schools" connected with our teacher-training instructions, until they have been proven effective.

In my experience, moving with preschoolers has never presented any problems, psychological or social or academic! As long as the little one is aware that the family unit is intact, and he has his pet gerbil and his one-eared teddy bear and his security blanket with the frayed satin binding, he is content. Thank goodness for that! Wouldn't it be great if things stayed that simple?

On the other hand, the child of elementary school age may resort to attention-getting devices in the new neighborhood and the new school. He may suddenly discover his comedic talents and become the class clown, or he may become overly rambunctious on the playground, or he may start using some words you didn't know he had overheard.

Many times a child will take to telling whoppers about his previous experiences and family connections to impress his new associates. When I attended the PTA Open House at my third grader's new school a few years ago, I was amazed and chagrined to discover that his teacher thought I was the wife of a general on duty in Vietnam! No wonder she viewed the man with me with curiosity and suspicion. She was taken aback when Blaze, a business executive in blue pinstripes, introduced himself to her. We were quickly able to set the record straight in that case, and later, when Junior boasted to the class that the lineman working on the power pole outside the school was his uncle, she took it with more than a grain of salt.

Try to help your child gain recognition in more acceptable ways. You could provide lessons in piano, guitar—even drums, if absolutely necessary. Enroll your child in the Cub Scouts or Brownies, or some of the various "Y" activities available in most towns. You might think about horseback-riding lessons, if this is something he craves, or some other activity that will set him apart in the crowd. Make sure he gets plenty of praise from all quarters to bolster his fragile ego.

Let's summarize some of the positive steps that you as a loving and caring parent can take to help your child's adjustment.

MAINTAIN COMMUNICATIONS WITH YOUR CHILD   Be there when your child needs you. When he arrives home from a "hard day at school" have a snack ready for him and a cup of tea for yourself. Sit down together and talk over the day's events, bad or good. Try to restrain yourself from the platitudes that we parents resort to so often. Be his sounding board when he opens up to you. He needs a sympathetic ear along with your warmth, your support and your understanding.

ESTABLISH LINES OF COMMUNICATION WITH THE SCHOOL   Remember that you and the counselor or teacher are observing your child through two different sets of eyes. She may be aware of something that you have not noticed at home, and you, no doubt, will have insight into your child's more private feelings. Don't delay too long in letting the school know if your child is miserable! The longer a problem is ignored, the deeper and more serious it becomes. It may be advantageous for you to think about doing some volunteer work at the school. This is an excellent means of getting to know teachers and school personnel on a personal basis, and it enables you to become acquainted with the customs, mores, and inhabitants of your child's new world. However, this should not be substituted for in-depth conferences with teachers and counselors.

HANG LOOSE! If your maternal instinct is working overtime, you must stop yourself from indulging in "smother love." You hate to see your son or daughter unhappy, but it is much better and more constructive for you to try to remain objective. Let your kids choose their friends in their own time and way. Encourage them to assume a friendly manner and to be open and receptive to overtures from others, but don't push!

It's a good idea to hold off on buying too many clothes before the child has a chance to reconnoiter the dress situation. Teenagers, especially girls, are very fad-conscious as far as clothing is concerned, and these fads are liable to differ from town to town. Kids want to conform with their peers, and you should allow your child to decide, within reason certainly, what mode of dress he desires. Have faith in his judgment and hold your tongue, if you can.

When at last your youngster has made a friend, encourage him to bring him home. Ask the friend to stay for dinner or to spend the night. This is also a great way for you to size things up.

THE FAMILY PLAN   After the major settling-in process has been completed, the family deserves a break. Time may hang heavy on your hands, and boredom is likely to set in. Nip it in the bud, and get out and do things as a family. Chances are in a few weeks or months everyone will become so involved in his new activities that it will be difficult to get the whole group together for a family outing. Set out to explore your new city en masse. Unless the majority are so inclined, skip the intellectual field trips, and do some fun things that you can all enjoy. Allow each member of the family to plan "his day." You may spend a lot of hours at the local amusement park topped off with a dinner of chili dogs, but what the heck! Go to a ball game, visit the zoo, and take in the local tourist attractions. There are lots of things to see and do when you are new to an area, and when you explore with the people you love best in the world you're bound to have fun, even if your feet are killing you.

VISITATION RIGHTS If you have older children, it's helpful to allow them a visit back to the old homestead for a special occasion such as Homecoming Weekend or a special dance. If it's too far, this may be financially impossible; if so, explain the situation to your child. Perhaps he can earn the money to help pay for the trip himself. It's not smart, however, to allow your child virtually to commute back and forth. He has got to make the adjustment to the new locale, and if he feels that he can see his old chums whenever he likes, his efforts to meet people in the new town will cease. Suggest to him that he invite his very best buddy to your new home during a school vacation. Junior can act as tour guide, and you may discover that he is developing some pride in his new home-town. Glory be! Maybe he's even beginning to like it here!

If you have done everything you can to ease your child's transition to your new community, you must be patient and let nature take its course. Children are actually quite adaptable. After living several years in Massachusetts, our kids all spoke in broad Bostonese—this in spite of the pure Midwestern accents intoned by the parents in the home! I decided the preschoolers picked it up in the milk when even the toddler, who spent all her waking hours in my company, demanded that we go for a ride in the "cah" to the "stoah." When we moved to Wisconsin, the neighbors were entranced with the children's accent—but not for long. Within a month it disappeared without a trace. A year or so later we were transferred to Connecticut, where we moved next door to a family from Boston, and within hours the whole tribe once again sounded like a clutch of Kennedys. At some age, however, we must pass a point of no return when our accent becomes fixed. No matter where we move, and what strong regional dialects I am exposed to, my pure Midwestern tones persist. In spite of their seeming fragility, perhaps it *is* easier to transplant a seedling than a mature specimen.

SMILE AND SAY YOU LOVE IT!

The art of coping Post-moving blues Reorganization of your life Society and the newcomer Self-help suggestions Dealing with the natives.

A few months ago while watching one of the network talk shows I learned from four or five of the better-known creative-type panelists that their feelings regarding life and its ups and downs could be summed up in one word—cope. What a terrific word that is. Certainly any of us involved in the human condition copes, whether it's by being a fascinating and stimulating guest of Merv or Mike, or by simply entertaining the weekly bridge club. We members of the much-maligned *Sisterhood of Wives and Mothers United* cope almost every day of our lives. It may be potty-training little Billy, getting Sue Ellen to clean up her clothes-strewn, cyclone-swept room, or pleading with the washer repair man to come as soon as possible and not a week from Tuesday, bathing the dog's wounded paw, and on and on. We cope a dozen times a day in a dozen different ways—with very little acknowledgment or cooperation from those whom we are coping for, I might add.

When we're involved in a moving expedition across the country or just around the corner, whether it be a company-sponsored move or a "U-Haul special," a happy, long-anticipated move or one that we dread more and more with every passing day, we have to cope with uncounted crises and details. Maybe you are a Golda Meir type who handles every situation with style and flair, accompanied by fanfare and headlines around the world, but if you are like most of us you won't hear thunderous applause nor will you be the recipient of testimonials and accolades. No one may ever be more deserving of the Nobel Peace Prize, but you will have to settle for the satisfaction of knowing that you have done your job in the best possible way. You have coped!

"Adjust" is another key word, and as defined in *Webster's New World Dictionary* it means "to settle or arrange rightly." "Cope," from the same source, means, "to fight or contend with successfully." Beginning with the day you first learned that a move was in the picture for you and your family, you have had to do a lot of both. From the moment you step over the threshhold of your new home, an adjustment begins to take place. You and every other member of the family will be adjusting in almost all you do, individually and as a group. Everyone participates. The family dog will reconnoiter the yard and the neighborhood canine residents and claim his territorial bush. The family cat will cautiously search out a new perch from which she can survey her own personal world, and even your plants will do or die in their new location. Moving can be a shock even to a plant's system, and they may appear to be on their last legs or roots, but don't despair— with tender loving care and soft-spoken words of encouragement they will survive (a bit of sage advice that also applies to weary women).

For the first few days after moving into your new home, you will be calling upon superhuman strengths and resources that you never realized you possessed to see you through. You will be busy unpacking, arranging and rearranging, hanging pictures and draperies, moving a chair from this corner and back to that, a table next to the sofa and then under the window, and then moving it all back where it was when you started. You'll spend endless hours waiting for servicemen who never arrive at the designated time—men to hook up the washer and dryer, men to install the phone, men to resod the neighbor's yard where the moving van didn't cut the corner sharply enough, and all the various humdrum details that it takes to make your household sing!

A few days after your move, you will begin to see order rising out of chaos like a phoenix from the ashes. The kitchen doesn't resemble the battle of Gettysburg nearly as much as it did yesterday. You are able to fix yourself a cup of coffee without going through too many contortions, and someone actually braved the disaster area to fix a toasted cheese sandwich for a snack last night. With the aid of your husband and kids, the place is really shaping up and beginning to look like a real live home. The children have cautiously and tentatively ventured out into the neighborhood to size up the kid population, and slowly communication lines are being opened up. Your kids are discovering that the children living in Ohio play ball, listen to rock, ride tricycles and minibikes, despise solid geometry, and love faded blue denims just as much as the kids in California.

Your husband is into his new job and running with every challenge he encounters. His new office, though it doesn't have its own executive washroom, is spacious and has a nice window; his secretary is, of course, rather plain and middle-aged but most competent (reminds him a bit of old Aunt Harriet, or so he says), and yes, he definitely made the right decision and already has a "handle on the situation."

Let's get back to the little woman of the house, good old what's-her-name. During these last few days or weeks you have been so physically exhausted and completely involved in the settling-in process that you barely had time to think. The days don't hold enough hours, and each night you have crawled into bed in a state of total fatigue. All at once the turmoil is over. Life is beginning to settle once again into near normalcy. It is completely within reason for you at this time to retire to the privacy of your beautiful new bedroom or the gleaming bathroom with the his and hers sinks, or even to the garage with the convenient automatic door opener, and quietly indulge yourself in a good old-fashioned, body-wrenching, sorry-for-yourself cry. And you really should give in to it. You deserve the luxury. You've earned every tear!

After the initial euphoria and feeling of accomplishment that result from doing a difficult job well, you can expect to experience, to some degree, a feeling of depression. In the case of an overseas move, the experts term this culture shock, but you will probably be aware of it even if your move was just across the state line.

It was said in our great-grandmothers' day that two moves were as destructive as one fire. Now the horse-drawn moving wagon has been replaced by Bionic Van Lines with all kinds of specialized packing materials and techniques, and the damage today is not to our household goods but to our psyches. Psychiatrists equate the trauma of a long-distance move to that of a death in the family. This may be a bit strong, but once the frenzied activity is finally over a period of "grief" does begin to set in. This feeling may take hold two weeks after the move or four months later, and its duration depends upon the individual and the speed with which he or she is able to replace friends and confidants. Vance Packard in *A Nation of Strangers* cited a study done by Robert S. Weiss at the Department of Psychiatry of the Harvard Medical School. The study showed that people have a basic need to have certain kinds of relationships with other people in order to enjoy a feeling of well-being. We need to know someone who will give us assistance if we need it; we need to have intimate friends with whom we can exchange confidences; we need the reassurance of our own worth that is given by friends who respect us; and we need the sense of community provided by knowing people who share our social concerns.

These are all needs that are frustrated when we move until we are able to locate new friends who will fill the void. It's this finding of people-replacements that comes hard, especially if you have moved several times and are out of your adventurous twenties. It doesn't take long to locate a good supermarket and an adequate hairdresser, but it may take months or years to locate a friend you can depend on to help you out in a pinch. When you enroll your kids in a new school, you are usually asked to fill out an emergency information card. The school requires the name of a friend or neighbor who will take charge of your child in the event of an emergency, if you can't be reached. I know this is necessary information, but when you've been in town for two days you generally don't know who your doctor is, let alone a friend who would help you out in that way, or *any* way! The school secretary usually makes me feel as though we are some kind of gypsies or migratory workers—which I guess in many ways we are!—when I tell her that I'll have to leave that space blank for awhile.

I'll never forget the way a friend of mine described her loneliness after moving into a beautiful home in Westchester County. She had an elderly carpenter coming in to build some bookcases and cabinets, but she kept him so busy chatting and having cups of tea that he was having difficulty getting any work done. She said that she realized later that her subconsicous didn't want him to finish because then she would be alone again. I've learned since from many other women that this is a common phenomenon. (Makes you wonder how many transplanted wives have taken up with their paperhanger or plumber when they were new in town.)

My friend Judy confessed that after one move she was so lonely she found herself making two or three trips to the bank every week because the teller in the drive-in window called her by name. "Good morning, Mrs. Guilderstern," he'd say. "How are you today?"

"Of course, he probably read it off the withdrawal slip," she said, "but he was the only person in town who took the trouble."

Another girl I know took to stopping off for a cup of coffee at the local diner every morning after the children were in school just to chat with the waitress there. That sounds pathetic, but it's true. I myself once took to shopping two or three times a week at a fancy neighborhood market, even though I am ordinarily a thrifty once-a-week-and-when-we're-out-of-it-we're-out-of-it shopper. The lure? A friendly checkout clerk who "visited" with me as she rang up my asparagus tips and hearts of palm.

Another friend told me that she spent most of her first months in one new town walking around a big shopping center because she yearned for companionship, and a salesclerk was better than no one. She'd try on shoes, look at washers and attend every sale—all with no intention of buying. When I asked her how she managed to stay solvent, she said she pretended the stores were museums, and nothing was really for sale!

In a couple of towns, I've even become addicted to certain radio programs with DJs who came across the air waves as sincere and friendly. You know you're in bad shape when you won't turn on the vacuum or the dishwasher for fear of drowning out the voice on the radio! All this is known as *The Any-Friendly-Face-or-Voice-Will-Do Syndrome.*

There are other syndromes that any veteran mover will recognize. For instance, the *I've-Had-It Syndrome:* This is the direct result of too much pressure being brought to bear on the movee. You can never predict when she will blow, but blow she will! One of my friends had endured a pregnancy that spanned three states and five different doctors. She had moved gracefully twice in six months and managed to keep her two preschoolers and her sanity under control. When she finally entered the hospital in labor a week after moving into another new house, she was devastated when the contractions stopped. The current doctor pronounced it false labor and said, "You can go home now, little lady, and come back when your baby is ready." "The hell I will!" said she. She turned to her husband and snapped, "*You* can go home and take care of those kids, and hang the curtains, and seed the lawn. I'm staying here in this bed until this baby is born, even if it takes a month!"

THE-GRASS-IS-ALWAYS-GREENER SYNDROME
Friends and relatives who have lived their entire lives in one town are inclined to look at the mobile family with envy. Our lives appear to be a round of sophisticated, stimulating change and travel. Not for us the obligatory Sunday dinners at the in-laws', the same old faces at the country club, and the New Year's Eve party. We're the lucky ones who enjoy new towns, new friends, new houses every couple of years or so. On the other hand, the mobile family casts green eyes at those with roots, with Grandma for a baby-sitter, with status in the community, with a solid circle of old friends, with a doctor who knows their name without resorting to a peek at the chart, and with an extended family to gather around the festive board at holiday time. Friends, it appears to me that it's six of one and half-a-dozen of the other.

THINGS-ARE-NOT-ALL-THEY-WERE-CRACKED-UP-TO-BE SYNDROME
It's hard to get a good fix on the new town in the week you may have been allotted for house-hunting, and if you move often enough, the odds are that you will occasionally make a boo-boo in your choice of housing or suburb or schools or something. Usually time resolves these doubts, yet I have known women who to all intents and purposes are settled but who continue to devour the real estate ads in search of a more suitable property. Looking at it another way, this becomes sort of a hobby with them, and it does bring them into contact with the locals—albeit real estate agents—and gives them something to occupy their days. Their husbands stand for it because *they* are suffering from the *Mea-Culpa-Syndrome*, but more about that later.

I suffered from *Things-Are-Not-All-They-Were-Cracked-Up-To-Be* myself on one notable occasion when, shortly after moving day, I realized that our nice new house was located just a couple of miles from the state penitentiary—a little detail the realtor had neglected to mention. I was nervous and upset about it and suggested to Blaze that we put the house back on the market. "Don't be silly," he said. "It's one of the best prisons in the country."

It was November when we moved to this brand-new subdivision, and things weren't quite finished yet. The street hadn't been paved, and there were no sidewalks or street lights. Our little house was the first one finished, and the skeletons of two others under construction were the only sign of human activity that could be seen from our windows. Beyond them lay the woods. Darkness fell early on those late Fall afternoons, and I was just starting dinner when I heard the voice on the radio announcing the break at State Prison in the urgent, sepulchral tones that announcers affect when they have something more exciting than the weather to report. Three convicts were loose, and troopers were combing the woods and setting up roadblocks in an effort to track them down.

Frantically, I dialed Blaze's office in the city. He wasn't in. I hurried through the house, pulling the window shades down to the sills. I dragged the baby's playpen into the kitchen and told the two-year-old to come and help Mommy fix supper, like a pioneer woman circling the wagons in preparation for the Indian attack. We were scraping carrots at the kitchen sink when there was a loud BANG!

From the sudden constriction in my chest, I was sure I had been shot, but in a moment my eye was caught by the shade, whirling around its roller at the top of the kitchen window. The mechanism was wound so tight on the brand-new shade that the spring had sprung!

That was enough for me. Ransacking the closet, I found the pistol that Blaze had brought home from the service. I couldn't find the clip that held the ammunition, but I took the gun to the kitchen anyway, and put it on the shelf next to the coffee cups.

In this state of siege I managed to throw a meat loaf together and put it in the oven, listening all the while to radio bulletins about the ongoing search for the convicts. Soon it was completely black outside, and I prayed that Blaze would be along any minute. I was shakily feeding the baby mashed carrots when I heard a footstep on the back porch and then a knock at the kitchen door. Blaze never knocks. A long moment passed, during which scenes from my life flickered before my eyes, and then I scrambled to the cupboard and grabbed the gun. In one simultaneous motion, I lifted the shade on the door window and pointed the pistol at the intruder. (Blaze always says the best defense is a good offense.)

The neighbor who was standing there was quite startled. He had come by to see if we were all right, but now he declined my fervid invitation to come in. In fact, he was always a little standoffish after that. We lived there four years, and there was never another prison break. I got so used to driving past the prison on the way to town that I seldom even saw it. You can get used to anything.

THE MEA-CULPA SYNDROME   Husbands rarely seem to be affected by the aforementioned syndromes. They are usually busy and challenged by the new job and they may be enjoying a promotion and its accompanying feelings of elation and prestige. So it can be very surprising and upsetting for a man to come home from the office on this high and find his wife hitting rock bottom. She may have been fine when he left the house that morning—humming as she rearranged the cupboards and looking forward to a day of shopping for new carpeting for the family room. Now she is sobbing that she is miserable here and they never should have moved!

When Blaze left on a business trip shortly after our last move the whole family was doing fine. When he returned a few days later he said he could sense the change in the air as soon as he put his key in the lock. He found all of us huddled in front of the television set in the tiny den, the depression so thick he could have cut it with a knife. The postpartum moving blues had set in. This depression can make the husband feel uncomfortably guilty. He's the one responsible for the move, and he wonders if he may have been selfish—putting his career ahead of the feelings of the rest of the family. Of course, what's good for the breadwinner is generally good for those whose bread he is winning, but still the guilt lingers. Husbands have been known to wear out their wallets in an effort to bring joy and gladness back into the household, but this is not recommended. Better to be depressed than bankrupt. Again, the only real antidote is time.

After one devastating move that brought us halfway across the country I was feeling pretty sorry for myself. When the preliminary unpacking had been taken care of, and Blaze was busily embarked on his new job and the children enrolled in their new schools, I stood in my new home and stared at the remaining boxes surrounding me. Where was I to put all these books? Should I line all the kitchen shelves before unpacking the dishes and just make do with paper plates for the time being? What had become of the toaster? And where was the serviceman who was supposed to be here the day before yesterday to hook up the washer and dryer? I was drowning in dirty clothes and mounds of plastic pop wrap. Surely nothing was worth the hassle I was going through!

The phone's shrill ring in the silence caught me by surprise. It really did work!—but who in the world could it be? There wasn't a soul within local calling range who even knew we existed. I immediately assumed the worst. One or all of the kids had run away from school and was hitchhiking back to Massachusetts! Or worse, my husband was either fired after the first week on the job or was being transferred again. I hesitantly reached for the phone. A sweet voice answered my Hello, with "Hi there, this is Lucy Goosey, and I just wanted to welcome you and your family to the neighborhood." My cup ranneth over! A lump formed in my throat and hot tears of gratitude stung my eyelids. Imagine! Someone actually knew that I was here. How very thoughtful of this lovely-sounding lady. After the conventional amenities had been exchanged, I began to gather the real purpose of this "friendly" gesture. Said Mrs. Goosey, "I understand that you have a darling eight-year-old daughter, and we would just love to have her join our Brownie troop." Since my daughter had been very unhappy about leaving her former troop and friends, I answered quickly and enthusiastically, "She'd love it! When will the meeting be?" She replied that they would gather the following Wednesday at 3:30 in Room 28 at the elementary school. I shouldn't have too much trouble finding it, but it would be a good idea to get there at least twenty minutes early so that the other leader could fill me in on what my job would be. There was dead silence on my end of the line. It was not my darling little eight-year-old that she was interested in—only *my* warm body to help keep the Brownies at bay! It seemed that the troop was short on volunteers, and in order to include my daughter, I would have to be the official co-leader! "Everyone must participate, don't you know," said good old Lucy. I have always considered myself to be an active and rather conscientious mother and I had in fact spent the past ten years doing my bit to help out with every children's program conceived by the mind of Man—certainly not the mind of Woman! (When you are the mother of five children in a span of six years, you truly don't miss out on a heck of a lot, especially when you have trouble saying no. It was this inability to say no that led me to have those five children in the first place!) Biting my tongue, I tried to explain to Mrs. Goosey in a pleasant and gracious manner that I could see no possible way for me to lead a troop of thirty Brownies this Wednesday. I told her that I would be happy to help in any possible way within a few weeks, as soon as we were a little more settled. She replied in a less syrupy voice that if that was the case, my daughter would just have to forget the Brownies this year! She also intimated that it was doubtful that she would be eligible for the Girl Scouts when the time came. I wouldn't recommend L.G. for a position with the Chamber of Commerce. This was not one of my all-time great welcomes to a new community. I forgot about the cartons piled around me and called the local Scouting headquarters and lodged a complaint. I was vindicated a short while later when another neighborhood leader called to invite my daughter to her troop meeting—no strings attached.

Everything in life is a matter of timing. Anyone who is even remotely aware of what moving with a family entails knows that you should not heap outside responsibilities on a newcomer, especially one just a few days old and still recuperating from the after-shock of the ordeal. The aforementioned lady, L.G., no doubt thought she had herself a patsy and would strike while the iron was steaming. I can only hope that her troop turned on her and administered Indian rope burns to her wrists! The second lady, who asked for no commitment from me and sincerely welcomed my daughter into her group, gladly gained whatever help I could provide, once I had settled into my new home and had gotten rid of those damned cartons. I was a standout later, regaling the little girls with my directions for superlative golden-sprayed orange-juice-can pencil holders. Many a father today is still grateful to me for that!

There seems to be a growing reluctance on the part of many an established community or neighborhood to welcome newcomers in the more "traditional" ways. Perhaps it's because we newcomers are not the novelty we once were. If you move into a house that has changed hands several times in recent years, the other neighbors will be inclined to leave you alone. I suppose they feel that it won't be long until you'll be gone too, so it's not worth the effort of getting to know you. Whatever the reason, it's been a long time since I've been welcomed with so much as a plate of cookies on moving day or thereafter. You may very often have to make the first move yourself. One exception to this trend is on streets where all the houses are brand-new. These are generally very friendly places because everyone is making a fresh start. But within three or four years when the houses start to change hands, this welcoming atmosphere slowly erodes, and newcomers won't be greeted with a coffee klatch or cocktail party any more. That really is too bad.

Some real estate agencies are right on the ball and are aware of the difficulties encountered by newcomers. They send an announcement to the immediate neighbors to inform them of the incoming family. They include the name of the family and the anticipated date of occupancy. Wouldn't it be nice if they added a few more pertinent facts, such as the children's ages and the family's former hometown? This would tend to break the ice for the new family in the neighborhood and make it easier for the old residents to come calling.

If you should find that you have become an "old-timer" in an area, be sure, as I've said before, to put yourself out for the newcomers. A simple gesture such as a friendly wave of the hand while retrieving your mail, a few words of recognition at the supermarket, a chat over the back fence while raking leaves can be a big thing to your new neighbor and can make her feel that she belongs. Many people who stay in one place allow themselves to become so insular and involved with their own lives that they tend to neglect the simple basic amenities. A smile has never cost its giver a cent. It's a very easy thing to give, and it may mean everything to someone who is feeling desperately alone.

It's a shame that, as you and your husband achieve a measure of success and become able to afford a home in a more substantial area, you will be even more likely to be ignored by the surrounding established native population. Transients usually fare better in the new subdivisions where there is no snobbery based, among other things, on stability, and you may choose to live in them even when you can afford older and better. But I sure do get tired of putting in lawns and planting trees whose shade I'll never be around to sit in! I've landscaped so many yards that I feel like Johnny Appleseed!

If you find, however, that you are not completely happy and content with the changes in your life as far as neighborhood and city are concerned, there are constructive courses to be followed. The most important factor in learning to make the best of the situation is probably to stop feeling sorry for yourself. Keep in mind that you really do have something to offer to the people you meet.

In his book *Corporate Wives—Corporate Casualties?*, Dr. Robert Seidenberg says, "In the inevitable moves of successful businessmen, while the male's identity is usually enhanced, the female's is shredded because of the vast inequity between the one and the other in ability to *transfer credentials*." No one in a new town knows that you were an untiring volunteer in the hospitals. Your years of teaching little boys and girls to make shell trees out of styrofoam and macaroni did not make national headlines. The hundreds of miles that you have driven car pools to dancing lessons, school sports events, and field trips are unknown by your new townsfolk. No one is aware that you received great personal rewards by working with a brain-damaged little girl two afternoons a week. Your new neighbors didn't see the spectacular rose garden that you created, nurtured and tended out of sandy, rocky soil. They are unaware that your Shrimp Creole recipe is nectar of the gods and that you threw the best New Year's Eve party in town. You arrive in a new community as clean and as pure as a mountain spring. A friend of mine, a most resourceful and intelligent woman who loves to be doing and involved, suggests that there should be résumés for wives to be sent along to all the local agencies in the new town. (Woman's clubs and the Junior League organizations do have reciprocal agreements with other cities and states.) It seems a shame that a woman should have to start all over again to establish herself within the community every time she moves. This gets harder as the lady gets older! There seems to be no simple solution to this problem except to say that a woman must rely on her own initiative. If people are not acknowledging your presence in their town, you will have to take the bull by the horns and join whatever activities interest you, remembering all the while to walk the fine line between being too pushy and too retiring.

When we were newcomers to one midwestern city, I was informed by TV and the newspapers that there would be one of those enormous auctions held to raise money for the local educational TV station. When the call went out through the city for volunteers I decided to step into the breach and offer my services for the cause. I had worked on a similar project in another city and knew that these auctions were worthwhile—and a great way to meet people.

I called one of the chairpersons named in the newspaper, and my services were happily accepted. Not too many chairmen will turn down a willing volunteer. I was told where to meet and the time and the date and looked forward to the job and the hope of some adult company. I arrived on the designated day, full of pep and vinegar, and received my assignment. I was to report to the warehouse out back. O.K. So I wouldn't be on one of the more glamorous committees, but there were bound to be lots of other workers in the warehouse. Wrong!

My volunteer service turned into six grueling hours of unpacking and sorting and marking of all the castoffs of the city. I unpacked smelly rubber hip-length fishing boots, hockey pucks, tattered wedding gowns, yellowed baby clothes, and forgettable potty chairs and a myriad of miscellaneous junk. After a few hours four ladies arrived for their shift. Mine was to continue. I said "Hi" to my coworkers. They said "Hi," walked on by and sat down and ate a picnic lunch, and spent time laughing and chatting and ignoring the work to be done—and me. I drove home later in the day in tears, muttering all of the obscenities I could muster, hating my new home in "pit city." When I had calmed down and returned to my normal rational state, I realized my mistake was in not thoroughly explaining my situation to the chairperson—I never did meet the lady. I should have told her that I was new to the city and wanted to work, but preferably with other people in order to meet and perhaps get to know some of the residents of the city. As I have learned through the years, moving entails a certain amount of selectivity and a great deal of pushiness, carried forth with good taste, of course. Now if I can only remember these sage words the next time around, I'll be in good shape.

The corporate wife that Dr. Seidenberg speaks of in his book is generally past the age of baby- and toddler-rearing. Her children are more than likely in their teens or older and thus relatively independent. Because of her age, it is sometimes more difficult for her to make a satisfying adjustment to a new environment. She has no baby to wheel in a stroller every afternoon when she will invariably run into other young mothers doing the same. Her children are past the age of playing in the neighborhood. She can't even meet the ten-year-old street bully's mother. Believe it or not, some really fast friendships have started when little Jodie has been bitten by little Bradley! The older woman will have to make an extra effort to establish herself in a new community for the umpteenth time.

Often, when you find yourself in new surroundings, you tend to lose all initiative to begin the process of meeting others once again. It's very easy to get into a rut, and it really is necessary to force yourself to get out of the house and seek new activities. Staying wrapped in your safe cocoon busy with family and housework can be satisfying for a time, but it can lead to eventual unhappiness and depression. A woman needs to relate to another woman, to exchange ideas and feelings, to share her interests, to be and to have a friend.

For months after one move we made, I busied myself in my spare time with needlework and reading. I turned out pillow after pillow, and quickly lined the bookshelves with current paperbacks. I suddenly realized that I had become a colossal bore to everyone around me. I had nothing to offer. I was dull, dull, dull. Eagerly awaiting the daily mail delivery, the newspaper boy, a favorite quiz show on TV, my children's return at the end of the school day, and my husband's homecoming in the evening, I hung on their every word. I had nothing to contribute to the conversations. I was living vicariously through the lives of my family, a state that was fast becoming detrimental to all of us. With my husband's prodding and my children's letting me know in not so subtle ways that I was becoming a drag, I decided to get busy and do something constructive with my life.

After you've shed the tears, it's time to bring out the pad and pencil again, and make one more list. This one concerns you and only you. First, list all the activities you participated in before your move. Include *everything*—your weekly bridge game, bowling with the girls, working for the PTA, helping at the school library, or whatever. Now take a good hard look at the list. Have any of these activities lost their appeal? Did the Wednesday morning bowling give you a migraine? Have you served your sentence with the Cub Scouts? Now is your big chance to start fresh! Ruthlessly cross from your list any of those activities that you really have had it with, and promise yourself that *no way* will you be drawn into that particular chore again. Too often we transients go from town to town doing the same old unpopular jobs that no one else wants any part of, just to gain a foothold. Recognize that for the trap it is, and don't fall into it again. Your outside activities should give you pleasure and fulfillment, not headaches and shattered nerves.

Now add to the whittled-down list some things you've always wanted to do. How about learning backgammon, writing poetry, or flying a plane? Live dangerously, at least on paper. Maybe you've always wanted to try oil painting, or to take a course in interior decorating or French cooking. Put it on the list.

Draw a line down the middle of the paper, and opposite each old activity you want to retain and each new activity you'd like to try, put down a possible contact—a person or organization that could get you started. For instance, almost all schools today have adult education programs, and this is a fine way to meet people while satisfying your own intellectual cravings. I joined a sculpture class, and it was great therapy to pound that clay. If ladies' groups are your thing, get in touch with Welcome Wagon or New Neighbors Club, if they don't find you first, and ask about golf groups and bridge clubs. In many cities Welcome Wagon sponsors wonderful fashion show luncheons, gourmet cooking classes and even weekend trips for couples. One of the nicest aspects of these clubs is discovering that you are not alone in this situation. There is comfort in numbers, and it makes for a healthier outlook when you can talk to someone who is going through a similar experience. In comparing notes, you can help one another and learn from those you meet. Many times close friendships begin in just this way.

It can be a big help to the mobile family if you cultivate hobbies and interests that necessarily involve meeting other people. Reading is nice, but it's not too sociable. Showing dogs, playing bridge, working in political organizations, joining clubs of any kind—gardeners, philatelists, golfers, environmentalists—all are a help in providing contacts with people who share your interests. Iris growers, coin collectors, cat fanciers, needlepointers have banded together in organizations all over the country, and they almost always welcome new members. Don't wait for people to find *you* though. You will have to seek out actively these avenues for your interests. After all, tennis is much more invigorating when played with two.

You might think about enrolling yourself and your husband in tennis lessons, or how about a course in Yoga or Transcendental Meditation? This could be a fine way to meet other couples while soothing the savage beasts that live within. How about taking a French course? That could come in handy if you are ever transferred abroad. Brush up on your typing, take a fling at glassblowing or creative writing or sewing. Public libraries offer book clubs and book review groups that you might attend, and of course your church or synagogue can be a great help in making friends in a new community. Churches are a veritable anthill of activity for all ages—youth groups, ladies' circles, men's discussion clubs, couples' clubs, nursery schools, Sunday school, choirs, and on and on. The main difficulty may be in finding the right church for you. There is quite a bit of variation in the practices and flavor of individual churches of the same denomination throughout the country. Sometimes you won't even be able to recognize them as *being* the same denomination. When we moved from a little old white-clapboard New England Methodist church to one in a large metropolitan city in the Midwest, it was quite a change. The first Sunday our eight-year-old son looked around with awe at the stained glass windows and the high cathedral ceiling and the large impressive altar. When the first hymn began and the choir in their red robes began the processional, the sound reverberated from the lofty rafters and he looked up at me, amazed, to whisper, "Mommy, what *are* we?"

It may take a little shopping around to find the right church for your family, and if you try too many you may find all your spare time taken up with entertaining ministers who come to call, but it's worth the search if you find a congenial group that shares your beliefs.

If you are interested in volunteer work, hospitals, schools, and public service groups always need help, so don't be shy about calling to volunteer.

If you are still tied down to house and hearth with small children, most of your activities will have to be confined to evenings when a good husband can be called upon to do the baby-sitting honors, or else a sitter will have to be found. Local churches and high schools are often able to put you in touch with reliable sitters at reasonable rates. Churches often operate play-schools where you can leave preschoolers for a few hours for a nominal fee.

There are lots of things you can do to speed up your period of adjustment. You'll find many good tricks yourself, but here are a few that have worked for me.

1. Pin up your map of the area in the kitchen or another prominent place, and use it to orient yourself to places you hear mentioned on the radio, on TV, in newspapers, and in conversation. If the traffic helicopter keeps reporting tie-ups on the Vandeventer Overpass, look at your map and see where it is, so you can avoid it.

---

2. Use your Yellow Pages and "let your fingers do the walking" when you can. Keep a copy in your car along with another map. It will come in handy when you need to locate a second greenhouse or lumberyard when you are out doing errands.

3. Don't be afraid to be adventurous when you're driving in the new city. There's always a policeman or service station attendant to show you the route back home. If you miss the right exit, just drive to the next one and reverse your course and ask for directions. Don't let the mysteries of the local geography keep you home. And don't be unnerved by the natives honking at you or be intimidated by their obscene gestures when you are trying to find your way around. It would be great to have a bumper sticker on your car saying, "Patience—I'm new around here." That would be a really helpful addition to the basket of goodies distributed to newcomers by the Welcome Wagon.

4. Latch on to any pamphlets or booklets available giving information on things to do in your new city. In many cities good guidebooks are available at reasonable prices, listing local attractions, their hours, admission prices, locations etc. They can be a big help in getting acquainted with your town.

One of the things that I dread most in any move is the trip to the auto license bureau for the state auto registration and my new driver's license. This may be because I had the misfortune to suffer the indignities of flunking the test twice in view of two of my sniggering teenagers. Rules and regulations, and even the time period allowing you to use your out-of-state license varies from state to state. It seems incongruous that it is a simple matter to obtain an international license which permits you to drive almost anywhere in the world, while South Dakota refuses to recognize your skills as certified by North Dakota. Think of the man-hours wasted in re-examination of competent drivers with a license from another state! Perhaps it's time for a national driver's license and car registration. This would certainly eliminate a lot of the hassle and trauma and expense inflicted upon the mobile American—and those of us who go to pieces at the thought of any kind of test.

Be sure to see the local sights. It will give you something to do as well as something to talk about when you do meet someone new. The natives are proud of their city and its attractions, even though they may not have actually seen them themselves. Several years ago, when we lived briefly in Philadelphia, we rented a row house where neighborly relations were close, and the residents came out to wave goodbye one Sunday as we headed downtown to see the historic section of the city. They were thrilled and excited to think that we were actually going to see Independence Hall and the Liberty Bell. "Tell us what it's like," they said. Not one of them had visited these landmarks himself. "Too many tourists," they said. I never visited the U.S.S. Constitution while living in Boston. My excuse was "Too many babies!" Take the time to see the sights while you have the opportunity. Tomorrow you may find yourselves transferred to East Podunk, where the main tourist attraction is the massage parlor on the outskirts of town.

In many cities books are now available rating the local restaurants and giving a sample menu, as well as a price list. Ask for these at your newsstand or bookstore. You might also consider joining one of the dining club plans that offer discounts at various restaurants about town. This is a good prod to get you and your husband out of the house and into the night life of the community. You may want to sign up for season tickets to the local concert series or repertory theater or professional hockey games. This will give you something to put on your calendar until your social life picks up.

5. If you meet another newcomer, suggest lunch, shopping, or cooperative touring of the kind that your kids don't want to do, such as antiquing, bargain-hunting, etc.

When they hear that you're moving to Walla Walla, friends and relatives alike will tell you to "be sure to look up" so-and-so. It may be Great Aunt Minnie, Cousin Sally's college roommate, or Brother-in-law Ralph's old army buddy. You will be reluctant to phone these people to announce, "Here I am!" but any port in a storm! Don't sit back and wait for them to throw a party in your honor, though. Invite them over for coffee or cocktails, or suggest that you meet for lunch. Nine out of ten of these contacts may be a disaster, but that one call could turn up a friend worth having.

6. If you have family connections in a far-off city or state, it's worthwhile to keep the ties strong—even with your in-laws! Try to nurture in your children a feeling of having roots by visiting and encouraging visits by aunts and uncles and cousins. Grandparents in particular are very special, so arrange to see them as often as possible. Kids need to know where they are from and that there are people besides their parents who love them. Thank goodness our relatives stay put so we always know where to find them, even if the opposite is not always the case!

7. One mobile family I know vacations every summer in the same Cape Cod cottage that they have rented for years. No matter where they happen to be living, they all look forward each summer to making the trek back to the Cape and the sand and the sea that have become their "roots." It can give children, as well as parents, a sense of continuity and security if you can manage to vacation in a favorite spot year after year.

8. It won't be too long after your arrival in the new town before you will be exposed to the native population. There is one important rule to remember when you are dealing with the natives. When they ask you how you like their town, *smile and say you love it*! Even if you are miserably lonely and wish you had never laid eyes on this particular part of the planet, even though you loathe the climate, the architecture, and the inflections of speech, find something about the place that you can admire. Remember Winston Churchill's famous remark when a pair of proud parents presented their incredibly ugly baby for his approval. He surveyed the baby gravely for a moment and then pronounced, "Well, that *is* a baby!" He had maintained his integrity without offending the parents. Try to find something about your new community that you can honestly compliment. It may be the shopping, the homes, or the major league ball team, but say it with as much conviction and even enthusiasm as you can muster.

An important corollary to this rule is this: Cool it on the glories of your former hometown. There is no surer way to turn off new friendships, whether it be in Dublin or Duluth, than going into ecstasies about the *superior* cultural opportunities, *perfect* climate, *fascinating* people, and *peerless* beauty of the town in which you used to live. Put that behind you as completely as you can, and explain the wisdom of this rule to your children, too.

Don't expect your life-style in your new home to be exactly as it was before. Wouldn't it be a bore to live the same kind of life in San Francisco that you did in Savannah? Absorb the flavor of your new community, enjoy its distinctive pleasures. I always thought I hated car racing until we moved to the Midwest and someone dragged me to the Indy 500. Don't moan about how you've always loved the mountains when you are living just a short drive from the beach. Long winters in your new state? Give winter sports a whirl. Skiing or snowmobiling could be a lot more fun than huddling by the radiator wishing you were back in Galveston. Observe the natives, and follow their example. You may find that you enjoy king crab and sourdough bread even more than soft shells and grits!

Smile and say you love it. It won't be long until you do!

Epilogue

Any family faced with relocation can't help weighing the pros and cons of moving. That there are negative aspects in a move is obvious, and we have touched upon many of them in these pages. Then why do people persist in venturing from their established homes and communities to new ones hundreds or thousands of miles away. Sometimes they have no choice, of course, but often they do, and still they move on. What makes them do so, plunging into these unknown waters again and again?

America's vitality has been attributed to the kind of people who settled her. It wasn't the timid and fearful who boarded those cramped wooden ships for a long and rough voyage to make new homes and lives in a wilderness peopled by savages. There weren't too many gutless wonders in Jamestown or Plymouth, or in the Conestoga wagons on the Oregon Trail. America was settled by risk-takers and visionaries, and we are their descendants. We are literally the movers and shakers of modern America, and we accept stagnation and the status quo no more than did our forebearers.

When a man is offered the challenge of a promotion or a better job, he and his family move into a new community bringing with them ideas and interests and concerns from other parts of the country. They bring vigor and a breath of fresh air to every group they touch—the PTA, garden club, men's prayer group, school board, local politics, as well as the business or industry they serve. They help keep America young, and prevent hardening of the arteries from developing in good old Uncle Sam.

Yes, families on the move do have to make compromises. Yes, there are indeed some obstacles and drawbacks. Yes, moving does create some problems. But it is the ultimate adventure available to the American family in our time, and when the day comes to start packing, we'll do it again.

APPENDIX

Countdown to Moving Day

Nothing can take the place of your own personal lists to organize your family's move, but I offer this timetable as a model for yours. Starting from the time you sell your house and buy a new one, these are some things you will want to remember ━━━━▶

Six Weeks to Go:

Contact moving companies to set up appointments with their representative. (Even earlier, if possible.)

Start using up frozen and canned foods.

Send change-of-address cards to:
credit card companies
periodicals
insurance company
personal correspondents
social security or companies from whom you receive dividends

Notify post office of new address and effective date.

Notify doctors and dentists, and have records prepared for transfer.

Have prescriptions filled.

Obtain referrals for new doctors.

Obtain eyeglass prescriptions.

See veterinarian for records, prescriptions, and a health certificate if you are planning to ship a pet.

Inform schools of your impending move and review your childrens' records.

Order new identification tags for pets.

Notify attorney, clergyman, and stockbroker.

Four Weeks to Go:

Close out local charge accounts.

Notify utilities of cut-off date.

Send rugs, draperies, other items out for cleaning.

Start packing if you are doing it yourself.

Clean out freezer.

Obtain maps you will need for your trip.

Make arrangements for care of small children on moving day.

Retrieve property on loan and return borrowed items.

Arrange for delivery of hometown newspaper if you wish to continue receiving it.

Start saying goodbye to friends.

Two Weeks to Go:

Make motel reservations specifying guaranteed late arrival.

Arrange for servicing of appliances just prior to moving.

Pick up items at cleaners.

Dispose of plants and pets not going with you.

Gather up warranties and operating instructions for appliances and put them in a conspicuous place for the new owners.

One Week to Go:

Have car serviced for trip to your new home.

Assemble lawn and garden equipment and items from the yard which are to go with you.

Empty lawn mower and dispose of all flammables such as paint, turpentine, charcoal lighter fluid.

Arrange to stop deliveries of milk, bakery, newspapers, etc.

Close out bank accounts and have funds transferred to new bank.

Retrieve items from safe deposit box and place in a strongbox to go with you.

Obtain cash or travelers' checks for your trip.

One Day to Go:

Clean out refrigerator and leave doors open so it can dry.

Establish which closet is Forbidden and label it boldly.

Store needed items in Forbidden Closet.

In winter see that walks and drive are cleared of ice and snow.

Set up color-coding system

Moving-Out Day:

Implement plan for care of young children.

Confine pets in a safe place.

Strip beds and pack bedding in well-marked boxes.

Activate color-coding system.

Go over inventory with mover when he arrives.

Put your copy of the inventory in the strongbox.

Point out to movers any items not to be loaded. Give them a list of these items.

Allow time to attend closing on old house if it has not already taken place.

Check closets, attic, garage, and yard to see that the movers loaded everything that is to go.

See that crib and vacuum are loaded last so they can come off first.

Load the car for your trip.

Clean rooms as they are emptied.

Give the driver directions to your new home and phone numbers where you can be reached in the interim.

Let relatives know where you can be reached in the event of emergency.

Leave your forwarding address with new owners.

Put names and telephone numbers of moving agents on both ends of your move in your purse.

Go to the weigh station to witness the weighing of your goods if you wish to do so.

Obtain certified check or cash to pay mover when he unloads your goods unless the move is to be charged to your company.

Day Before
Moving-In Day:

Get in touch with local moving agent as soon as you reach town and let him know how to reach you.

Attend closing on new house if not already done.

Arrange for baby-sitter on moving day if needed.

Arrange for telephone and utilities to be connected.

Moving-In Day:

Be at the house to let movers in when they arrive.

Confine pets in a safe place.

Check items off the inventory list and note any damage as they are unloaded.

Reactivate color-coding system.

Direct placement of furniture and other goods.

Have appliances reconnected.

Put linens on the beds as they are set up.

Clean bathrooms.

Organize kitchen.

Arrange for further unpacking if movers are to provide this service.

INDEX

Schools
  achievement test scores, 45, 90
  choosing of, 45-47
  course selection, 190
  experimental programs in, 197, 201
  first day, 27
  grade placement in, 198-99
  graduation credits, 189
  overseas, 159-60
  teacher-pupil ratio, 45
  teenage adjustment to, 186-94
  transferring records to, 90
  transportation to, 40
Seidenberg, Dr. Robert, 217, 219
Selling your house, *see also* Realtors
  advertising, 19-20
  by owner, 18-20
  corporate moving policies, 26
  determining price, 18
  furnished, 25
  multiple listing service, 21-22
  negotiable items in, 18-19
  open house, 22
  preparation for, 12-13
  showing of, 22-24
Shopping overseas, 158
Slipcovers, 177
Storage, furniture, 83

Tag sale, *see* Garage Sale
Teenagers, *see also* Schools
  adjustment to moving, 27, 186-96

Teenagers *(cont'd.)*
  discipline after a move, 194-96
  on moving day, 122
Telephone company, moving statistics from, 9
Telephone service, discontinuing, 91
Toddlers
  car of on moving day, 103, 117-18, 136
Traveling, *see also* Maps
  illness while, 126-28
  in two cars, 128-29
  with children in car, 124-26
  with pets, 110-15
Trailer rental, 145-46

Unemployment, 6-7
Unpacking service, 139
Utilities, disconnection of, 91

Veterans Administration (VA), mortgage, 61-62

Wallpaper, 179-82
Wall Street Journal, 3, 7, 89
Warranties, *see* Guarantees
Webster's New World Dictionary, 206
Weiss, Robert S., 208
Welcome Wagon, 221, 223
White House, on moving day, 105-06

Zip codes, 90